PEACEFUL COEXISTENCE

International Law in the Building of Communism

PEACEFUL COEXISTENCE

->>><<<-

International Law in the Building of Communism
by
Bernard A. Ramundo

The Johns Hopkins Press, Baltimore, Maryland

Published in cooperation with The Institute for Sino-Soviet Studies
George Washington University

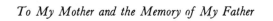

To My Mother and the Memory of My Father

PREFACE

This study, a commentary on the Soviet approach to contemporary problems of international law, was prompted by the desire to scratch beneath the surface of the frequently encountered generalization that the Soviet Union's use of international law is manipulative and self-serving. To indicate the correctness of the generalization, the author fashioned the title around the slogan-like formulation, "building of communism." The title, however eye-catching, is not accurate. It is meaningful only to the extent that it implies that the law of coexistence has an anti-Western bias. Its basic defect lies in the failure to reflect that Soviet preoccupation with the "building of communism" is catechismal and that practical domestic and foreign policy objectives and needs, vis-à-vis capitalist and socialist states, provide the substantive basis for the liturgical form. The author chose the title because the Soviets use this formulation in the socialist camp where the "building of communism" is considered to have persuasive force and is used exhortationally, with diminishing success, to gain support for Soviet positions on international law.

The study is divided into two parts. Part I is devoted to the Soviet approach to basic questions of international law under the law of peaceful coexistence. Principal focus is on the impact of peaceful coexistence upon traditional legal concepts. As Soviet jurists tend to ascribe socialist content to traditional concepts which they modify in the interest of the Soviet Union, the specific task is to identify the socialist content of contemporary international law. The focus in Part II continues to be on policy orientation in the Soviet approach to international law. The context is somewhat different, however, in that principal attention is directed to specific Soviet policies, and the manner in which legal positions provide for their support, in selected areas of contemporary concern. In effect, Part II is a selective survey of Soviet legal positions in their basic policy support role.

The author received generous assistance and encouragement from many quarters. Those to whom the author owes a special debt are Professor Samuel L. Sharp of the American University who sharpened (figuratively and literally) the author's perception of the Soviet scene; Susie Blankenship who, with limitless patience and great intuition, created a workable draft from notes frequently illegible and in disarray; Mary Louise McDaid who took in stride the mystery of transliteration; Mary Schlegel, whose dedication and personal loyalty produced the finished work; and, of course, the author's wife, Ellen Elizabeth Ramundo who, in encouraging him along the literary path, experienced the loneliness of the one who waits at its end.

The study, prepared as a doctoral dissertation at The American University, is a private effort of the author unrelated to his official position in the Department of Defense or his membership on the faculty of the George Washington University. Consequently, any errors contained in the study are the sole responsibility of the author and the views and conclusions stated by him do not reflect those of the Department of Defense or the George Washington University.

CONTENTS

I. INTRODUCTION................................ 1

PART ONE:

Soviet Positions on Basic Questions of International Law 3

II. CONTEMPORARY INTERNATIONAL LAW.... 5

Function and Purpose—The Role of Propaganda......... 7
Universality....................................... 18
Component Principles............................. 22
Definitions...................................... 24
Substantive Content............................. 28
Relationship to Domestic Law..................... 37

III. SOURCES OF INTERNATIONAL LAW......... 43

The Agreement of States.......................... 46
Treaties—The Charter of the United Nations........... 50
Custom... 60
General Principles............................... 64
Auxiliary "Sources"............................. 67

IV. SUBJECTS OF INTERNATIONAL LAW........ 73

The Nation-State................................ 73
International Organizations....................... 80
The Party....................................... 82
Individuals..................................... 85

V. SOVEREIGNTY................................ 87

Shield.. 88
Sword.. 98
Integrating Force............................... 103

->))·((<-

PART TWO

Soviet Positions on Basic International Legal Relationships . . .   109

VI. PEACE AND WAR   111
  The Policy   111
  "Law in the Service of Peace"   118
  Lawful War   121
    "Just" Wars   125
    The Right of Self-Defense   128
    Subversion, Insurgency and Counterinsurgency   133
    The Law of War   138

VII. COLONIALISM   141
  The Policy   141
  The Legal Position   143

VIII. COLLECTIVE SECURITY   151
  The Policy   151
  The Legal Position   153

IX. INTERNATIONAL ORGANIZATION   159
  Globalism   160
  Universalism   163
  Regionalism   170
  Functionalism   178

X. PEACEFUL SETTLEMENT OF INTER-
  NATIONAL DISPUTES   181
  The Policy   181
  The Legal Position   184

XI. ARMS CONTROL   193
  The Policy   194
  The Legal Position   200

XII. INTERNATIONAL RELATIONS   215
  International Collaboration   216
  Peaceful Change   224
  "World Peace through Law"   226

XIII. CONCLUSION   231
Bibliography   237
Index   255

CHAPTER ONE

INTRODUCTION

All states attempt to utilize international law to cloak their
foreign policies with the mantle of legality.[1] The intensity and extent
of a particular state's effort vary with its position in the family of
nations. A state which enjoys the reputation of being law-abiding
will, as a rule, strain for a legal rationale to support actions not
clearly covered by generally accepted principles.[2] On the other
hand, a state with a reputation for lawlessness and only partially
accepted by the family of nations has a lesser need to advance a
legal rationale for its actions.[3]

The Soviet Union, principally as a consequence of further
"nationalization" of its revolution, the normalization of its relations
with other states, and its increasingly status quo orientation, has
outgrown its earlier behavior as an "outlaw state"[4] and now mani-
fests an acute sensitivity to the aura of propriety and legality in
international relations.[5] Since 1956 the Soviet Union has made a
determined effort to (1) demonstrate its dedication to the "progressive development of international law and the strengthening of its

[1] See, generally, Percy E. Corbett, *Law in Diplomacy* (Princeton: Princeton
University Press, 1959), Chap. VIII.

[2] The concepts of "quarantine" and of "aggressive defense" and "hot pursuit"
advanced by the United States in characterizing its military operations during
the Cuban crisis and in Vietnam, respectively, are examples of such state effort.

[3] For example, the People's Republic of China has shown little interest in
justifying, under international legal principles, the occupation of border areas
in dispute with India.

[4] The Soviet Union was so characterized in 1952 by a leading Western authority (Herbert W. Briggs, *The Law of Nations* [2d ed.; New York: Appleton-
Century-Crofts, Inc., 1952], p. 870).

[5] Edward McWhinney, *Peaceful Coexistence and Soviet-Western International
Law* (Leyden: A. W. Sythoff, 1964), pp. 52, 118.

1

role in international relations"[6] and (2) win support for its formulation of peaceful coexistence as the progressive general international law of the present epoch.[7] The Soviets expect that acceptance of this formulation will provide the legal basis for flexibility in the conduct of foreign relations required by the conflicting demands of their practical need to support the status quo and their ideological commitment to support the forces of world revolution. The purpose of this study is to explore the Soviet position on basic international legal problems and relationships in the context of this ambivalent orientation to determine the manner in which the Soviet Union utilizes international law to support policy objectives, and whether Soviet use of international law differs essentially from that of other states.

[6] The Soviets claim that the socialist states and neutralist states of Asia, Africa, and Latin America are the prime movers and most active in this endeavor. (For example, A. P. Movchan, "O Znachenii Kodifikatsii Printsipov Mezhdunarodnovo Prava" [On the Importance of the Codification of the Principles of International Law], *Sovetskoe Gosudarstvo i Pravo* [Soviet State and Law, hereafter cited "*SGIP*"], No. 1 [1965] pp. 46-55; see p. 46). After the Twentieth Congress of the Communist Party of the Soviet Union (1956), there was a related emphasis upon "socialist legality" on the domestic scene.

[7] See, generally, Bernard A. Ramundo, *The (Soviet) Socialist Theory of International Law* (Washington, D.C.: Institute for Sino-Soviet Studies, The George Washington University, 1964), Chaps. 3, 4.

PART ONE

–»»)«««–

SOVIET POSITIONS ON BASIC QUESTIONS OF INTERNATIONAL LAW

CHAPTER TWO

·→≫⟫⟨⟨⟨←·

CONTEMPORARY INTERNATIONAL LAW

Aware of the psychological advantages of being able to invoke legal principles to support its policies, the Soviet Union has developed a "new" international law—the law of peaceful coexistence—designed to provide legal support for maximum flexibility in formulating its foreign policy. The present effort in behalf of such support is not unprecedented in Soviet international legal practice; the need to free policy makers from the restraints of the international legal order was recognized early in the history of the Soviet state. Although the law of peaceful coexistence shares the purpose of earlier formulations, it is a substantial departure in terms of the magnitude and ambitious nature of the effort behind it.

As an aspect of Stalin's nationalization of the revolution in the thirties (i.e., recognition of the need for some measure of international legal stability to implement the policy of "socialism in one country" which, in the international sphere, called for the pursuit of traditional, rather than revolutionary, goals),[1] the Soviet Union discarded revolutionary approaches to the problems of international law and order and began to operate within the framework of conventional international law.[2] Weak, "encircled," and feeling the need for greater acceptance by the family of nations, the Soviet Union was compelled by circumstances to adjust to the international law of the capitalist world. Soviet international legal specialists were called upon to provide a rationale of flexibility for policy makers

[1] Bernard A. Ramundo, *The (Soviet) Socialist Theory of International Law* (Washington, D.C.: Institute for Sino-Soviet Studies, The George Washington University, 1964), pp. 18, 19.

[2] *Ibid.* See also T. A. Taracouzio, *The Soviet Union and International Law* (New York: Macmillan Company, 1935), pp. 350, 351.

caught between the demands of Soviet national objectives and the constraints of a capitalist international legal order. The technique for achieving flexibility was simple. The Soviet Union firmly supported the doctrine of positivism[3] and, in addition, claimed "the right to reject or modify rules of law followed by the noncommunist states by the touchstone of supposedly objective principles of peace, equality, justice and liberty."[4] The rules of law acceptable to the Soviet Union on the latter basis were characterized as progressive. Thus, consent and unilateral characterization of the progressive were the foundations of the Soviet *modus vivendi* in coping with what was viewed as a hostile legal order.[5]

The Soviets claim that the international legal order is no longer hostile, because it has been influenced and shaped by the ever-growing forces of world socialism. Nevertheless, as will be demonstrated later, consent and unilateral characterization, which are the basic defenses against a hostile order, remain the keystones of the new law of peaceful coexistence. The apparently new ingredient, "peaceful coexistence," is intended as a formulation of all that is progressive (i.e., socialist-inspired) in international law. The campaign to secure its acceptance as the basic legal principle is an attempt to gain acquiescence in an "objective" standard which will actually facilitate unilateral characterization by the Soviet Union by providing a universally accepted "legal" basis for it.[6] The Soviet

---

[3] L. B. Shapiro, "The Soviet Concept of International Law," *Yearbook of World Affairs, 1948*, II, 272–310. See 273, where it is said: "Soviet theorists accept as an axiom consent as the sole basis of the validity of international law. . . ." (See also, *Ibid.*, p. 282.)

[4] *Ibid.*, p. 283. See also Oliver J. Lissitzyn, "International Law in a Divided World," *International Conciliation*, No. 542 (March 1963), pp. 22, 23.

[5] *Ibid.*, p. 287.

[6] See Lissitzyn, *op. cit., supra* note 4, p. 19. "The main difference is that by seeking Western acceptance of the principle of peaceful coexistence, the Soviet Union, the source of the concept, and therefore, presumably the most knowledgeable concerning it, seeks, in effect, formal acquiescence in its role as judge of the progressive development of international law." (Ramundo, *op. cit., supra* note 1, p. 28.) McWhinney sees this as the principal danger in Western acceptance of peaceful coexistence. (Edward McWhinney, *Peaceful Coexistence and Soviet-Western International Law* [Leyden: A. W. Sythoff, 1964], p. 36.); but cf. the apparent softening of this position in his view that moderate or "passive"and revolutionary approaches to peaceful coexistence exist within the Soviet Union with the principal differences being (a) the former's "patient quest for the

attempt to achieve this more acceptable lever of legal flexibility is cunningly conceived for it permits pursuit of a maximum position on the nature and operation of the international legal order (i.e., increasingly socialist in its orientation) without foregoing earlier, less cosmetic, techniques intended to achieve similar flexibility under a hostile order. Failure of the peaceful coexistence campaign will not affect the minimum Soviet defensive position based upon consent and unilateral characterization, since that position, basic to peaceful coexistence, will have been consistently maintained.

FUNCTION AND PURPOSE—THE ROLE OF PROPAGANDA

The Soviet approach to the function and purpose of international law reflects the communist tenet that law must be employed in the building of communism.[7] Specifically, Soviet international law positions must contribute to the world victory of socialism by providing legal support for the foreign policies and practices of the Soviet Union in pursuit of that goal. Throughout most of its existence, the Soviet state's position vis-à-vis the international legal order has been primarily defensive, a reflection of having to live with a legal order it had not made and could not shape. Soviet reliance upon consent and unilateral characterization as a means of

peaceful accommodation of contending systems of World Public Order" and (*b*) the latter serving as either "a temporary expedient by way of securing a breathing space until the Soviet Bloc's armed strength could more nearly match that of the West, or else . . . a [long range] stratagem to baffle and confuse Western leaders as to Soviet intentions to effectuate a revolutionary rewriting of international law doctrines in Marxist terms." (*Ibid.*, pp. 41 and 37–42.) Tunkin, whom McWhinney considers a proponent of the moderate or passive orientation, declares there is no such thing as "passive peaceful coexistence." See G. I. Tunkin, *Voprosy Teorii Mezhdunarodnovo Prava* [Problems of the Theory of International Law] (Moscow: State Publishing House of Legal Literature, 1962), p. 14. Since all approaches to peaceful coexistence are directed at the creation of an international legal order favorable to the realization of Soviet foreign policy objectives, it is difficult to appreciate the utility of McWhinney's distinction.

[7] See editorial "Za Vysokuiu Partiinost' v Sovetskoi Iuridicheskoi Nauke" [For a High Degree of Political Orientation in Soviet Legal Science], *SGIP*, No. 1 (1964), pp. 3–11. The Western view of "apolitical science and the special role of the scientist standing above politics" is severely criticized (p. 11).

avoiding legal restrictions upon state freedom of action represents a minimum use of international law to support foreign policy practices and objectives. The campaign for the new law of peaceful co-existence, on the other hand, represents a maximum use of international law to mold or create an environment favorable for world socialism. This move to the legal offensive[8] which commenced in 1956 reflects the assessment, made at that time, that the growing strength of the socialist camp had become the decisive factor in social development and, as a consequence, in the shaping of international law.[9] The current Soviet view requires full exploitation of international law in the building of communism, i.e., international law must be interpreted and developed to serve "the interests of peace and socialism."[10]

The basic Soviet position that international law should be used to complement and serve the foreign policy needs of the Soviet state[11] approaches the question of the function and purpose of international law, from the narrow, selfish point of view of national interest. Soviet jurists would deny that there is a national interest orientation behind the Soviet Union's approach to international law, since the foreign policies of the Soviet Union, being the policies of the leader of the forces of world revolution, are by definition international in their orientation. This semantic legerdemain reflects the view, not generally accepted outside the socialist world, that under the immutable laws of social development class interests in opposing imperialism and colonialism are more truly inter-

---

[8] See, generally, *Peaceful Coexistence, A Communist Blueprint for Victory* (Chicago: American Bar Association, 1964) and *Soviet Impact on International Law* [External Research Paper 156] (Washington, D.C.: U.S. Department of State, Bureau of Intelligence and Research, May 1964).

[9] G. Tunkin, "Vstupitel'naia Stat'ia" [Introductory Article], *Sovetskii Ezhegodnik Mezhdunarodnovo Prava, 1959* [The Soviet Yearbook of International Law, 1959, hereafter cited as "*Sovetskii Ezhegodnik,____*"] (Moscow: Publishing House of the Academy of Sciences of the U.S.S.R., 1960), pp. 11–15; see 12, 13.

[10] G. I. Tunkin, "The Twenty-second Congress of the CPSU and the Tasks of the Soviet Science of International Law," *Soviet Law and Government* (New York: International Arts and Sciences Press, Winter 1962/63), Vol. 1, No. 2, pp. 18–27, see 25.

[11] Tunkin states that the international law position of a state is "determined by the basic principles of its foreign policy" (Tunkin, "Vstupitel'naia Stat'ia," *op. cit., supra* note 9, pp. 12, 13).

nationalist than are conventional Western concepts of international law and order.[12]

Prior to discarding the Stalinist view of the inevitability of conflict between the forces of capitalism and socialism, the Soviets had no developed concept of international order beyond that of the *process* of "struggle and co-operation."[13] As a consequence, a very limited role could be assigned to international law in the maintenance of world order in the conventional sense. The changed position, which recognizes the possibility of the world victory of socialism without conflict and the impermissibility of conflict because of improved weapons technology, has produced a Soviet concept of interim world order ("peace and peaceful coexistence") and, with it, the feasibility of assigning to international law a definite role in the maintenance of that order, by regulating the "struggle and cooperation" of states toward that end.[14] In line with this approach it is now said that "ensuring peaceful coexistence between countries is the . . . chief function of international law."[15] The latest Soviet textbook on international law states that "effective maintenance of world peace, above all, peaceful coexistence," is the principal purpose of international law:[16] "The opinion has been firmly established in Soviet jurisprudence that modern international law is above all a law whose main aim is to insure peace and friendship between all states regardless of their social and economic systems."[17] Although the Soviets can present peaceful coexistence as international law in the service of world order, thereby enhancing its appeal

[12] Gleb Starushenko, "Internationalism—Steadfast Principle of Soviet Foreign Policy," *Moscow News*, No. 6 (February 5, 1966), p. 3.

[13] *Iuridicheskii Slovar'* [Legal Dictionary], ed. P. I. Kudriavstev (2d ed.; Moscow: State Publishing House of Legal Literature, 1956), I, 563.

[14] *Mezhdunarodnoe Pravo* [International Law], ed. D. B. Levin and G. P. Kaliuzhnaia (Moscow: Publishing House "Legal Literature," 1964), p. 8. See also Ramundo, *op. cit., supra* note 1, see p. 25.

[15] G. I. Tunkin, "Sorok Let Sosushchestvovaniia i Mezhdunarodnoe Pravo" [Forty Years of Coexistence and International Law], *Sovetskii Ezhegodnik, 1958* (Moscow: Publishing House of the Academy of Sciences of the U.S.S.R., 1959), pp. 15–49; see p. 48.

[16] *Mezhdunarodnoe Pravo* [International Law], ed. F. I. Kozhevnikov (Moscow: Publishing House "International Relations," 1964), p. 32.

[17] O. Vasilyev, "World Peace, an International Law," *International Affairs*, No. 1 (1965), pp. 107, 108.

and respectability, the type of order (the same *process* of "struggle and co-operation" of states with an indication, perhaps, of its protracted nature) and the dialecticism reflected in it indicate that foreign policy considerations remain uppermost in Soviet international legal formulations.

World order, in the Soviet view, has two principal planes of operation and two contexts—relations with capitalist states, and relations within the socialist camp. The former, reflecting the Marxist teaching of class struggle, involves conflict between capitalist and socialist states. The only world order which is desired is the minimum necessary to prevent mutual annihilation by a thermonuclear exchange.[18] In dealing with members of the socialist camp, on the other hand, a maximum of order is sought to achieve integration and the reduced importance of national boundaries which will produce a single socialist state and, following that, a world communist society. The basic thrusts of Soviet foreign policy are embodied in the Soviet statement of the two fundamental principles of contemporary international law: "peaceful coexistence" and "socialist internationalism." The former is said to be the basic principle regulating the international class struggle and relations between the capitalist and socialist camps; the latter is the basis upon which members of the so-called socialist commonwealth of nations achieve the fullest measure of co-operation and collaboration. Although these principles are mutually exclusive in their operation, they are subsumed under the general "law of peaceful coexistence."

It is apparent that Soviet commentators, displaying their Marxist predilection to observe all social relationships in class context, consider the capitalist and socialist states the principal actors in contemporary international relations. Although the existence of a third group of "neutralist" states is recognized, they say that no separate principle of international law develops out of relations with such states, since they are fraternal allies who support the

[18] The conclusion of the Limited Test Ban Treaty (1963) in the face of violent Chinese opposition and the split with China over the dangers of nuclear warfare as a tactic of world revolution reflect the depth of Soviet concern in this area.

socialist struggle for peace and against imperialism.[19] Despite an early flirtation with the view that the principles of socialist internationalism govern relations between socialist and neutralist states, the Soviets now say that the applicable principles are those of peaceful coexistence.[20] They claim, however, that the principles have a special democratic application which does not exist in other relationships governed by peaceful coexistence.[21] The special "democracy" allegedly reflects community of interest in fighting the forces of imperialism and colonialism which makes possible coexistence of a higher type. Many of the legal positions taken by the Soviet Union reflect the concept of, and desire for, an alliance between socialist and neutralist states in the international class struggle, recalling the alliance between the proletariat and peasantry in the internal struggle for socialism and communism. They are used as a means of harnessing neutralist states to the effort to build communism, a euphemism for policy objectives of the Soviet Union.

The current, specific task of Soviet international legal specialists is to support the progressive foreign policy of the Soviet Union by gaining acceptance of the new law of peaceful coexistence and its basic component principles: peaceful coexistence and socialist internationalism.[22] Despite their intention to reshape the international legal order, the Soviets understate their effort as simply one of seeking international legal support to justify their foreign policies.[23] In keeping with the Soviet views that no single state can make

[19] Ramundo, *op. cit., supra* note 1, p. 45. See *Ibid.*, pp. 43–45. See also D. I. Fel'dman, *Priznanie Gosudarstv v Sovremennom Mezhdunarodnom Prave* [The Recognition of States in Contemporary International Law] (Kazan': Publishing House of Kazan' University, 1965), p. 34, where it is said that neutralist states "play an important role in international life. Together with the other peace and freedom-loving forces of the world, these states strive to direct the development of international relations in the direction of peaceful coexistence. . ."

[20] *Ibid.*, p. 44. See also Tunkin, Voprosy Teorii, *op. cit., supra* note 6, p. 316.

[21] Tunkin, Voprosy Teorii, *op. cit., supra* note 6, p. 316.

[22] Tunkin, "The Twenty-second Congress of the CPSU," *op. cit., supra* note 10, p. 20. See also G. A. Nekrasova, "Deviatoe Ezhegodnoe Sobranie Sovetskoi Assotsiatsii Mezhdunarodnovo Prava" [The Ninth Annual Meeting of the Soviet Association of International Law] *SGIP*, No. 16 (1966), pp. 133, 134; and V. Trukhanovsky, "Proletarian Internationalism and Peaceful Coexistence," *International Affairs*, No. 8 (1966), pp. 54–59.

[23] Tunkin, Voprosy Teorii, *op. cit., supra* note 6, pp. 239, 240.

international law or impose its will in this regard upon other states[24] and that "the mobilization of world public opinion is one of the greatest services of the communist parties in their struggle for peace and international legality,"[25] propaganda is relied upon as an essential element in their campaign. Although propaganda has always been an eye-catching tool of Soviet international legal specialists, its use in support of peaceful coexistence is, like the law itself, more ambitious than earlier efforts to attain the international legal objectives of the Soviet Union. The special dependence upon propaganda assures it a prominent place in the statement of Soviet legal positions.

The current propaganda effort, complemented by diplomatic initiatives, stresses the acceptance of the new law, its progressive character, the necessity for it under contemporary conditions, and its "scientific" basis in Marxist-Leninist terms. These basic themes are utilized in a two-pronged offensive on behalf of peaceful coexistence. The Soviets seek, most of all, voluntary acceptance of the law of peaceful coexistence because such acceptance is considered the best practical guarantee of compliance and is in accord with the dominance of positivism in their international legal formulations. The first three propaganda themes are part of the main effort to obtain the consent of target states. The fourth reflects a natural-law type of approach of limited practical effectiveness under which Marxism-Leninism is the scientific basis of a supreme law of social development which demands observance of the principles of coexistence as *jus cogens*. In effect, the Soviets claim special correctness for their international legal formulations because of their scientific character: "Only socialist international law is truly scientific because it is based upon the timeless teachings of Marxism-Leninism."[26] In both the consent and *jus cogens* routes to coexistence the role of propaganda is basically the same: to gain acquiescence in Soviet legal characterizations through consent to the open-ended,

[24] *Ibid.*, p. 243.
[25] B. I. Melekhin, "Vozdeistvie Mirovovo Obshchestvennovo Mneniia na Sovremennoe Mezhdunarodnoe Pravo" [The Influence of World Public Opinion on Contemporary International Law], *SGIP*, No. 2 (1964), pp. 75–83; see 79.
[26] *Mezhdunarodnoe Pravo* (Kozhevnikov), *op. cit., supra* note 16, p. 60.

peaceful coexistence formulation, or by recognition of a scientific basis for such characterizations.

Soviet international legal specialists claim that the principles of peaceful coexistence are embodied in the Charter of the United Nations and have, therefore, become generally accepted principles of international law—for members of the United Nations, through their acceptance of the Charter, for nonmembers, as a customary principle.[27] Despite the alleged acceptance and entry into force of the law of peaceful coexistence, the Soviets are pushing for codification of its general principles.[28] To ensure that codification is a move in the direction of peaceful coexistence, the Soviets say that the Charter of the United Nations must serve as the general legislative framework:

...every codification of the principles of international law, in whole or in part, is possible only on the basis of the Charter of the U.N. The further progressive development of contemporary international law at variance with the Charter of the U.N. as desired by representatives of the imperialist states is unthinkable.[29]

The need for codification is rationalized on the general basis that the new international law "is far from perfect and needs to be further developed" in order to "bring the content of the principles and rules of international law in line with contemporary social development" (i.e., "along the lines of consolidating peaceful coexistence").[30] Codification, whether of treaty or customary law,

[27] Ramundo, op. cit., supra note 1, p. 30, citing Tunkin, Korovin, and the 1960 Soviet textbook on international law; and Nekrasova, op. cit., supra note 22, p. 133.

[28] A. P. Movchan, "Kodifikatsiia Mezhdunarodnopravovykh Printsipov Mirnovo Sosushchestvovaniia" [Codification of the International Legal Principles of Peaceful Coexistence], Sovetskii Ezhegodnik, 1963 (Moscow: Publishing House "Science," 1965), pp. 15–30; see 28. See also Movchan's article "O Znachenii Kodifikatsii Printsipov Mezhdunarodnovo Prava" [On the Importance of the Codification of International Law], SGIP, No. 1 (1965), pp. 46–55.

[29] V. M. Chkhikvadze, "Voprosy Mezhdunarodnovo Prava na XX Sessii General'noi Assamblei" [Problems of International Law at the 20th Session of the General Assembly], SGIP, No. 3 (1966), pp. 67–78; see 72. It is said that the imperialist states oppose the progressive development of international law (p. 71).

[30] Movchan, op. cit., supra note 28.

is considered beneficial as it provides an opportunity for socialist and neutralist states to combine their efforts in furtherance of the progressive development of international law.[31]

In addition to the Charter of the United Nations, resolutions of the General Assembly and multilateral declarations, agreements, and practices are adduced as further evidence of the general acceptance of the principles of peaceful coexistence.[32] Similarly, the binding character of the principles of socialist internationalism is said to be based upon treaty as well as customary law.[33] Soviet commentaries note that multilateral declarations of the socialist countries[34] have affirmed socialist internationalism to be the guiding principle in relations between socialist states, and the principles of socialist internationalism are reflected in all such relations, bilateral as well as multilateral.[35]

In demonstrating the progressive character of the law of peaceful coexistence, the Soviets play their traditional game of characterization in the Soviet interest. Peaceful coexistence is described as "law in the service of peace."[36] They say that the law of peaceful coexistence, the result of the progressive inititative of the Soviet Union, provides for the preservation of peace and the averting of a nuclear world war, the peaceful settlement of international disputes, an end to the arms race through general and complete disarmament, support for national liberation movements against colonialism and imperialism, and achievement of the world victory of socialism

[31] *Ibid.*, See also *Mezhdunarodnoe Pravo, op. cit., supra* note 14, p. 95.

[32] *Mezhdunarodnoe Pravo, op. cit., supra* note 14, pp. 58–60. The 1966 Havana Tricontinental Conference endorsed peaceful coexistence. (See "Documents of the First Conference of Solidarity of the Peoples of Asia, Africa and Latin America," *Moscow News*, Supplement to No. 6 [February 5, 1966], pp. 2–29.)

[33] Tunkin, Voprosy Teorii, *op. cit., supra* note 6, p. 313.

[34] See the Declaration of the Twelve Communist Parties in Power (November, 1957) and the Declaration of Representatives of the Eighty-one Communist Parties (November-December, 1960) in *The New Communist Manifesto*, ed. Dan N. Jacobs (2d ed.; Evanston, Illinois and Elmsford, New York: Row, Peterson and Company, 1962), pp. 169–182 and 11–47, respectively.

[35] *Mezhdunarodnoe Pravo, op. cit., supra* note 14, pp. 62–78.

[36] See I. I. Karpets, "Pravo na Sluzhbu Mira" [Law in the Service of Peace], *SGIP*, No. 6 (1964), pp. 71–77; see 77; and F. I. Kalinyshev, "Pravo Narodov na Mir" [The Right of Nations to Peace], *SGIP*, No. 3 (1961), pp. 3–15.

through peaceful competition.[37] As such, "it serves the interests of the people of the socialist countries and all the people of the world."[38] The coexistence formulation is designed to enlist all possible support in the struggle against the capitalist camp.

The Soviet Union and the countries of socialism are taking concrete steps to defend the peace. . . The firm and consistent struggle of the Soviet Union for peace, for general and complete disarmament, for the prohibition of nuclear weapons tests, for the implementation of practical measures aimed at clearing international relations of the remnants of World War II enhance the prestige of socialism, of the communist movement, in the eyes of the peoples. The banner of peace help [sic] the Marxist-Leninist parties rally the masses to speed up the transition from capitalism—which is the source of bloody wars—to socialism which stands for eternal peace on earth, for friendship and cooperation of peoples. *The policy of peaceful coexistence is aimed at mobilizing the masses against the enemies of peace.*[39]

In effect, the Soviet Union has combined the struggle for peace, national liberation, and socialism, seeking to achieve support for its foreign policy-oriented legal objectives by using the general appeal of those formulations as an attractive cover.

The Soviet claims that the law of peaceful coexistence is in effect and is progressive law are bolstered by showing that, under contemporary conditions, international law as the regulating mechanism of international class struggle can only be couched in terms of coexistence. Except for general references to the interdependence of capitalist and socialist states resulting from technological advances and their common interest in avoiding thermonuclear warfare, Soviet commentaries prefer Marxist-Leninist litany to considerations of interdependence when rationalizing the present need for

[37] N. A. Ushakov and E. P. Meleshko, "Novyi Uchebnyi Kurs Mezhdunarodnovo Prava" [The New Text on International Law], *SGIP*, No. 10 (1964), pp. 153–155; see 153. See also *Mezhdunarodnoe Pravo, op. cit., supra* note 14, p. 54; and Professor G. Zadorozhny, "What Is Peaceful Coexistence" *Moscow News,* No. 17 (April 23, 1966), p. 6.

[38] *Mezhdunarodnoe Pravo, op. cit., supra* note 14, p. 54.

[39] "Peaceful Coexistence and Revolutionary Struggle" trans. from *Kommunist* [Communist] (March, 1963), in *The Daily Review* (Moscow), IX, No. 22, (March 26, 1963), p. 14. See also Yu. Zhilin and V. Zagladin, "The Anti-War Tradition of the Workers' Movement" translated from *Pravda* (September 5, 1965), in the *Current Digest of the Soviet Press* (hereafter cited "*CDSP*"), XVII, No. 38, pp. 8, 9.

coexistence.[40] In the Marxist-Leninist "scientific" view of contemporary international relations, peaceful coexistence is "an objective necessity for the further development of mankind."[41] Shades of Marxist concepts of base and superstructure appear in the additional rationale that "international law is only the juridical expression of the objective fact of the peaceful coexistence of the countries of the two systems."[42] Peaceful coexistence is said to be "the political basis of general international law and its development determines the possibilities of the development of general international law."[43] A recent commentary combines all of the foregoing in this terse statement: "peaceful coexistence is an historical fact, an objective reality, the natural process of social development and the basic international legal norm."[44] Although the objective laws of social development are invoked, the heart of the matter is the impermissibility of nuclear warfare, producing the non-Marxist result that interdependence based upon technological advances in weaponry, rather than Marxism-Leninism, has dictated the policy and law of coexistence.

In the case of the socialist countries, there is a similar predilection for litany. The existence of the socialist commonwealth of nations is said to reflect the great community of interest within the socialist camp. Soviet commentaries, however, prefer to use Marxist-Leninist terms for the new type of international relations claimed for the commonwealth. Reliance is placed upon the common economic base of socialism and the identity of class interest in the conducting of international relations. Thus, a "scientific" basis is stated for the new principles of socialist internationalism[45] which, with the growing strength of the forces of world socialism, are destined to replace the

[40] Ramundo, *op. cit.*, *supra* note 1, pp. 3–7.

[41] Ushakov and Meleshko, *op. cit.*, *supra* note 37, p. 153.

[42] V. M. Shurshalov, Review of N. M. Minasian, *Sushchnost' Sovremennovo Mezhdunarodnovo Prava* [The Essence of Contemporary International Law] (Rostov: Publishing House of Rostov State University, 1962), *SGIP*, No. 5 (1964), pp. 158–160; see 158. See also Tunkin, *Voprosy Teorii, op. cit., supra* note 6, p. 9.

[43] Tunkin, Voprosy Teorii, *op. cit., supra* note 6, p. 7.

[44] G. P. Zadorozhnyi, *Mirnoe Sosushchestvovanie i Mezhdunarodnoe Pravo* [Peaceful Coexistence and International Law] (Moscow: Publishing House "International Relations," 1964), p. 7.

[45] Tunkin, Voprosy Teorii, *op. cit., supra* note 6, pp. 302 and 327.

general law of peaceful coexistence as the nucleus of a new socialist international law.[46] Soviet legal rationalizations in Marxist-Leninist terms reflect the basic bias toward the view that "International Law, like any other law, pertains to the superstructure and is of a class character."[47]

The total propaganda effort in support of the policy and law of peaceful coexistence is complemented by related diplomatic initiatives. The close co-ordination and relationship between propaganda and diplomacy justify treating these two efforts as mutually supporting aspects of the campaign for peaceful co-existence. Generally, Soviet diplomatic initiatives in such forums as the United Nations and the Eighteen Nation Disarmament Committee are intended to demonstrate adherence to peaceful co-existence in action. Included among these initiatives are Soviet plans for nuclear and general and complete disarmament; proposals for nuclear-free zones, peaceful settlement of boundary disputes, and complete cessation of nuclear testing; and recent calls in the United Nations for a summit conference on arms control and for acceptance of proposed treaties to prohibit intervention in the internal affairs of states and the proliferation of nuclear weapons.[48] Many of these appealing, general propaganda-diplomatic initiatives of the Soviet Union are not regarded in the West as meaningful negotiating commitments. The failure of the West to accept these initiatives is usually described by Soviet commentators as part of a continuing effort to block progress towards peaceful coexistence. The Soviet Union emerges from the propaganda-diplomatic smoke screen as the patient proponent of peace, national liberation, and disarmament; the capitalist states are seen as an aggressive, colonial, obstructionist force.

[46] *Ibid.*, pp. 325–326. See also Ramundo, *op. cit., supra* note 1, pp. 51–52.

[47] *International Law* (Moscow: Foreign Languages Publishing House, n.d.), p. 10.

[48] S. Viskov, *Za Mir bez Oruzhiia, za Mir bez Voin* [For a World Without Arms and War] (Moscow: Publishing House of Social-Economic Literature, "Thought," 1964), pp. 40–105; "Gromyko Proposes World Arms Summit, *The Evening Star* (December 7, 1964) p. A-1; "The General Assembly," *New Times*, No. 40 (October 6, 1965), pp. 1, 2; and "Reds Offer Guarantee to Limit A-Arms Use," *The Washington Post* (February 3, 1966), p. A-14. In connection with Gromyko's speech to the plenary session of the General Assembly on December

The Soviet legal offensive in support of the policy of peaceful coexistence involves mutually supporting propaganda and diplomatic efforts to gain acceptance of the proposition that contemporary international law is the law of peaceful coexistence. The nature and extent of the Soviet commitment to this offensive reflect the great reliance placed upon the persuasive force of law in pursuing foreign policy goals. As the proponent of a new international law favorable to "the cause of socialism," the Soviet Union can afford to discard its defensism vis-à-vis the international legal order and become the champion of international legality:

> The socialist states call for strict observance of the principles and rules of international law. At the same time they fight unswervingly for the incorporation into international law of new progressive principles and rules furthering peaceful coexistence.[49]

In championing international legality, however, the Soviets reserve their support for the "progressive" and "democratic" law of peaceful coexistence.

UNIVERSALITY

Soviet international legal specialists formally recognize the universality of international law, that is, the concept of a single general international law binding on all states:[50] "contemporary

---

7, 1964, the Soviet Government circulated a memorandum enumerating the following measures "for the further relaxation of international tensions and limiting the arms race": (1) reduction of military budgets, (2) recall or reduction of foreign based troops, (3) liquidation of foreign bases, (4) prevention of further proliferation of nuclear weapons (and, of course, the NATO multilateral force), (5) prohibition on the use of nuclear weapons, (6) creation of nuclear-free zones, (7) destruction of bombers, (8) prohibition of underground nuclear testing, (9) conclusion of a nonaggression pact between the NATO and Warsaw Pact countries, (10) prevention of surprise attack, and (11) reduction of the overall strength of the armed forces ("Memorandum Sovetskovo Pravitel'stva o Merakh po Dal'neishemu Smiagcheniiu Mezhdunarodnoi Napriazhennosti i Ogranicheniiu Gonki Vooruzhenii" [Memorandum of the Soviet Government Concerning Measures for the Further Relaxation of International Tensions and Limiting the Arms Race], *Pravda* [December 8, 1964], pp. 1 and 4).

[49] Tunkin, Vstupitel'naia Stat'ia, *op. cit., supra* note 9, pp. 22, 23.

[50] McWhinney, *op. cit., supra* note 6, p. 32. See also Ramundo, *op. cit., supra* note 1, pp. 21, 22 and 25.

international law is a universal, general law; i.e., a law for the states of all continents."[51] Support for this concept is a necessary part of the proponency of the law of peaceful coexistence, both in seeking its acceptance and deriving benefits from its operation. The Soviets claim that there can be only a single international law which reflects the general nature of the international relationships it regulates. As the peaceful coexistence of capitalist and socialist states is the principal, objective fact of contemporary international life, they claim that the law regulating the varied and diverse relationships between such states can be only the law of peaceful coexistence.[52] In effect, universality is used to enhance the credibility of peaceful coexistence as a normative system.

Soviet international legal specialists are confronted with a dilemma in coping with the problem of universality. Although the law of peaceful coexistence must be universal in the sense of binding all states to meet Soviet foreign policy needs in dealing with capitalist and socialist states, it must, at the same time, allow for different operation in relationships within the socialist camp. Given the difference in the nature of the relationships desired between socialist states and between socialist and capitalist states—close collaboration and eventual integration versus limited co-operation and struggle—the Soviets feel a practical and ideological need to distinguish between these relationships. They are concerned, however, that fragmentation of the international legal order may result in a reduced area of operation for the law of peaceful coexistence, thereby adversely affecting its capability to lend persuasive support to Soviet foreign policies. Soviet jurists realize that their position that contemporary international law can be only the law of peaceful coexistence is premised upon the principle of universality, and derives much of its persuasiveness from this principle. In short, the law of peaceful coexistence must be fragmented in the Soviet interest without destroying the over-all claim of universality.

Burdened with this difficult task, the Soviets have put a wrinkle in the mantle of universality of the law of peaceful coexistence by

[51] Shurshalov, Review of Minasian, *op. cit., supra* note 42, p. 158.

[52] *Ibid.* See also *Mezhdunarodnoe Pravo, op. cit., supra* note 14, pp. 5–9. This approach reflects the Soviet view that any system of law must reflect the most important aspects of the social relationships governed by it.

holding that it is composed "of socially different components, . . . general international law, the principles and norms which have a general democratic nature, and socialist principles and norms that have come into being or are coming into being in the relations between the countries of the world system of socialism."[53] In the Soviet view, contemporary international law is composed of two basic principles which are mutually exclusive in their operation.[54] These principles, peaceful coexistence and socialist internationalism, regulate international relations between socialist and nonsocialist states and between socialist states, respectively.[55] This departure from universality is rationalized as follows:

Socialist international law does not contradict general international law: rather, in reflecting the special nature of the relations between socialist states, it broadens and deepens the democratic character of general international law.[56]

Socialist principles and norms relate to the principles and norms of general international law as a new and higher quality does to an older quality. As is the case with every higher stage of development, they constitute not naked negation of the generally recognized principles of international law, but negation as a moment of connection, as a moment of development, with retention of what is positive. . . . While they incorporate positive factors and go further than the principles and norms of general international law in assuring friendly relations among states, the socialist principles and norms do not conflict with general international law.[57]

. . . the existence of principles of socialist internationalism and other socialist principles and norms in the relations between countries of the socialist system in no way contradicts the needs of a general international law.[58]

---

[53] Tunkin, "The Twenty-second Congress of the CPSU," *op. cit., supra* note 10, p. 25. See also, Lissitzyn, *op. cit., supra* note 4, pp. 21, 22.

[54] *Mezhdunarodnoe Pravo, op. cit., supra* note 14, p. 76.

[55] Ramundo, *op. cit., supra* note 1, p. 25; Lissitzyn, *op. cit., supra* note 4, pp. 21, 22; and *Mezhdunarodnoe Pravo, op. cit., supra* note 14, pp. 8, 9. The socialist states are said to be "united in a commonwealth by the class character of their social orders and their common interests in international matters" (*Mezhdunarodnoe Pravo, op. cit., supra* note 14, p. 9).

[56] *Mezhdunarodnoe Pravo, op. cit., supra* note 14, p. 9. See also Lissitzyn, *op. cit., supra* note 4, pp. 21, 22.

[57] Tunkin, "The Twenty-second Congress of the CPSU," *op. cit., supra* note 10, p. 26. Tunkin's rationale reflects the dialectical approach to the process of legal development.

[58] Ushakov and Meleshko, *op. cit., supra* note 37, p. 154.

It is obvious that emphasis upon the lack of inconsistency between general and "socialist" international law[59] establishes the compatability of these principles rather than their unity. In apparent recognition of this defect of logic, Tunkin, the leading Soviet international legal specialist, introduces a changed concept of universality to meet Soviet needs in this area.

...the basic principles of contemporary international law are binding and states cannot establish in their bilateral or regional multilateral relationships norms which would conflict with the basic principles.

Nevertheless, states can create principles and norms binding upon a limited number of states, if these principles and norms do not conflict with the mentioned basic principles, especially if they go further than these principles of general international law in furthering friendly relations and securing the peace. Such are the international legal principles of socialist internationalism.[60]

Under Tunkin's definition of convenience, only socialist fragmentation of the international legal order is permitted in that the local principles and norms contemplated are those which are compatible with the law of peaceful coexistence or more progressive "in furthering friendly relations and securing the peace." Although the attempts to deny the departure from universality in Soviet formulations or to change the concept of universality suffer from a lack of logic and consistency, the "explanations" and characterizations devised do provide a rationale for the policy needs of the Soviet Union. Since satisfaction of these needs is the paramount consideration, logic and consistency become luxuries reserved for situations permitting such indulgence.

To designate contemporary international law "the law of peaceful coexistence" appears a misnomer in view of the duality in formulating the basic component principles of contemporary international law (peaceful coexistence and socialist internationalism);

[59] See Ramundo, *op. cit.*, *supra* note 1, pp. 17–24, for a discussion of the wavering course in Soviet pronouncements concerning the existence of socialist international law.

[60] Tunkin, Voprosy Teorii, *op. cit.*, *supra* note 6, p. 325. The recasting of international legal concepts in the Soviet interest has always been a preoccupation of Soviet jurists. Therefore, the campaign to obtain general acceptance of peaceful coexistence as the new contemporary international law represents a difference in scope, rather than basic orientation, of effort.

21

the mutual exclusivity of the operation of the component principles; and the claim of an ever-expanding scope of operation of the principle of socialist internationalism as a consequence of the growing strength of the camp of socialism.[61] The Soviets justify their peaceful coexistence designation by noting that the international relationships governed by the principles of peaceful coexistence far outnumber those under socialist internationalism at the present time. Under these conditions, they consider it appropriate to refer to contemporary international law as the law of peaceful coexistence.

COMPONENT PRINCIPLES

As already indicated, in the Soviet view contemporary international law is composed of two basic principles, peaceful coexistence and socialist internationalism, under each of which are subsumed appropriate subordinate principles. Although these principles govern international relationships that are basically different, they are said to be complementary components of a universal system of international law. It is repugnant to Soviet ideological sensitivity, however, to associate, without some distinguishing rationale, the principles of socialist internationalism and peaceful coexistence under the contemporary international law of coexistence. The Soviets seek to preserve the qualitative difference between the two basic principles —socialist internationalism as a more advanced form of international law is to provide the nucleus of the socialist international law of the future—by dividing the alleged universal international legal order into general international law and the special principles of socialist internationalism.[62] General international law, the equivalent of the principle of peaceful coexistence and its subordinate principles, represents an artful Soviet fragmentation of international law which incorporates the principle of universality while maintaining the essential separateness of peaceful coexistence and socialist internationalism.

[61] Ramundo, *op. cit.*, *supra* note 1, p. 25. The present epoch is officially described as the period of transition from capitalism to socialism, the increasing influence of the socialist system of world development, and the decline of the colonial system of imperialism (*Mezhdunarodnoe Pravo, op. cit., supra* note 14, p. 20).

[62] See R. L. Bobrov, "Mezhdunarodnoe Pravo i Istoricheskii Progress" [International Law and Historical Progress], *SGIP*, No. 12 (1963), pp. 3–11; see 11.

⇥⇥✵⇤⇤

The Soviet approach in this area has resulted in formulations which blur the distinction between "contemporary international law" and "general international law." For example, it is usually said that "international law" is composed of three types of principles and norms: (1) reactionary, bourgeois principles which have resisted the progressive forces unleashed by the Great October Revolution, (2) bourgeois democratic principles which have become more progressive under the influence of these forces, and (3) new, progressive principles introduced by the forces of socialism.[63] The commentary accompanying such statements clearly indicates that, despite the reference in the introductory language to the whole of contemporary international law, what is actually being described is "general international law," i.e., the principles subsumed under peaceful coexistence. As indicated earlier, these do not include the special principles of socialist internationalism governing relations between socialist states.[64] A somewhat different statement in mid-1964 reflects the same lack of preciseness of definition:

Contemporary international law is composed of (a) progressive international legal norms and principles created by mankind in the course of social development and (b) progressive principles sponsored by the Soviet state and other socialist states and recognized by other [i.e., nonsocialist] states.[65]

The condition that the principles sponsored by socialist states be recognized by nonsocialist states indicates that what is being discussed is general international law. The latest (1964) Soviet textbook on international law attempts to meet the problem by describing the component principles of international law as the "generally recognized principles and norms" which regulate relationships between subjects of international law on the basis of

[63] Tunkin, "The Twenty-second Congress of the CPSU," *op. cit., supra* note 10, pp. 23, 24.

[64] *Ibid.* See also Shurshalov, Review of Minasian, *op. cit., supra* note 42, p. 160, criticizing Minasian's treatment of the component parts of international law to bring it in line with Tunkin's. One of the specific errors attributed to Minasian is his inclusion of the socialist norms and principles which operate in relations between socialist states as new progressive principles introduced by socialism in general international law.

[65] *Mezhdunarodnoe Pravo, op. cit., supra* note 14, p. 16.

"peaceful coexistence, in some cases, and socialist internationalism in others."[66] This latest approach, although it suffers from the defect of purporting to claim general recognition of the principle of socialist internationalism, corrects the obvious inaccuracies of earlier formulations of "international law" by indirectly including socialist internationalism as a component principle. Actually it finesses the need to distinguish between the basic governing principles by casting the statement in terms of the totality of international relationships. The difference in formulation, however, is more cosmetic than real, for the distinction between the principles of general international law and the special principles of socialist internationalism is maintained throughout the text.[67] Although not clearly stated in all formulations, the Soviet view is that contemporary international law is composed of general international law (the principles of peaceful coexistence) and "the socialist principles and norms [which] replace in relations between countries of the world system of socialism the corresponding principles and norms of general international law."[68] Again, policy needs (e.g., to support the principle of universality and socialist internationalism as a more progressive international law) have required Soviet international legal specialists to devise new formulations of the component principles of international law in order to gloss over the essentially fragmented approach to the international legal order. Their inventiveness has produced "general international law" (the *principles* of peaceful coexistence) which is not to be confused with the *principles* of socialist internationalism or "contemporary international law" (the *law* of peaceful coexistence). Contemporary international law encompasses both general international law and the principles of socialist internationalism.

DEFINITIONS

Soviet definitions of international law have been adjusted through the years to reflect policy changes in the basic approach to the international legal order. Prior to the announcement of the policy

[66] Ushakov and Meleshko, *op. cit., supra* note 37, p. 153.
[67] *Ibid.*, p. 154.
[68] *Ibid.*

of peaceful coexistence in 1956, the standard definition of international law reflected Stalin's and Vyshinsky's emphasis upon class struggle and the use of force in international relations. (This was subsequently denounced as a distortion connected with the cult of the individual.) International law was then defined as "the aggregate of norms governing the relations between states in the course of their struggle and co-operation, reflecting the will of the ruling classes of these states and enforced by the states collectively or individually."[69] The promulgation of the new policy at the Twentieth Congress of the Communist Party of the Soviet Union and its supporting legal rationale required a change in definition to reflect the new emphasis upon negotiated settlement in lieu of force, the existence of special socialist principles of international law, and the emergence of the Soviet state of the entire people to which the concept of a ruling class is alien.[70] The following definition, reflecting the new emphasis, is standard in most Soviet commentaries:

The aggregate of norms which are established by the agreement of states, including those with different social orders; express the wills of these states; regulate their struggle and collaboration on the basis, and in the interest, of the effective maintenance of peace and peaceful coexistence; and enforced when necessary, by collective or individual state action.[71]

The reference to the agreement of states, peace and peaceful coexistence, the exceptional nature of the reliance upon force and absence of the ruling class-concept were express accommodations of the earlier Vyshinsky definition to the new policy of peaceful coexistence. Special principles governing relationships between socialist states are handled indirectly by limiting the standard definition to the "essence" of the law of peaceful coexistence (general international law) and treating separately the existence of special

[69] *Iuridicheskii Slovar'*, *op. cit.*, *supra* note 13, I, 563.

[70] Ramundo, *op. cit.*, *supra* note 1, pp. 26, 27.

[71] *Mezhdunarodnoe Pravo*, *op. cit.*, *supra* note 14, p. 8. See also Tunkin,Voprosy Teorii, *op. cit.*, *supra* note 6, p. 211; and *Entsiklopedicheskii Slovar' Pravovykh Znanii* [Encyclopedic Dictionary of Law], ed. V. M. Chkhikvadze (Moscow: Publishing House "Soviet Encyclopedia," 1965), pp. 221, 222. In 1962,Korovin defined international law as "the international code of peaceful coexistence in the sense of the competition and struggle of the two systems of socialism and capitalism by exclusively peaceful means" (*Mezhdunarodnoe Pravo* [Kozhevnikov], *op. cit.*, *supra* note 16, p. 32).

principles of socialist internationalism.[72] Apart from the incorporation of the flavor of peaceful coexistence, the definition retains much
of its earlier substance.

Some of the very recent commentaries contain variations of the
standard definition which seem to foretell the changes that may
be expected in the future. These variations relate primarily to the
omission of any reference to class struggle and the use of force in
international relations, although the existence of struggle and the
possibility of force are acknowledged elsewhere in the commentaries.
The new definitions also more fully and appealingly present the
policy of peaceful coexistence. For example, Zadorozhnyi, in his
1964 work, defines international law as the "totality of generally
recognized (in treaties or custom and legally binding on all states)
international norms and principles, which express the interests of all
mankind and prescribe an international legal order under which
mutual relations between nations and states of different social-
economic systems are maintained on the basis of the principles of
peaceful coexistence."[73] His definition incorporates the concept of
peaceful coexistence as a law serving the interests of all mankind, and
reflects the view that nations as well as states have international
legal personality. The latest Soviet textbook, said to reflect the current international legal practice of the Soviet Union, contains a new
definition of international law which follows the general pattern of
the Zadorozhnyi definition (i.e., in omitting the reference to class
struggle and the use of force) with the addition of an explicit
reference to socialist internationalism.[74] The textbook defines
international law as:

. . . those generally recognized principles and norms which regulate the many
aspects of sovereign relationships between subjects of international relations on the basis, and in the interest, of the effective maintenance of international peace, and, above all, of peaceful coexistence, on the one hand, and
socialist internationalism on the other.[75]

[72] *Ibid.*, pp. 8, 9. See also Tunkin, Voprosy Teorii, *op. cit., supra* note 6, pp.
211, 212. It is said that "in defining the essence of contemporary international
law, Soviet science proceeds from the fundamental teachings of Marxism-
Leninism" (*Mezhdunarodnoe Pravo* [Kozhevnikov], *op. cit., supra* note 16, p. 30).

[73] Zadorozhnyi, Mirnoe Sosushchestvovanie, *op. cit., supra* note 44, p. 359.

[74] Ushakov and Meleshko, *op. cit., supra* note 37, p. 153.

[75] *Mezhdunarodnoe Pravo* (Kozhevnikov), *op. cit., supra* note 16, p. 32. It is said
that the absence of the reference to force does not mean that compulsion has
disappeared from international relations. It means only that compulsion has a

The coverage of socialist internationalism reflects a basic departure from the approach since 1956 to define only general international law and treat the special socialist principles and norms separately.

These variations in the standard definition appear to herald a new one in the making since they fully reflect current Soviet emphasis upon abstention from the use of force in international relations, the reduction of the class struggle to a clash of ideologies which does not inhibit agreement in areas of common concern, increased international collaboration, and the growing importance and consequent equality of socialist relationships. Both the variations and the standard definition, however, retain the basic features of positivism as the juridical basis of international law and the subordination of the international legal order to Soviet concepts of world order. These features—in effect, consent and unilateral characterization—can be expected to remain constant in Soviet definitions of international law.

Although private international law is not specifically included under the general definition of international law, it is said to be part of it.[76] Soviet jurists are careful to note, however, that public and private international law are separate, distinct branches of international law, lest confusion on this score undermine their firm position that individuals cannot enjoy international legal personality.[77] As this study is principally concerned with Soviet positions on basic questions of public international law, it is noted only in passing that state management of the economy, especially the monopoly of foreign trade, necessarily colors Soviet thinking in drawing the line between public and private international law.[78] Similarly, new interstate relationships in the socialist commonwealth of nations which result from the requirements of international socialist division of labor under socialist internationalism affect the traditional parameters of public and private international law.[79]

---

more limited role in socialist and capitalist interrelationships and, of course, no place at all in socialist relationships.

[76] *Mezhdunarodnoe Pravo, op. cit., supra* note 14, p. 20.

[77] *Mezhdunarodnoe Pravo* (Kozhevnikov), *op. cit., supra* note 16, p. 27.

[78] See, for example, Ushakov and Meleshko's criticism of the statement "not all economic relations between states are in the field of public international law" contained in the most recent Soviet textbook on international law (Ushakov and Meleshko, *op. cit., supra* note 37, p. 154).

[79] *Mezhdunarodnoe Pravo* (Kozhevnikov), *op. cit., supra* note 16, p. 28.

->>|<<-

SUBSTANTIVE CONTENT

Because the dichotomy of peaceful coexistence and socialist internationalism is the principal feature of the Soviet approach to contemporary international law, the substantive content of these principles will be considered separately.

Peaceful Coexistence. Soviet commentators are not in complete agreement concerning the specific component principles of peaceful coexistence.[80] This lack of agreement stems from the two spheres of operation attributed to the basic principle. Peaceful coexistence is the general term which reflects all that is progressive in contemporary international law, and at the same time, the kernel of future progressive development.

The principle of peaceful coexistence . . . is a reflection in international law of the practice of the peaceful coexistence of states of the two opposing social systems. . . . It is a general summary of the development of international law after the October Revolution reflecting in a general way the changes in international law which became the law of peaceful coexistence.
The principle of peaceful coexistence assumes the presence of other important, closely related principles of international law. It expresses in general form the content of these principles but does not constitute a simple summary of them. Enriching the future development of international law, it at the same time contains the potential for a whole program of progressive development of international law, of many new principles and norms which are dictated by life and can be logically deduced from the principle of coexistence but which are still not generally recognized principles of international law.[81]

The dualism of this concept, combining law in being and law in the making, results in diverse formulations of component principles, either because of lack of agreement concerning the principles

[80] Ramundo, *op. cit.*, *supra* note 1, p. 29.

[81] G. I. Tunkin, "Printsip Mirnovo Sosushchestvovaniia—General'naia Liniia Vneshnepoliticheskoi Deiatel'nosti KPSS i Sovetskovo Gosudarstva" [The Principle of Peaceful Coexistence—The General Line of the Foreign Policy of the CPSU and the Soviet State], *SGIP*, No. 7 (1963), pp. 26–37; see 32. See also, Tunkin, Voprosy Teorii, *op. cit.*, *spura* note 6, p. 52 and Bobrov, "Mezhdunarodnoe Pravo," *op. cit.*, *supra* note 62, p. 6. This approach explains the apparent lack of logic of such statements as "Peaceful coexistence is the basic principle from which all others stem—even those which in point of time preceded it" (D. B. Levin, *Istoriia Mezhdunarodnovo Prava* [The History of International Law] [Moscow: Publishing House of the Institute of International Relations, 1962], p. 130.)

deemed to have been accepted, or the intent to enumerate "accepted" as well as desired principles.[82] This dualism also "explains the apparent anomaly of. . . Soviet formulation[s] of peaceful coexistence, in which the basic principle appears to include among its component elements the basic principle itself."[83] The potential for variation thus built into peaceful coexistence provides an element of flexibility which, although explainable ideologically in terms of the dialectics of legal development, actually and practically provides the legal basis for coping with the changing needs of foreign policy.

As will be demonstrated below, changes in the principles of peaceful coexistence are made whenever necessary to provide legal support for new policy positions.[84] Such changes are rationalized on the basis of the self-serving principle that the binding character of an international legal norm depends upon its continued compatibility with the basic principle of peaceful coexistence.[85] Soviet reasoning in the expansion of the foregoing is noteworthy because of its circularity and its potential for mischief. The law of peaceful coexistence must reflect, in Marxist terms of base and superstructure, the policy of peaceful coexistence dictated by the immutable, scientific laws of social development derivable from the basic tenets of Marxism-Leninism. Thus, either because the foreign policy of the Soviet Union presumptively is consistent with peaceful coexistence,

[82] After surveying the differing statements of the principles of peaceful coexistence, a competent Western observer concludes that "peaceful coexistence is nothing but a general term for a number of principles and rules of international law, partly already recognized partly only *de lege ferenda*" (Ivo Lapenna, "The Legal Aspects and Political Significance of the Soviet Concept of Co-existence," 12 *International and Comparative Law Quarterly* 737–777 [1963], pp. 762–765).

[83] Ramundo, *op. cit., supra* note 1, p. 26.

[84] For example, the rejection of aggressive war is said to have made possible the conversion of the political need for disarmament into a legal norm in R. L. Bobrov and S. A. Malinin, Review of O. V. Bogdanov, *Vseobschee i Polnoe Razoruzhenie (Mezhdunarodnopravovye Voprosy)* [General and Complete Disarmament (International Legal Problems)] (Moscow: Publishing House "International Relations," 1964), *SGIP*, No. 8 (1964), pp. 152–154; see 152).

[85] Y. Korovin "International Law Today," *International Affairs*, No. 7 (1962), pp. 18–22; see 19 and 21. Fel'dman holds that all norms which are inconsistent with peaceful coexistence have no juridical force—only those which serve to strengthen and develop peaceful coexistence further have such force. (Fel'dman, *op. cit., supra* note 19, p. 238.)

or because the Communist Party of the Soviet Union enjoys papal-like authority in interpreting the basic laws of social development when formulating Soviet policy, the basis is laid for an international legal order responsive to the policy needs of the Soviet Union.[86]

Soviet statements of the principles of peaceful coexistence generally are based upon the *Pancha Shila*, or five principles contained in the Sino-Indian Agreement of 1954 concerning Tibet: (1) mutual respect for territorial integrity and sovereignty, (2) nonaggression, (3) noninterference in internal affairs, (4) equality and mutual benefit, and (5) peaceful coexistence.[87] The formulations of other component principles of peaceful coexistence differ to such an extent that a Soviet international legal specialist commented in 1963: "there is no agreement in Soviet literature as to the number and identity of the basic principles of international law."[88] Soviet jurists still appear to be groping for a definitive statement of the component principles of peaceful coexistence.

In 1962 Tunkin enumerated the following as "new principles of peaceful coexistence": peaceful settlement of disputes, self-determination of nations, disarmament, and prohibition of propaganda for war.[89] Other Soviet commentators add such principles as "the equality of the socialist and capitalist systems," "the illegality of colonialism," "the inviolability of diplomatic representatives," and "freedom of the high seas."[90] One 1964 Soviet commentary redundantly enumerates fifteen generally-recognized principles of peaceful coexistence.[91] Although this enumeration depends upon the *Pancha*

[86] See Tunkin, Voprosy Teorii, *op. cit.*, *supra* note 6, pp. 8, 9; Bobrov, Mezhdunarodnoe Pravo, *op. cit.*, *supra* note 62, p. 4; and P. N. Demichev, "Leninism Is the Scientific Foundation of the Party's Policy," trans. from *Pravda* (April 23, 1965), in *CDSP*, XVII, No. 17, pp. 3–8.

[87] Lapenna, "Legal Aspects of Co-existence," *op. cit.*, *supra* note 82, pp. 759–761. See also *Mezhdunarodnoe Pravo*, *op. cit.*, *supra* note 14, pp. 58, 59. McWhinney characterizes these as the "five *primary* principles of peaceful coexistence." (McWhinney, *op. cit.*, *supra* note 6, pp. 33, 34.) In *Mezhdunarodnoe Pravo* they are described as "the five principles of peaceful coexistence" (p. 59).

[88] R. L. Bobrov, Review of G. I. Tunkin, *Voprosy Teorii Mezhdunarodnovo Prava* [Problems of the Theory of International Law] (Moscow: State Publishing House of Legal Literature, 1962), *SGIP*, No. 5 (1963), pp. 167–170; see 169.

[89] Tunkin, Voprosy Teorii, *op. cit.*, *supra* note 6, pp. 26–65.

[90] Ramundo, *op. cit.*, *supra* note 1, p. 29.

[91] Zadorozhnyi, Mirnoe Sosushchestvovanie, *op. cit.*, *supra* note 44, pp. 399–402.

Shila and other principles of peaceful coexistence for the derivation of "additional" principles, it does include some noteworthy principles not contained in other formulations. Those are the illegality of regional and collective security arrangements not compatible with the Charter of the United Nations (e.g., Western military blocs); "the illegality of the arms race"; unity of action and unanimity of the permanent members of the Security Council in maintaining peace and security; and "active collaboration of the states of the two systems to eliminate all that interferes with peaceful coexistence."[92] Another Soviet commentary of the year 1964 augments the *Pancha Shila* with only the following principles: peaceful settlement of disputes, self-determination of nations, and disarmament.[93]

Still undefined, the component principles of peaceful coexistence are said to supplement the democratic principles of traditional international law (i.e., those which support the peaceful coexistence of states with different social systems) to form general international law.[94] The indefinite criterion, "democratic," used to describe the principles of traditional international law included under peaceful coexistence, adds another element of uncertainty to the over-all formulation of coexistence. The Soviet view that the law of peaceful coexistence operates differently in relations between socialist and newly independent "neutralist" states (allegedly because of their community of interests in peace and socialism) than it does in relations between capitalist states and between capitalist and socialist states further contributes to the unclear situation.[95]

In spite of the absence of a definitive formulation, the Soviets are seeking codification of the law of peaceful coexistence in various international forums.[96] They claim that near-universal adherence to the Charter of the United Nations reflects general acceptance of

[92] *Ibid.*

[93] *Mezhdunarodnoe Pravo, op. cit., supra* note 14, pp. 59, 60.

[94] Tunkin, Voprosy Teorii, *op. cit., supra* note 6, pp. 63–65.

[95] *Ibid.*, p. 316.

[96] John N. Hazard has recorded the problems of codification of the principles of peaceful coexistence in "Legal Research on 'Peaceful Coexistence,'" 51 *American Journal of International Law* (hereafter cited as *AJIL*), 63–71 (1957); "Codifying Peaceful Co-existence," 55 *AJIL* 109–120 (1961); and "Coexistence Codification Reconsidered," 57 *AJIL* 88–97 (1963); see also McWhinney, *op. cit., supra* note 6, p. 36.

the principle of coexistence, leaving codification as the sole remaining task. An intensive propaganda effort to demonstrate world opinion in support of peace, national liberation, and disarmament, the keystones of the policy of peaceful coexistence, has been mounted to obtain Western acquiescence in the effort to codify this law.[97] The West tends to reject peaceful coexistence as the basis for a meaningful normative system and to treat it as a political slogan, "a powerful instrument of Soviet foreign policy widely utilized for fortifying the position of the Soviet Union in the world and for promoting Soviet interests in general."[98]

Socialist Internationalism. In the Soviet view, relationships between socialist states have progressed beyond the minimum collaboration required under peaceful coexistence.[99] United in a commonwealth based upon a community of political, social, and economic aims, these states are said to be subjects of a new, higher type of fraternal international relations.[100] These relations are regulated by the new socialist legal principles and norms encompassed by socialist internationalism, "the juridical expression of the international collabora-

[97] See, for example, Soviet coverage of the Helsinki World Congress for Peace, National Independence, and General Disarmament (July 10–15, 1965) (V. Chkhikvadze, "Outlook for the Peace Movement," *New Times*, No. 27 [July 7, 1965], pp. 1–3; "Helsinki: A Great Movement of our Time," *Moscow News*, No. 28 [July 10, 1965], pp. 3 and 7; "Forum Narodov Otkryt" [The Peoples' Forum Has Opened], *Pravda* [July 11, 1965] pp. 1 and 4) and the Havana Tricontinental Conference (January 3–15, 1966) of the "hundreds of people whose lifework is the fight against imperialism and colonialism" (D. Volsky, "Tricontinental Conference," *New Times*, No. 52 [December 27, 1965] pp. 3, 4; see 3; T. Gaidar and Iu. Pogosov, "Solidarnost' Bortsov Trekh Kontinentov" [Solidarity of the Fighters of Three Continents], *Pravda* [January 5, 1966], pp. 1 and 4; Latif Maksudov, "Havana Forum of Unity," *Moscow News*, No. 5 [January 29, 1966], p. 3; and Yuri Bochkaryov, "Three Continent Organization," *New Times*, No. 4 [January 26, 1966], pp. 4, 5).
[98] Lapenna, "Legal Aspects of Co-existence," *op. cit., supra* note 82, p. 774. Lapenna suggests the following as the Soviet ends sought to be achieved:

". . .(i) popularity because of the strong appeal of the idea of peace; (ii) attaining political maxima in foreign policy without being involved in a world war; (iii) further internal development of the Soviet Union for which a long period of peace is an essential condition." (*Ibid.*)

[99] V. M. Shurshalov, "Mezhdunarodno-pravovye Printsipy Sotrudnichestva Sotsialisticheskikh Gosudarstv" [International Legal Principles of the Collaboration of Socialist States], *SGIP*, No. 7 (1962), pp. 95–105; see 96, 97.
[100] Ushakov and Meleshko, *op. cit., supra* note 37, p. 154.

tion of socialist states. . . . in the struggle for the victory of socialism and communism."[101] General international law operates in the relations between socialist states only to the limited extent that it has not been replaced by socialist internationalism and the socialist principles and norms subsumed under it. Even where general international law is operative it reflects, at the very least, the "new spirit" of the guiding principle of socialist internationalism.[102] The "new spirit" is said to impart to general international law a special socialist content which makes possible the applicability of that law to the higher relationships within the commonwealth.

The legal principles and norms which govern socialist relationships are described as (1) new socialist principles "arising from the base of socialism" and (2) general democratic principles "which, in the setting of the socialist commonwealth, are not only more fully and consistently observed but also acquire a new content in the process of their application."[103] The basic principle, socialist internationalism, is vaguely stated as follows:

> . . . the comradely reciprocal assistance of socialist countries in many different activities . . . fraternal friendship, the voluntary combining of forces in the cause of building socialism and communism, genuine equality with no country enjoying or being able to enjoy special rights or privileges, the impermissibility of any forms of compulsion, a community of vital interests and unity of purpose in the common struggle for the building of communism and general peace and security of nations.[104]

The principle is said to serve both the national interest of socialist states as well as their common interest in the building of communism: "Socialist internationalism has two aspects: on the one hand, recognition and upholding the equality, freedom, and independence of socialist states and nations; on the other, recognition and upholding of the need for their unity, friendship, and mutual

[101] E. T. Usenko, "Osnovnye Mezhdunarodnopravovye Printsipy Sotrudnichestva Sotsialisticheskikh Gosudarstv" [The Basic International Legal Principles of the Collaboration of Socialist States], *SGIP*, No. 3 (1961), pp.16–29; see 29. See also Tunkin, Voprosy Teorii, *op. cit., supra* note 6, pp. 311–313.

[102] Tunkin, Voprosy Teorii, *op. cit., supra* note 6, pp. 326, 327. See also *Mezhdunarodnoe Pravo* (Kozhevnikov) *op. cit., supra* note 16, pp. 106–117.

[103] Shurshalov, Mezhdunarodno-pravovye Printispy, *op. cit., supra* note 99, p. 95. See also Usenko, *op. cit., supra* note 101, p. 27.

[104] *Ibid.*, pp. 96, 97.

assistance in the struggle for the victory of socialism and communism."[105] Yet, Tunkin notes the primacy of common interest in stating that the principle of socialist internationalism "includes, above all, fraternal friendship, close collaboration, and mutual assistance" in all aspects of international relations.[106] Other commentators confirm that implicit in socialist internationalism are the requirements that (1) "national interests, on occasion . . . be subordinated to more important, international interests of the whole socialist commonwealth"; (2) "the new *function* . . . of each socialist state of fraternal friendship, sincere collaboration, and unselfish, reciprocal assistance" be discharged; and (3) "state sovereignty must be exercised with consideration of the general interests of the entire socialist camp as well as the national interest."[107] Also, "in its international legal aspect, the principle of socialist internationalism means the obligation of each socialist state to collaborate with other socialist states in the struggle against imperialism and in the cause of socialist and communist construction."[108]

There is no single formulation of the component principles of socialist internationalism. Tunkin notes that the principles of respect for sovereignty, noninterference in internal affairs, and equality of states have a new socialist content as a result of the influence of socialist internationalism and, therefore, have become new socialist principles.[109] A commentary in 1964 formulates the component principles of socialist internationalism as "voluntary association, equality, sovereignty, noninterference in internal affairs, respect for territorial integrity, mutual advantage, and comradely mutual

[105] *Mezhdunarodnoe pravo, op. cit., supra* note 14, p. 64.

[106] Tunkin, Voprosy Teorii, *op. cit., supra* note 6, pp. 319, 320–322.

[107] Shurshalov, Mezhdunarodno-pravovye Printsipy, *op. cit., supra* note 99, pp. 96 and 103. The use of the word "function" appears to complement the reduced emphasis upon national interest in the formulation of socialist internationalism. ". . . the principles of socialist internationalism make possible the harmonious combination of the interests of the whole socialist commonwealth and the national interests of the member states." (Tunkin, Voprosy Teorii, *op. cit., supra* note 6, p. 323.)

[108] *Mezhdunarodnoe Pravo, op. cit., supra* note 14, p. 64.

[109] Tunkin, Voprosy Teorii, *op. cit., supra* note 6, pp. 316 and 319. For example, in the economic field, the essence of this socialist content is the "combining of national interests with those of the entire socialist system."

assistance.''[110] This commentary accepts Tunkin's view that democratic principles of general international law changed under the progressive influence of socialist internationalism should be treated as new principles of international law (i.e., component principles of socialist internationalism).[111] Shurshalov, another Soviet international legal specialist, rejects the characterization of democratic principles influenced by socialist internationalism as new socialist principles in an attempt to safeguard the concept of the universality of international law.[112] His concern in this area appears to be a bit belated in view of the fact that recognition of the existence of special principles of socialist internationalism is sufficient, of itself, to undermine the unity of the international legal order. The fact that more or fewer principles are included under socialist internationalism is of little significance in the preservation of the universality concept. Shurshalov lists (1) everlasting, permanent peace, (2) popular (i.e., serving the true interests of the people) character of international legal norms, and (3) the leading and directing role of the communist and workers' parties in the development of relations of a new type, as the new socialist principles included under socialist internationalism.[113]

The Soviets have also failed to arrive at a definitive formulation of socialist internationalism because they are attempting to create a normative system—in this case for members of the socialist camp—which by its very nature and purpose cannot be specific in content. This effort, paralleling that of the campaign for peaceful coexistence, is to create the concept of a general legal obligation to serve the

[110] *Mezhdunarodnoe Pravo, op. cit., supra* note 14, p. 65. A detailed discussion of these principles follows on pages 66–76.

[111] *Ibid.*, pp. 76, 77. It is said that these democratic principles under peaceful coexistence serve only to ensure peace amongst nations—under socialist internationalism, they go further to ensure "the closest collaboration of socialist states in the cause of building a new society." Further on, it is noted that observance of socialist internationalism, *ipso facto*, includes compliance with the lesser requirements of peaceful coexistence.

[112] Shurshalov, Mezhdunarodno-pravovye Printsipy, *op. cit., supra* note 99, p. 102. See discussion of Soviet divergence of views on this point in Ramundo, *op. cit., supra* note 1, pp. 37–41.

[113] *Ibid.*, 98, 100. See Ramundo, *op. cit., supra* note 1, pp. 34–37, for a discussion of these principles.

changing needs of the common or "public" weal as defined by the Soviet Union. In effect, socialist internationalism is expected to provide a legal basis for the unity of effort said to be required for the world victory of socialism. The Soviet Union regularly issues clarion calls for socialist unity in an effort to obtain support for its policy goals within the camp, without the need to rely upon great power restraint upon the pursuit of national goals by client states. As a substitute for a more traditional means, socialist internationalism is a convenient, cosmetic device for ordering intracamp relationships in the name of a common, as distinguished from national, interest. In this sense, the effort to convert socialist internationalism into an effective normative principle represents the maximum Soviet legal position in its relations with socialist states. Despite idealization of relationships within the socialist commonwealth and, in Marxist terms, the absence of the root cause of antagonism and the existence of a community of interest, polycentric tendencies resulting from increased emphasis upon national interest indicate that realization of the Soviet maximum position will be increasingly difficult.

Soviet proponency of peaceful coexistence and socialist internationalism as the fundamental principles of contemporary international law has not produced a normative system. More political than legal, these principles have been resisted in the West and are generating resistance in the socialist commonwealth because they are considered to be devoid of meaningful, substantive content, except, perhaps, "to provide license for Soviet freedom of action in . . . relations with members of the capitalist and socialist camps."[114] The basic Soviet approach to view the function and purpose of international law as an adjunct of foreign policy confirms the view that peaceful coexistence and socialist internationalism were formulated to provide such license.[115]

[114] Ramundo, op. cit., supra note 1, p. 57.

[115] "It has been correctly suggested that the Soviet Union fundamentally prefers two distinct sets of law and two models of international behavior—one for the orbit it seeks to control, the other for the outside world it does not control." (Alexander Dallin, *The Soviet Union at the United Nations* [An Inquiry into Soviet Motives and Objectives] [New York: Praeger, 1962], p. 8.)

⇢⟩⟩⟨⟨⟨

RELATIONSHIP TO DOMESTIC LAW

The Soviets reject both the dualist and monist approaches to the relationship between international and domestic law.[116] The former approach is said to be disruptive of the international legal order because, in recognizing the equality of the two bodies of law, it overemphasizes the freedom of states to enact domestic law without regard to the requirements of international law. The latter is objected to because, in according pre-eminence to international law, it infringes upon state sovereignty and the conduct of internal affairs.[117]

Although not going into a critical detailed discussion of both tendencies in bourgeois science [of international law] we only note that, while the dualist theory to a certain extent reflects international practice, it overly stresses the formal legal aspect of the matter and ignores the actual interrelationship between international and domestic law. The theory of the primacy of international law [monism] grossly distorts reality in the interest of imperialist circles who seek, under color of this theory, a basis for political and economic hegemony and interference in the internal affairs of other states.

The socialist science of international law criticizes the juridical dogmatism of the "dualists" and resolutely condemns the anti-scientific and reactionary schemes of the "monists."[118]

The third possibility, the primacy of domestic over international law, attributed to German writers of the Nazi era and to Vyshinsky, is roundly condemned because it negates the existence of an international legal order to which the Soviet Union is strongly committed as a necessary concomitant of its proponency of the law of peaceful

[116] D. B. Levin, "Problema Sootnosheniia Mezhdunarodnovo i Vnutrigosudarstvennovo Prava" [The Problem of the Relationship between International and Domestic Law], *SGIP*, No. 7 (1964), pp. 86–95; see 86, 87.

[117] *International Law, op. cit., supra* note 47, p. 14.

[118] Levin, Problema Sootnosheniia, *op. cit., supra* note 116, pp. 86, 87. But cf. V. I. Lisovskii, *Mezhdunarodnoe Pravo* [International Law] (2d ed.; Moscow: State Publishing House "Higher School," 1961), p. 7, where, in apparent agreement with the dualist theory, it is said that "international and domestic law are separate and independent bodies of law."

coexistence. This possibility is dismissed as another legal distortion produced by the cult of the individual.[119]

International and domestic law are of equal juridical significance in the Soviet view—they must not "contradict each other or have primacy one over the other."[120] There is, however, an indivisible link between them in the form of the international obligation to conform, as necessary, domestic legislation to international legal norms to which consent has been given. The Soviet view only slightly modifies the dualist approach by the addition of the obligation to implement domestically international principles and norms. This modification complements the greater deference to international law in support of the policy of peaceful coexistence.[121] It does not, however, unduly restrict Soviet sovereign prerogatives as is apparent from the following rationale:

---

[119] *International Law, op. cit., supra* note 47, p. 14; *Mezhdunarodnoe Pravo, op. cit., supra* note 14, p. 10; and E. Korvin, "Likvidirovat' Posledstviia Kul'ta Lichnosti v Nauke Mezhdunarodnovo Prava" [Eliminate the Consequences of the Cult of the Individual in the Science of International Law], *Sotsialisticheskaia Zakonnost'* [Socialist Legality], No. 8 (1962), pp. 46–49; see 48.

"The Soviet concept of the relationship of an international treaty and a national law differs from the concept of the bourgeois doctrine of international law. It denies both the theory of primacy of an international treaty over a national law and the theory of primacy of a national law over an international treaty, because both of them do not correspond to the actual correlation of force of a treaty and a law. Moreover, ultimately both theories lead to the negation of a prime principle of international and national law, the principle of state sovereignty." (N. V. Mironov, "Sootnoshenie Mezhdunarodnovo Dogovora i Vnutrigosudarstvennovo Zakona" [The Relationship Between an International Agreement and Domestic Law], *Sovetskii Ezhegodnik, 1965, op. cit., supra* note 28, pp. 150–170; see 169.)

[120] *International Law, op. cit., supra* note 47, p. 15. See also Mirnov, *op. cit., supra* note 119, p. 157.

[121] Korovin, Likvidirovat' Posledstviia, *op. cit., supra* note 119, p. 48.

". . .The Soviet position is by no means a mere reproduction of the dualistic theory which proclaims the legal equality of a treaty and a law in the way this theory is usually understood by the bourgeois doctrine which recognizes the principle of division of authority and the absence of any connection and interdependence between a treaty and a law." (Mironov, *op. cit., supra* note 119, p. 170.)

Every state is bound to implement its international obligations domestically, but the manner or method of implementation is a matter of sovereign prerogative.

. . . .

A state must ensure fulfillment of its international legal obligations by means suited to it. If legislative measures are necessary, they must be taken. Of course, those measures must take account of the peculiar social and political order of every state. This principle is especially important under conditions of the coexistence of states with two antagonistic social systems.[122]

The ambivalence of the Soviet position is reflected in the statement that "socialist states stoutly support observance of the norms of international law, but firmly reject the use of reference to international law as a means of negating state sovereignty."[123]

The three basic methods of reference, reception, and transformation are recognized as techniques of domestic implementation of international law.[124] Although transformation provides the maximum flexibility and is said to be the general practice, the Soviets do not accept the view of some Western writers that it is the best or only method.[125] For greater flexibility, they endorse the method which best suits a given situation.[126] "States must have at their disposal all methods and use them in accordance with the demands of their state policy."[127]

[122] Levin, Problema Sootnosheniia, *op. cit.*, *supra* note 116, at 92 quoting Tunkin.

[123] *Ibid.*, p. 95.

[124] As understood by the Soviets, in "reference," implementing domestic legislation is enacted based upon the existence of international legal principles and norms; in "reception," the international legal norm is accepted as a part of domestic law without the need of domestic legislation; and in "transformation," the international norm is converted into domestic law by a special enactment which may change the substantive content of the former (*Ibid.*, p. 93). Cf. Usenko's view of transformation (i.e., ratification of an agreement *ipso facto* gives it domestic legal force) which, in effect, is equated to reception. See the criticism of this view in L. A. Lunts, "Ob Odnoi iz Vazhneishikh Problem Mezhdunarodnovo Prava" [Concerning One of the Most Important Problems of International Law], Review of E. T. Usenko, *Formy Regulirovaniia Sotsialisticheskovo Mezhdunarodnovo Razdeleniia Truda* [Methods of Regulating Socialist International Division of Labor] (Moscow: Publishing House "International Relations," 1965), *SGIP*, No. 8 (1965), pp. 136, 137; see 137.

[125] *Ibid.*

[126] *Ibid.*

[127] *Ibid.*

-»»«⟨-

In at least one area, the Soviets have apparently limited their freedom of action. Article 129 of the Fundamental Principles of Civil Legislation for the U.S.S.R. and the Union Republics and corresponding Article 64 of the Principles of Civil Legal Procedure provide that treaties or international agreements establishing regulations in conflict with the civil legislation and procedure of the U.S.S.R. and the Union Republics supersede the latter and are effective as domestic law.[128] The existence of these articles is said to attest "to the Soviet Union's loyalty [*sic*] to the international obligations it assumes."[129] There is, however, a compensating, inherent flexibility in the domestic legal order under the principle of "socialist legality," which mitigates the effect of the commitment to give pre-eminence to those treaties and agreements which conflict with Soviet civil law and procedure. As the overriding principle in domestic law, "socialist legality" ensures that law is administered consonant with the policy of the Communist Party in directing the building of communism. The Civil Code reflects the primacy of this principle as follows: "Civil law rights are protected by law except where their enjoyment contradicts the purpose of these rights in a socialist society building communism."[130] As legislation must give way before this overriding principle, so too must treaty provisions which would otherwise have full force and effect as domestic law. The domestic operation of "socialist legality" is of special interest in the context of the Soviet campaign to gain acceptance of peaceful coexistence and socialist internationalism as overriding international principles, because it demonstrates a penchant for institutionalized flexibility in bending law to the needs of policy.

In the absence of legislative provisions similar to those in the Civil and Civil Procedural Codes, it is not entirely clear whether a treaty norm takes precedence over inconsistent domestic law. Soviet jurists are split on the extent of the formalities necessary to

[128] T. P. Grevtsova, "Mezhdunarodnyi Dogovor v Sisteme Istochnikov Sovetskovo Vnutrigosudarstvennovo Prava" [International Agreements as Sources of Soviet Domestic Law], *Sovetskii Ezhegodnik*, 1963, *op. cit., supra* note 28, pp. 171–179; see 179.

[129] *Ibid.*

[130] *Grazhdanskii Kodeks, RSFSR* [Civil Code of the RSFSR] (Moscow: Publishing House "Legal Literature," 1964), Art. 5, p. 8.

supersede inconsistent domestic legislation. The majority view is said to be that upon ratification and publication a treaty becomes effective as domestic law and supersedes existing inconsistent law.[131] Under the minority view, ratification and publication must be followed by a special legislative or governmental act before a treaty norm can be effective as domestic law and, therefore, affect inconsistent law.[132] All Soviet jurists agree, however, that subsequent, inconsistent domestic legislation takes precedence over extant treaty norms. In cases of tug-of-war between international and domestic law, the former is expected to provide the "give" factor:

> If a conflict between norms of international and domestic law cannot be satisfactorily resolved on the basis of the provisions of domestic law and with the assistance of methods contemplated by it, then its resolution must be sought in the international sphere with resort to those methods by which international disputes are usually settled, i.e., diplomatic negotiations, agreements, mediation, arbitration and the court [International Court of Justice].[133]

It is said that there is less possibility of conflict between international and domestic law in a socialist state because, with the absence of the separation of powers or other divisive institutional framework, the unity of government power ensures greater consistency in external and internal policy.[134] Moreover, the harmony in relations between socialist states tends to minimize these conflicts, as it

---

[131] Grevtsova, *op. cit.*, *supra* note 128, pp. 172, 173. See also Jan F. Triska and Robert M. Slusser, *The Theory, Law and Policy of Soviet Treaties* (Stanford, California: Stanford University Press, 1962), pp. 106–111.

[132] Mironov, *op. cit.*, *supra* note 119, p. 158, where it is said:

> Soviet law does not hold that an international agreement automatically is converted into domestic law. Even a ratified agreement which has been published in an official publication does not *ipso facto* become domestic law in the U.S.S.R. It can have that effect only after the publication of an appropriate legislative act transforming the norms of the agreement into domestic law. Soviet socialist law does not recognize the *general transformation* of norms of agreements into domestic law. Transformation occurs only as a result of special legislative or governmental acts.

The minority view makes for greater certainty as the requirement for special legislative or governmental action avoids the problem of implied repeal or modification of existing legislation.

[133] Levin, Problema Sootnosheniia, *op. cit.*, *supra* note 116, p. 95.

[134] *Ibid.*, pp. 93, 94.

is claimed that the character of international relations directly affects the extent of conflict between international and domestic norms. "Socialist internationalism and socialist democracy which permeate these [socialist] relations ensure the harmony of internal needs and interests of each state and common international interests."[135] The implication here is that the conflict between international and domestic law is a problem only because of the governmental practice of capitalist states and the existence of international class struggle.

The Soviets claim that under the law of peaceful coexistence the need for flexibility in the domestic implementation of international norms is greater than before because the states of both systems must not be inhibited in the struggle to demonstrate system supremacy. In taking formal, rather than substantive, issue with the dualists, the Soviets effectively preserve maximum freedom of state action without sacrificing their commitment to the need for a strengthened international legal order as part of the proponency of peaceful coexistence. In stating their position, Soviet commentators inject the familiar propaganda themes of defects in the capitalist world versus an idealized socialist commonwealth.

[135] *Ibid.*, p. 95.

CHAPTER THREE

SOURCES OF INTERNATIONAL LAW

The Soviet Union is a party to the Statute of the International Court of Justice, and presumptively is bound by the traditional sources of international law enumerated in Article 38: treaties, international custom, and general principles of law. Notwithstanding Article 38, however, there is, under the Soviet view, a single source of all international legal norms—the agreement of states. This view limits the formal sources of international law to treaties, where agreement of the parties is express, and to those customary principles which have been agreed to (i.e., the "tacit agreement" theory) and, then, only as to states which have agreed and so long as they continue to agree.[1] Treaties are considered the principal source of international law, favored over customary norms because of the unambiguous character of the consent of the signatory states.[2] The broader coverage of Article 38 of the Statute of the International Court of Justice is explained on the ground that it enumerates legal principles to be applied by the Court, and not the sources of international law.[3]

[1] It is said that the key element in the binding nature of international custom is the consent of the state concerned. *Mezhdunarodnoe Pravo* [International Law], ed. D. B. Levin and G. P. Kaliuzhnaia (Moscow: Publishing House "Legal Literature," 1964), p. 19.

[2] *Ibid.*, pp. 19 and 79, and *International Law* (Moscow: Foreign Languages Publishing House, n.d.), pp. 247, 248.

[3] *International Law, op. cit., supra* note 2, p. 12. See also P. I. Lukin, *Istochniki Mezhdunarodnovo Prava* [Sources of International Law] (Moscow: Publishing House of the Academy of Sciences of the U.S.S.R., 1960), pp. 52–55.

->>><<<-

The Soviets distinguish between man-made, formal, international law resulting from the agreement of states, and a higher law, the scientifically correct laws of social development derivable from Marxism-Leninism. The latter, reflected in the material conditions of society, is said to be the substantive basis of law; the former, the juridical forms (i.e., treaty and customary norms) which correspond to those conditions. In the Soviet view, valid man-made law, as part of the superstructure, must be compatible with the social base resulting from the operation of the laws of social development.[4] The invocation of a higher law serves many purposes. Apart from paying lip-service to ideology and giving greater credibility to the law of peaceful coexistence, the higher law based upon Marxism-Leninism provides a more fundamental basis than the law of man for flexibility vis-à-vis the international legal order. Although the Soviets reject the Western concept of natural law, they appear to embrace the mechanics of that concept with an appropriate substitution to provide for the unhampered pursuit of foreign policy objectives. The Soviet effort to control the international legal order would be considerably more complicated if the higher law were not socialist in character.

The laws of social development are relied upon to support the whole system of the law of peaceful coexistence, and to provide flexibility within that system. These laws prescribe that the present epoch is that of the peaceful coexistence of socialist and capitalist states, thereby requiring contemporary international law to be the law of peaceful coexistence.[5]

The special fundamental juridical force of these principles [of peaceful coexistence] is their compatibility with the objective requirements of international relations, and especially the objective requirements for the ensuring of peaceful coexistence.[6]

---

[4] *Mezhdunarodnoe Pravo* [International Law], ed. F. I. Kozhevnikov (Moscow: Publishing House "International Relations," 1964), p. 41.

[5] G. I. Tunkin, "Organizatisiia Ob'edinennykh Natsii: 1945–1965 (Mezhdunarodnopravovye Problemy)" [The United Nations: 1945–1965 (International Legal Problems)], *SGIP*, No. 10 (1965), pp. 58–68; see 60, 61.

[6] *Mezhdunarodnoe Pravo* (Kozhevnikov), *op. cit., supra* note 4, p. 46.

→»)«←

Similarly, individual basic laws derivable from the laws of social development (e.g., respect for sovereignty, national liberation, and the illegality of colonialism) are invoked as the basis for judging man-made international law resulting from the agreement of states.[7] In relying upon the existence of basic laws, Soviet jurists have developed their own concept of *jus cogens* (i.e., the fundamental nature of certain norms, the possibility of the misuse or abuse of fundamental norms, and the inherent illegality of other norms) which is unaffected by the agreement of states "in the sense that two states or any group of states cannot affect [by agreement] . . . [its] applicability to their mutual relations."[8] Paradoxically, the content of the *jus cogens* is said to be established through the agreement of states.

. . .in contemporary international law there are norms and principles of an imperative character, arising from the agreement of states, the operation of which cannot be affected by the local [local'nyi] agreement of these states.

The presence of imperative norms in no way interferes with the progressive development of international law. They do not bar the creation of new norms which go further than old ones in the direction of securing peace and friendly relations among states.[9]

In international law there are generally binding norms which cannot be violated or changed by individual states in their agreements. There is a *jus cogens* (a generally binding law). But the generally recognized norms which should be observed by all states are not eternal. They can be changed by the wills of all states. But as long as they exist, treaties must not violate them. Treaty norms which contradict the generally binding norms have no legal force. Such generally binding norms are the basic principles of international law.[10]

---

[7] G. P. Zadorozhnyi, *Mirnoe Sosushchestvovanie i Mezhdunarodnoe Pravo* [Peaceful Coexistence and International Law] (Moscow: Publishing House "International Relations," 1964), pp. 365, 366.

[8] G. I. Tunkin and B. I. Nechaev, "Pravo Dogovorov na XV Sessii Komissii Mezhdunarodnovo Prava OON," [The Law of Treaties at the 15th Session of the International Law Commission of the U.N.], *SGIP*, No. 2 (1964), pp. 84–92; see 87–88. The misuse of international law is actually the domestic concept of abuse of law. It is conceded that the "concept still has not received sufficient [international law] definition and even is in dispute." (*Mezhdunarodnoe Pravo* [Kozhevnikov], *op. cit., supra* note 4, p. 53.)

[9] G. I. Tunkin, *Voprosy Teorii Mezhdunarodnovo Prava* [Problems of the Theory of International Law] (Moscow: State Publishing House of Legal Literature, 1962), p. 120.

[10] Lukin, *op. cit., supra* note 3, p. 75.

The Soviet assertion that the agreement theory of norm formulation applies to the imperative norms is misleading, because it conveniently leaves unstated the underlying position that certain fundamental legal principles exist a priori in every historical period by the mandate of social development. The imperative norms of the present epoch are said to be the principles of peaceful coexistence, with codification and the progressive development of these principles the only matters left for the agreement of states. Thus, the Soviet Union has a basis for claiming the existence of the law of peaceful coexistence in spite of its rejection by Western states as an effort to transform "international law into a body of communist principles which will serve as important weapons in waging peaceful coexistence."[11]

Although the Soviet Union continues to seek consent as the best practical means of ensuring observance of the principles of peaceful coexistence, it has in the concept of *jus cogens* a means of obviating the need for capitalist consent through the claim that these principles exist a priori. *Jus cogens* also provides the basis for claiming the effectiveness of new fundamental principles which are not acceptable to capitalist states. On the other hand, unpalatable new principles or changes in existing principles can be resisted on the basis that the consent of a majority of states of both systems is a necessary precondition for agreements which change fundamental principles. The Soviets protect themselves against a similar nullification of socialist consent by rejecting natural law and other nonsocialist *jus cogens* bases for international law. In effect, the Soviet concept of *jus cogens* provides the Soviet Union with a convenient lever of flexibility against its own formulation that the agreement of states is the single source of international law.

THE AGREEMENT OF STATES

The agreement theory of international norm formulation, including customary rules,[12] reflects emphasis upon negotiation and

[11] Summary of Robert Crane's remarks in *Soviet Impact on International Law* [External Research Paper 156] (Washington, D.C.: U.S. Department of State, Bureau of Intelligence and Research, May 1964), p. 2.

[12] G. I. Tunkin, "Remarks on the Juridical Nature of Customary Norms of International Law," 49 *California Law Review* 419–439 (1961), pp. 423, 428, and 430.

compromise in the peaceful coexistence formulation. Recognition of the possibility of agreement between the two camps is actually premised upon interdependence and the existence of "certain general (coinciding) interests" which transcend ideological differences.

When States agree on recognition of this or that norm as a norm of international law they do not agree on problems of ideology. They do not try to agree on such problems, for instance, as what is international law, what is its social foundation, its sources. . . . They do agree on rules of conduct. . . . So States may profoundly disagree as to the nature of norms of international law, but this disagreement does not create an insurmountable obstacle to reaching an agreement relating to accepting specific rules as norms of international law.[13] . . . in solving problems of consent in contemporary international law one should take into account that: (1) the social class conflict of states does not in any way preclude certain general (coinciding) interests in the sphere of interstate relations; (2) the necessity of peaceful coexistence of the socialist and capitalist systems dictates the necessity of certain compromises. And this applies equally to the formulation of international legal norms as well as to the resolution, on the basis thereof, of disputes between states.[14]

Agreement and compromise in the international class struggle are said to be possible only if the contending parties are sovereign equals. International inequality resulting in an exploitative relationship precludes agreement and compromise as is the case in the class struggle within a single country:[15]

. . .contemporary international law requires that agreements be freely entered into with full observance of the legal equality of all parties. Unequal

---

[13] Edward McWhinney, "Peaceful Coexistence and Soviet-Western International Law," 56 *A.J.I.L.* 951–970 (1962); see 962, quoting Tunkin in his Hague lectures of 1958. See also, to the same effect, G. Tunkin, "The Soviet Union and International Law," *International Affairs*, No. 11 (1959), pp. 40–45; see 40; and Tunkin, Voprosy Teorii, *op. cit., supra* note 9, pp. 6–7.

[14] R. L. Bobrov, Review of G. I. Tunkin, *Voprosy Teorii Mezhdunarodnovo Prava* [Problems of the Theory of International Law] (Moscow: State Publishing House of Legal Literature, 1962), *SGIP*, No. 5 (1963), pp. 167–170; see 169. See also V. M. Shurshalov, Review of N. M. Minasian, *Sushchnost' Sovremennovo Mezhdunarodnovo Prava* [The Essence of Contemporary International Law] (Rostov: Publishing House of Rostov State University, 1962), *SGIP*, No. 5 (1964), pp. 158–160; see 158.

[15] Shurshalov, Review of Minasian, *op. cit., supra* note 14, p. 158.

treaties in which these principles are not observed contravene the basic principles of international law.[16]

Thus, the peaceful coexistence of socialist and capitalist states requires full recognition of sovereign equality.

The Soviets logically deduce from the agreement theory of norm formulation that contemporary international law (i.e., the law of peaceful coexistence) "cannot be socialist [nor can it be capitalist] since agreement on this basis is impossible between socialist and capitalist countries."[17] In effect, contemporary international law is considered neither socialist nor capitalist (that is, an inter-class, law), although the Soviets claim for it a special socialist content essence, and purpose.[18] This claim is based upon the view that the principles of peaceful coexistence, as *jus cogens*, are in full accord with the Marxist-Leninist laws of social development.

The same legislative process is applicable to the principles and norms included under socialist internationalism. However, the absence of ideological struggle in socialist relationships makes possible broader agreement on the law governing collaboration and cooperation:

...in describing socialist principles and norms of international law, it is necessary to proceed from the fact that they are created through agreement and express the coordinated wills of socialist states of a similar type. Their function is to regulate inter-state relations of a new, higher, socialist type, relations within the framework of the social, economic, and political collaboration of free and sovereign peoples proceeding along the path of

---

[16] B. B. Ganiushkin, Review of A. N. Talalaev, *Iuridicheskaia Priroda Mezhdunarodnovo Dogovora* [The Legal Character of International Agreements] (Moscow: Publishing House of the Institute of International Relations, 1963), *SGIP*, No. 7 (1964), pp. 167–169; see 167.

[17] G. I. Tunkin, "Sorok Let Sosushchestvovaniia i Mezhdunarodnovo Prava" [Forty Years of Coexistence and International Law], *Sovetskii Ezhegodnik, 1958* (Moscow: Publishing House of the Academy of Sciences of the U.S.S.R., 1959), pp. 15–49.

[18] A. P. Movchan, "O Znachenii Kodifikatsii Printsipov Mezhdunarodnovo Prava" [On the Importance of the Codification of the Principles of International Law], *SGIP*, No. 1 (1965), pp. 46–55; see 54, where it is said that, as a result of the influence of socialism, new principles (e.g., peaceful coexistence and disarmament) have become a part of international law, obsolete principles (e.g., capitulations and colonialism) have been eliminated, and older democratic principles (e.g., sovereignty and peaceful settlement of disputes) enriched.

socialism and communism, united by a community of interests and goals and by the close bonds of international socialist solidarity.[19]

The principles and norms resulting from the community of interest and purpose in the building of socialism and communism constitute the basis of a new socialist international law which in time will replace contemporary international law.[20]

Although the agreement theory of norm formulation is characterized as a "new concept,"[21] it is in fact quite old, both in Soviet formulations and practice. As early as 1952, Tunkin had propounded the theory of the agreement of states as the sole method by which international legal norms are "enacted."[22] Similarly, Soviet practice always has reflected the position that the Soviet Union's consent to a norm is an indispensable condition to its being bound by it. This is a basic element in the Soviet minimum approach to international law. The essence of this position is maintained in the broader context of peaceful coexistence, the Soviet maximum position, by the formulation that "only norms accepted by the states of the two systems. . .can become norms of general international law."[23] Since contemporary international law is, as a matter of *jus cogens*, the law of peaceful coexistence and the socialist camp has a veto in the norm formulation process, the agreement of states can have meaningful application only as the formal means of ratifying *jus cogens* or of effecting the further progressive (socialist) development of international law. To ensure the availability of the socialist veto, the Soviets have advanced the concept (which has great appeal to the small, neutralist states) that all states have the right to participate in the formulation of international legal norms.

[19] G. I. Tunkin, "The Twenty-second Congress of the CPSU and the Tasks of the Soviet Science of International Law," *Soviet Law and Government* (New York: International Arts and Sciences Press, Winter 1962/63), Vol. 1, No. 2, pp. 18–27; see 25.

[20] Bernard A. Ramundo, *The (Soviet) Socialist Theory of International Law* (Washington, D.C.: Institute for Sino-Soviet Studies, The George Washington University, 1964), pp. 19–22.

[21] Tunkin, "The Twenty-second Congress of the CPSU," *op. cit., supra* note 19, p. 21.

[22] D. A. Gaidukov, Review of *Mezhdunarodnoe Pravo* [International Law] (Moscow: State Publishing House of Legal Literature, 1951), *SGIP*, No. 7 (1952), pp. 67–77; see 69.

[23] Tunkin, "The Twenty-second Congress of the CPSU," *op. cit., supra* note 19, p. 23.

From these principles [respect for sovereignty and the equality of states] it follows that, on the one hand, states are free to choose their treaty partners, and, on the other, all states have the right to participate in general multilateral agreements which are intended to regulate relationships of interest to all states.[24]

Furthermore, the Soviets claim that "norms of contemporary international law should be created not on the basis of the agreement and will of the ruling classes of imperialist states, *but on the basis of consideration of the sovereign interests of the peoples of all countries* [i.e., the realization of the peaceful coexistence of states]."[25] In effect, the Soviets are attempting to limit "legislation" under the agreement theory to progressive norms.

TREATIES: THE CHARTER OF THE UNITED NATIONS

Influenced by the agreement theory of norm formulation, Soviet writers reject as "of no practical significance" the distinction made by some Western writers between "law-making" and "contract" treaties.[26] In the Soviet view, all treaties establish norms in the sense that binding obligations are created by the parties; however, a distinction in the importance of treaties as "legislation" is made in terms of the parties, subject matter, and relationship to existing norms.[27] In order for a treaty to qualify as a legislative enactment, the parties must intend to create legal norms, and the norms created cannot violate the basic principles of peaceful coexistence.[28] If valid as international legal enactments, treaties may confirm existing law, develop it further, create new norms, or eliminate outdated ones.[29]

[24] G. I. Tunkin and B. I. Nechaev, "Pravo Dogovorov na XVII Sessii Komissii Mezhdunarodnovo Prava OON" [The Law of Treaties at the Seventeenth Session of the International Law Commission of the U.N.], *SGIP*, No. 4 (1966), pp. 56–62; see 59.

[25] M. I. Lazarev, "Mezhdunarodnopravovye Voprosy Dvizheniia Narodov za Mir" [International Legal Aspects of the Peoples' Movement for Peace], *Sovetskii Ezhegodnik, 1963* (Moscow: Publishing House "Science," 1965), pp. 45–69; see 63.

[26] Tunkin, Voprosy Teorii, *op. cit.*, *supra* note 9, pp. 66–72.

[27] *Ibid.*, p. 72.

[28] Lukin, *op. cit.*, *supra* note 3, pp. 12 and 140. Lukin states, "Treaties which contradict the basic principles of international law are illegal. They do not have juridical force and cannot be sources of international law." (*Ibid.*, p. 142.)

[29] Tunkin, Voprosy Teorii, *op. cit.*, *supra* note 9, p. 73. See also *International Law*, *op. cit.*, *supra* note 2, p. 22.

The Soviets single out the Charter of the United Nations as the most important piece of international legislation because it embodies the principles of peaceful coexistence. They claim that this enactment confirms contemporary international law as the law of coexistence. The Charter, the formal pillar of the law of peaceful coexistence, is described as "the charter of contemporary international law, its most important source."[30] Using the Charter as a point of departure, the Soviets are active proponents of codification as a means of implementing and developing the law of peaceful coexistence. They claim that the earlier effort was to obtain general acceptance of the law of coexistence; whereas now, "the struggle" is to codify the specific norms of the new law. The United Nations is expected to assist in, and serve as the forum for, the struggle for codification. "One of the important tasks of the United Nations is the codification and progressive development of the principles of peaceful coexistence."[31] In view of their expectation that codification can be achieved through the United Nations, the Soviets actively participate in the codification work of the International Law Commission of the General Assembly.[32]

The Soviets still appear to prefer bilateral to multilateral agreements, presumably because of the greater influence and situational control inherent in the negotiation of the former.[33] There is, however, a growing appreciation of the compensating advantages of multilateral agreements, both within the socialist commonwealth

[30] V. M. Chkhikvadze, "Voprosy Mezhdunarodnovo Prava na XX Sessii General'noi Assamblei OON" [Problems of International Law at the 20th Session of the General Assembly of the U.N.], *SGIP*, No. 3 (1966), pp. 67–78; see 71.

[31] *Mezhdunarodnoe Pravo* (Kozhevnikov), *op. cit.*, *supra* note 4, p. 92. See also *Ibid.*, p. 90.

[32] Tunkin and Nechaev, *op. cit.*, *supra* note 8, pp. 84–92. See the authors' commentary on the Sixteenth Session under the same title in *SGIP*, No. 3 (1965), pp. 70–77, and on the Seventeenth Session, cited *supra* note 24. The work of the International Law Commission is said to reflect the struggle of the progressive and reactionary lines of legal development (*Mezhdunarodnoe Pravo* [Kozhevnikov], *op. cit.*, *supra* note 4, p. 57).

[33] Edward McWhinney, *Peaceful Coexistence and Soviet-Western International Law* (Leyden: A. W. Sythoff, 1964), pp. 66–68.

and in dealing with capitalist states.[34] As a result, Soviet treaty practice has become more diversified and places greater emphasis upon multilateral agreements.

In the Soviet view, contemporary international law is, basically, treaty law.[35] Preference for treaties as the principal formal source of international law reflects the Soviet Union's basic positivist approach and is an important element in its bid for Western acceptance of the law of peaceful coexistence.[36] The Soviets consider "law by treaty" an extremely flexible and useful device for achieving minimum and maximum international legal goals; defending against a hostile order, in the first instance, or transforming the international order, in the second. For the former purpose, a claim of lack of consent constitutes a universally accepted, traditional bar to the enforcement of a challenged norm; for the latter, acceptance of the principles of peaceful coexistence in treaty form would provide a universally recognized legal basis for the new law. Thus, the Soviets claim, the Charter of the United Nations embodies the principles of coexistence.

Soviet treaty practice generally follows that of the West, principally because the Soviet state had to accept the institution as a condition of membership in the family of nations. Later, no fundamental changes were attempted as the law of treaties was expected to serve as the "bridge between the traditional and revolutionary systems."[37] "Soviet treaty law, on the whole, is not widely different from Western treaty law. They both shared one cradle, and this common origin still shows."[38] Where differences in the Soviet approach to treaties exist, they are "profound. . .politically oriented

[34] V. I. Morozov, "Mnogostoronnie Soglasheniia—Deistvennaia Forma Ekonomicheskovo Sotrudnichestva Sotsialisticheskikh Stran" [Multilateral Agreements—An Effective Form of Economic Collaboration of Socialist Countries], *SGIP*, No. 12 (1963), pp. 75–85. Soviet extolling of the Limited Test Ban Treaty of 1963 as an example of the triumph of peaceful coexistence reflects the new appreciation for multilateral arrangements with the West.

[35] *Mezhdunarodnoe Pravo, op. cit., supra* note 1, p. 80.

[36] Jan F. Triska and Robert M. Slusser, *The Theory, Law and Policy of Soviet Treaties* (Stanford, California: Stanford University Press, 1962), pp. 9–29.

[37] *Ibid.*, p. 28.

[38] *Ibid.*, p. 172. See Part II, "The Soviet Law of Treaties" in *Ibid.*, pp. 34–172 for a detailed statement of Soviet treaty law. See also, *International Law, op. cit., supra* note 2, pp. 247–282.

and . . . sharpened by hostile, purposeful ideology."[39] The differences
in Soviet treaty practice—primarily, the creation of legal loopholes
which permit relief from the burden of a treaty arrangement no
longer compatible with the interests of the Soviet Union—reflect a
bid for flexibility as a counter to the fervent lip-service paid to the
principle of *pacta sunt servanda*. Soviet writers vehemently react to this
treatment of the treaty practice of the Soviet Union, attacking it as
an "anti-Soviet falsehood and an attempt to discredit the Soviet
Union as a treaty partner."[40] They seek to counter such treatment
by extolling the Soviet Union's fulfillment of international obligations as an integral part of the law and policy of peaceful coexistence.

Following the legacy of V. I. Lenin, the Soviet Union has always con-
scientiously fulfilled its international obligations. In the international legal
practice of the U.S.S.R. there has not been a single instance of an arbitrary
breach of an agreement or a violation of generally accepted norms of
international law.[41]

The need for the loyal [*sic*] performance of international treaties (*pacta
sunt servanda*) is a vital generally recognized principle of International Law.
Without the recognition of the principle of adherence to treaties there can
be no intercourse between nations or any International Law. The U.S.S.R.
and the other socialist countries are waging a constant struggle for the
observance of international treaties. But the imperialist states frequently
repudiate undertakings which they have assumed.[42]

While creating its own loopholes, the Soviet Union has attempted to
limit the operation of traditional principles such as *rebus sic stantibus*
[changed conditions] which could be the basis for flexibility hostile
to its interests:[43]

. . . this clause [*rebus sic stantibus*] is frequently interpreted broadly by capitalist states, in the sense that any change in the international situation gives
the right to annul a treaty. Such an interpretation has been used by aggressor countries to justify expansionist foreign policies.

---

[39] *Ibid.*

[40] See the review of Triska and Slusser's work in A. N. Talalaev, "Eshche
Odna Antisovetskaia Fal'shivka" [Another Anti-Soviet Falsehood], *SGIP*,
No. 5 (1964), pp. 142–144; see 143, 144.

[41] *Ibid.*, p. 143. Further on, Talalaev quotes Churchill's wartime comment
about the Soviet Union: "Never has any state fulfilled its obligations more
exactly." See also Zadorozhnyi, Mirnoe Sosushchestvovanie, *op. cit., supra*
note 7, p. 270.

[42] *International Law, op. cit,. supra* note 2, p. 282.

[43] McWhinney, *op. cit., supra* note 33, p. 65. See also Tunkin and Nechaev
(1964), *op. cit., supra* note 8, p. 91, 92.

Only a fundamental, radical change in the international situation can constitute grounds for the application of the clause *rebus sic stantibus*.

The unilateral, arbitrary dissolution of international treaties contradicts International Law. Nevertheless, it is a frequent phenomenon in the practice of capitalist States, particularly in the period of imperialism. . . . The U.S.S.R. unswervingly champions the stability of international treaties concluded on the basis of the sovereign equality of the parties.[44]

The ambivalence of the Soviet approach is described by a competent Western observer as follows:

Thus, Soviet writers uniformly tend to reject the more avant-garde Western theories as to the necessity for the novation or dissolution of treaties according to changed historical and political situations; and in particular they would reject the *clausula rebus sic stantibus* doctrine. Yet the Soviet jurists would retain for themselves, so to speak, a unilateral right of repudiation or denunciation of those treaties that they themselves do not particularly like.[45]

The Soviets seek to enhance their own flexibility vis-à-vis the international legal order by the creation of *sui generis* bases for the modification of international undertakings, and, at the same time, to inhibit similar flexibility on the part of capitalist states by narrowing the scope and application of traditional bases for modification of international commitments.

The Soviet effort to attain flexibility involves insistence upon consent as the condition of a state being bound by an international undertaking, and the principle of the illegality of certain types of agreements (e.g., unequal treaties and those colonial in character), thereby providing a basis for unilateral characterizations of legality. For example, the Soviets counter capitalist use of *rebus sic stantibus* as a "pretext for 'legalization' of capricious violations of international agreements" by insisting upon the need for the consent of all parties to a treaty before it can be reviewed or modified. This includes modification by practice or custom.[46] Consent is also relied upon to resist loss of control over a treaty arrangement through interpretation.

[44] *International Law, op. cit., supra* note 2, p. 281.

[45] McWhinney, *op. cit., supra* note 33, p. 65.

[46] *Mezhdunarodnoe Pravo, op. cit., supra* note 1, p. 93. See also Tunkin and Nechaev (1965), *op. cit., supra* note 32, pp. 73–76.

->>><<<-

An international agreement can be interpreted only by the parties themselves or, with their consent, by an international organ. . .Analogy cannot be used in interpreting a treaty as it is not possible to impose obligations upon a sovereign state. Nor can a broad or narrow construction be utilized to expand or reduce the rights and obligations of the parties.[47]

Consent is similarly central to the Soviet positions on nonparty, third-state relationships and the effectiveness of reservations to multilateral agreements.[48] The Soviets are more flexible, however, on the question of consent when their interests so require. Their concept of *jus cogens* is, in effect, a negation in the Soviet interest of the necessity for state consent. A recent Soviet commentary reflects this approach in discussing Article 2, paragraph 6, of the Charter of the United Nations which provides that the Organization shall ensure compliance of nonmember states with Charter principles when it is necessary for the maintenance of peace and security. The operation of paragraph 6 is said to be only an apparent contradiction of the principle that a state must consent to be bound. The principles of the Charter, the embodiment of the law of peaceful coexistence, become operative as part of *jus cogens* without regard to the consent of states. Therefore, the lack of consent of nonmember states is irrelevant.[49]

The principle of overriding illegality is invoked in the interest of policy flexibility in order to undermine hostile or undersirable arrangements.

The most varied aspects of inter-state relations may constitute the content for treaties. But their object can be only that which is legitimate.

---

[47] *Ibid.*, p. 91.

[48] *International Law, op. cit., supra* note 2, pp. 269–271. Although the Soviets state the general rule to be that a treaty is binding only as between the parties to it and as to the terms agreed upon, they do recognize that treaties may have legal consequences for nonparty, third states.

"Strictly speaking, it would be incorrect to say that obligations of third states are based upon a treaty to which the state is not a party. [However]. . .certain treaties can impose obligations upon third states. For example, the agreement concerning Germany concluded at the end of World War II by the allied powers undoubtedly impose obligations upon the two states presently existing on German territory. The basis of these obligations is the responsibility of an aggressor-state." (Tunkin and Nechaev [1965], *op. cit., supra* note 32, pp. 74.)

[49] Lukin, *op. cit., supra* note 3, pp. 69, 70.

The voluntary expression of the will of the parties and equality and mutual advantage must be the basic legal principles underlying international treaties.[50]

In brief, the Soviets hold the position that treaties cannot contradict the generally recognized principles of contemporary international law.[51] The generally recognized principles invoked for this purpose are those included under peaceful coexistence and socialist internationalism. Of the latter, they say that the harmonious relationships between, and the strict observance of the principles by, socialist states make unnecessary any special guarantees of legality in their treaty practice.[52]

Thus, treaties deemed to conflict with the policy of peaceful coexistence can be claimed to be invalid as contrary to the law of peaceful coexistence.[53] The relationship of the overriding principle to the basic principles of treaty law is stated by Korovin as follows:

Another example is the theory of an international treaty and the conditions for its legal validity. Certainly all the classical requirements for the validity of an international treaty, pertaining to its form, the full powers of the parties, the expression of will, etc., retain their importance. But now the most important feature in appraising a treaty is the question of whether it promotes, and is in accordance with, the principles of peaceful coexistence, or, on the contrary, is designed to undermine these principles. Constation [sic] of the latter is in effect equivalent to denying that the treaty concerned has any legal force.[54]

For example, treaties which are "unequal," "colonial," or which violate the "legal conscience of the peoples" of the states which are

[50] International Law, op. cit., supra note 2, p. 247.

[51] Mezhdunarodnoe Pravo, op. cit., supra note 1, p. 83.

[52] The treaties between states of the socialist camp are a new type of international agreement which reflects the specific features of the new social order and the principles of socialist international relations (Tunkin, Voprosy Teorii, op. cit., supra note 9, p. 324).

[53] Triska and Slusser, op. cit., supra note 36, pp. 24, 25.

[54] Y. Korovin "International Law Today," International Affairs, No. 7 (1962), p. 22. It is said that "Treaties which contradict the generally accepted principles of international law such as equality of states, noninterference in internal affairs, right of self-determination are illegal (S. V. Chernichenko, "Pravo Natsii na Samoopredelenie i Voprosy Grazhdanstva" [The Right of National Self-determination and Problems of Citizenship], SGIP, No. 1 [1964], pp. 110–114; see 113).

parties to a treaty are said to be invalid. The latter concept is included in a new socialist principle of international law, "popular sovereignty," under which the legality of state acts depends upon compatibility with the desires of the masses (i.e., presumptively, in the Soviet view, to advance the cause of peace and socialism).[55]

Unequal treaties are invalid from the point of view of present-day international law and are not binding.[56]

Many of the articles proposed . . . are clearly colonial in character. Provisions dealing with applicability of a treaty in a State's territory and in all other territory for which it is responsible is contrary to present international law [because it sanctions or is premised upon colonialism].[57]

An international treaty has for its juridical basis the voluntary agreement of the states-parties to the treaty. Such sovereign act of agreement, however, cannot contradict the general principles of international law or the legal conscience of the peoples of such states.[58]

Western military base agreements, collective security agreements, and economic assistance agreements are cited as prime examples of agreements which violate these general criteria:[59]

[55] See Ramundo, *op. cit.*, *supra* note 20, pp. 35, 36. It is said that the true interests of nations are "invariably realized in the treaty practice of the socialist countries where real popular sovereignty has triumphed." (V. M. Shurshalov, "Mezhdunarodno-pravovye Printsipy Sotrudnichestva Sotsialisticheskikh Gosudarstv" [International Legal Principles of the Collaboration of Socialist States], *SGIP*, No. 7 (1962), pp. 95–105; see 99.)

[56] A. N. Talalaev and V. G. Boiarshinov, "Neravnopravnye Dogovory kak Forma Uderzhaniia Kolonial'noi Zavisimosti Novykh Gosudarstv Azii i Afriki" [Unequal Treaties as a Form of Prolonging the Colonial Dependence of the New States of Asia and Africa], *Sovetskii Ezhegodnik, 1961* (Moscow; Publishing House of the Academy of Sciences of the U.S.S.R., 1962), pp. 156–170; see 170.

[57] Tunkin and Nechaev (1965), *op. cit.*, *supra* note 32, p. 71.

[58] N. M. Minasian, *Istochniki Sovremennovo Mezhdunarodnovo Prava* [Sources of Contemporary International Law] (Rostov: Publishing House of Rostov University, 1960) quoted by V. N. Durdenevskii and M. I. Lazarev in their review of Minasian's work in *SGIP*, No. 1 (1962), pp. 125–127; see 125. See also O. Khlestov, "International Law is on the Side of Panama," *International Affairs*, No. 4 (1964), pp. 92, 93; see 93, where it is said: "It is now generally recognized that an international treaty which runs counter to the basic principles of international law is invalid."

[59] Triska and Slusser, *op. cit.*, *supra* note 36, pp. 24, 25 and Talalaev and Boiarshinov, *op. cit.*, *supra* note 56, p. 170.

...the author considers inoperative agreements which contravene the basic principles of international law, including in this category various agreements of imperialist states concerning aggressive military blocs, military bases, unequal treaties, agreements of economic "assistance" with harsh conditions imposed by the imperialists upon developing countries, etc.[60]

The Soviet effort, in effect an attempt to establish a basis for excluding certain types of arrangements from the principle *pacta sunt servanda*, is well described by two Western specialists:

...having seen its [the Soviet Union's] advocacy of treaties as a primary source of international law gradually win the assent of the non-Soviet world, Soviet international law and in particular Soviet treaty law is now ready to move to the more advanced position of establishing its own "basic principles" on the strength of which it can judge and condemn the treaties of the non-Soviet world.[61]

The technique used for this purpose is the familiar propaganda line which juxtaposes Soviet support for legality and equality of all states before the law with the lawlessness and neo-colonial policies of the great Western powers. For example:

The Soviet Union, like the other socialist countries, stands for the strict observance of obligations assumed under international agreements, as has been demonstrated by the entire history of Soviet foreign relations.
The imperialist states frequently refuse to fulfill their obligations, and make international treaties mere scraps of paper.[62]
Offensive [Western] alliances cannot be considered as legally valid.
The treaties of alliance which the Soviet Union has concluded with other countries are genuine instruments of peace.[63]
Clearly that principle [*pacta sunt servanda*] cannot be applied to those predatory or one-sided treaties which imperialist powers impose and try to impose upon developing countries.[64]
It is well known that imperialist states always strive to impose one-sided, unequal treaties upon weak countries and peoples.[65]
All international legal acts to which the signature of the U.S.S.R. or any other country of the socialist camp is affixed, correspond to the interests of all peoples and promote the cause of peace, although in a number of cases, due to the opposition of the capitalist parties to these acts, they cannot fully, and completely, reflect these noble aims.

[60] Ganiushkin, *op. cit.*, *supra* note 16, p. 168.
[61] Triska and Slusser, *op. cit.*, *supra* note 36, p. 25.
[62] *International Law*, *op. cit.*, *supra* note 2, pp. 248, 249.
[63] *Ibid.*, pp. 254, 255.
[64] *Mezhdunarodnoe Pravo*, *op. cit.*, *supra* note 1, p. 84.
[65] *Ibid.*, p. 85.

᠅᠊᠊᠊᠊᠊᠊᠊᠊᠊᠊

In all cases where the Soviet Union or some other socialist state is a party to an agreement, the agreement by its very nature cannot be contrary to the popular will or aggressive. This is an indication of the progressive influence of the U.S.S.R. on international treaty practice and the democratic development of international law. [66]

As is apparent from the foregoing, Soviet legal writing is more polemical than reasoned.

In recognizing the existence of certain fundamental principles before which inconsistent treaty obligations fall, the Soviets rely upon their concept of *jus cogens*. Soviet commentators criticize Western jurists who reject this concept, as well as those who find the content of *jus cogens* in natural law. [67] Soviet jurists who use as fundamental principles nonlegal concepts such as the laws of social development are also subjected to criticism. [68] Although it is said that the basic laws of social development of the base do control the content of the legal superstructure, nevertheless "the validity of an agreement must be determined on the basis of international legal criteria." [69] The laws of social development must be converted into usable legal concepts, for the obvious reason that the fundamental laws of themselves can have no persuasive, operative effect as part of international law.

The Soviet approach to the law of treaties constitutes an artful bid for flexibility. Although it pays fervent lip-service to the principle of *pacta sunt servanda*, the Soviet Union, in effect, claims that there are preconditions basic to the legality, and therefore enforceability, of all treaties: agreements must (*1*) be consented to and (*2*) not conflict with the basic principles of "peaceful coexistence" and, in the socialist camp, "socialist internationalism." Only those agreements which

[66] *Mezhdunarodnopravovye Formy Sotrudnichestva Sotsialisticheskikh Gosudarstv* [Forms of International Legal Collaboration of Socialist States], ed. V. M. Shurshalov (Moscow: Publishing House of the Academy of Sciences of the U.S.S.R., 1962), p. 26.

[67] Tunkin, Voprosy Teorii, *op. cit,. supra* note 9, pp. 114–117.

[68] *Ibid.*, pp. 118, 119. See I. I. Lukashyk and V. A. Vasilenko, "Pol'skii Uchebnik po Mezhdunarodnomu Pravu" [Polish Textbook on International Law], *SGIP*, No. 5 (1966), pp. 140–142, for criticism of a Polish international legal specialist, A. Klafkovskii, for his failure to emphasize the significance of *jus cogens* derivable from the objective laws of social development.

[69] *Ibid.*, p. 119.

qualify (i.e., further the cause of "peace and socialism") are considered valid, and therefore, subject to the compliance requirement of the *pacta* formulation.

> The Soviet conception of the law of treaties renders the Soviet Union a difficult contracting party; it provides the Soviet government with formal as well as substantive loopholes which can be resorted to as Soviet foreign policy requires.[70]

The presence of these conditions or loopholes overshadows, for all practical purposes, Soviet affirmance of the general principles of treaty law.

CUSTOM

In Soviet literature on international law "there is a conscious depreciation of the role of historical practice between states (custom) as a source of international law."[71] Soviet writers reject as outdated the proposition advanced by certain Western jurists that custom, rather than treaties, represents true "general international law."[72] The growing number of multilateral arrangements and treaties codifying international law is adduced as convincing proof of the incorrectness of the Western view. Furthermore, the Soviets affirm that the swiftness of technological changes during the present epoch points up the special suitability of treaties to introduce the necessary, corresponding changes in international law.[73] The Soviet position on customary law reflects their decided preference for treaties as the principal source of international law.

The objectionable feature of customary law from the Soviet point of view is the potential for loss of control in the creation of binding norms. For many years after the formation of the Soviet state, custom was rejected as a source of international law because of the need to protect itself against hostile customary law. The recognition, however, that custom can be useful as a source of international law if properly controlled has resulted in acceptance of customary

[70] Triska and Slusser, *op. cit.*, *supra* note 36, p. 172.
[71] McWhinney, *op. cit.*, *supra* note 33, p. 62.
[72] Tunkin, Voprosy Teorii, *op. cit.*, *supra* note 9, pp. 104, 105.
[73] *Ibid.*, p. 106.

law with qualifications designed to meet Soviet foreign policy needs. Soviet attempts to control the scope and impact of customary law in the cause of coexistence are considered of great importance as it is recognized that:

...as a practical matter, it is difficult for a single state to insist upon its being excepted from the operation of a customary rule which is generally observed.

...force of circumstances compels the individual states in most cases to recognize as binding those norms which have already been recognized by the overwhelming majority of states belonging to both systems, including the Great Powers.[74]

The Soviets have rejected the Western supported doctrine that customary norms recognized as such by a considerable number of states are binding upon all as a concept which is dangerous in the epoch of coexistence. They have superimposed their concept of *jus cogens* and the agreement theory of norm formulation as controls upon the formation of customary law.[75] To be effective, a custom must be in accord with the *jus cogens* (the law of peaceful coexistence) and be accepted by the state which is to be bound.

As in the case of treaties, a departure from the *jus cogens* in customary law requires acceptance "by the states of both systems. . .[to] be regarded as a [universal] customary rule of international law."[76] Further assurance that international law will develop along progressive lines is contained in the view that the applicability of a customary rule is subject to continuing review to determine the extent to which it meets present-day requirements. This view provides still another basis for invoking the fundamental law of social development in the form of *jus cogens*.[77] The Soviet position on consent is based upon tacit agreement (i.e., that one state's acceptance or recognition of an international custom is deemed to constitute a tacit

[74] Tunkin, "Remarks on the Juridical Nature of Customary Norms," *op. cit.*, *supra* note 12, p. 428.

[75] *Ibid.*, p. 420.

[76] McWhinney, *op. cit.*, *supra* note 33, pp. 63, 64, quoting Tunkin. It is said that the *jus cogens* of customary law cannot be rejected by individual states. (Lukin, *op. cit.*, *supra* note 3, p. 86.) See, for example, Lukashyk and Vasilenko, *op. cit.*, *supra* note 67, pp. 141, 142.

[77] Tunkin, "Remarks on the Juridical Nature of Customary Norms," *op. cit.*, *supra* note 12, p. 425.

proposal to other states to regard the custom as a norm of international law). The acceptance by other states can be express, or indicated by a course of conduct. Once accepted, the custom becomes a customary norm of international law with the same force, effect and weight as a treaty norm.[78] The distinction made between a "custom" and a "customary norm of international law" is generally accepted in the West (i.e., the element of *opinio juris*) without the extreme positivism of the Soviet position.[79] The positivist strain is evident in the following:

Customary international law may be changed or abolished either by treaty or by a new customary rule. In either case there is a new agreement between states.[80]

Customary norms of international law being a result of agreement among states, the sphere of action of such norms is limited to the relations between the states which accepted these norms as norms of international law, i.e., the states participating in this tacit agreement. . . . As for the newly emerging states, they have the juridical right not to recognize this or that customary norm of international law. . . .The concept that customary norms of international law recognized as such by a large number of states are binding upon all states not only has no foundation in modern international law but is fraught with great danger.[81]

Soviet commentaries reject the position of many Western jurists that the principle of "majority rule" applies in the formulation of customary norms as a "crying contradiction to the basic generally recognized principle of modern international law, the principle of the equality of states, in particular."[82] In making this argument, the Soviets depict the socialist states and newly emerging states of Asia and Africa as victims of Western attempts to impose international norms under the guise of customary law.[83] The Soviet Union frequently courts the support of these nations for its positions on inter-

---

[78] *Ibid.*, pp. 422, 423 and Tunkin and Nechaev (1964), *op. cit., supra* note 8, p. 88.

[79] See Herbert W. Briggs, *The Law of Nations* (2d ed.; New York: Appleton-Century-Crofts, Inc., 1952), pp. 46, 47.

[80] Tunkin, Voprosy Teorii, *op. cit., supra* note 9, pp. 103, 104.

[81] Tunkin, "Remarks on the Juridical Nature of Customary Norms," *op. cit., supra* note 12, pp. 428, 429.

[82] *Ibid.*, p. 427.

[83] Tunkin, Voprosy Teorii, *op. cit., supra* note 9, p. 103.

->>><<<-

national legal questions by demonstrating their common plight or community of interest. The Soviet approach to customary law has great appeal to African and Asian states because they feel that they have not had a voice in the formation of the international legal order.

In insisting upon the agreement of states as the essence of the process or means of creating a customary norm of international law, Soviet commentators apparently reject the requirement under the traditional formulation that a customary norm, as distinguished from a regional rule, reflects a general or universal practice.

It is not at all necessary for a practice leading to the creation of a customary norm of international law to be "universal." A customary rule may be created by the practice of a limited number of states. Being recognized as a norm of law, it may at first be a customary norm with a limited sphere of application. This sphere of application may gradually expand, and the norm in question will then closely approximate a generally recognized norm of international law.[84]

This formulation provides a basis for the special, progressive, customary law of socialist internationalism and its development into the customary socialist international law of the future. Soviet recognition of the existence of local customary law is subject to the requirements of *jus cogens*, the effect of which is to preclude nonsocialist local rules and arrangements which, by definition, are nonprogressive.

As indicated previously, the reversal of the Soviet Union's initial position (which rejected custom as a source of international law) is based upon recognition of the utility of custom in serving Soviet needs in foreign relations.[85] The Soviets use custom as part of their campaign to win support for the law of peaceful coexistence. For example, it is claimed that the principles of peaceful coexistence already "have become, partly by custom and partly by treaty, generally recognized principles of modern international law."[86] Similarly, the principles of socialist internationalism are said to

[84] Tunkin, "Remarks on the Juridical Nature of Customary Norms," *op. cit.*, *supra* note 12, p. 425.

[85] Triska and Slusser, *op. cit.*, *supra* note 36, p. 28.

[86] Tunkin, "Remarks on the Juridical Nature of Customary Norms," *op. cit.*, *supra* note 12, p. 428.

63

have become international legal principles among the socialist states through customary law and treaties.[87] The Soviet approach to customary law also has a defensive aspect which attempts to retain control at two levels: the state, and the international legal order. As to the former, consent is posited as an indispensable condition of a state's being bound by a customary rule. In recognition of the fact that there will be instances where consent cannot be withheld because of the interdependence of states, an attempt is made to control the content of customary law by the concept of *jus cogens* and the requirement that any change in extant customary law must be accepted by the states of both camps.

Thus there . . . [can] be no danger that the Soviet Union . . . [will] find itself bound by the international custom to which it has not given specific approval, while any custom which it . . . [has] not so approved . . . [will] not enter into its concept of the sources of international law.[88]

The Soviet position on customary international law fits well the basic pattern of a bid for flexibility in the interest of foreign policies of the Soviet Union.

GENERAL PRINCIPLES

Paragraph 1 (*c*) of Article 38 of the Statute of the International Court of Justice authorizes the Court to apply "the general principles of law recognized by civilized nations" in deciding, in accordance with international law, the disputes submitted to it.[89] Various meanings have been attributed to this Article with the Western view being that "general principles" are a "true, if subsidiary, 'source' of international law."[90]

The paragraph then introduces no novelty into the [international legal] system, for the "general principles of law" are a source to which international courts have instinctively and properly referred in the past. But its inclusion is important as a rejection of the positivist doctrine, according to which international law consists solely of rules to which states have given

---

[87] Tunkin, Voprosy Teorii, *op. cit., supra* note 9, p. 313.
[88] Triska and Slusser, *op. cit., supra* note 36, p. 21.
[89] Briggs, *op. cit., supra* note 79, Appendix II, p. 1077.
[90] *Ibid.*, p. 48.

their consent. It is an authoritative recognition of a dynamic element in international law, and of the creative freedom of the courts which administer it. [91]

Soviet adherence to the positivist doctrine and the general reluctance to expand the competence and importance of international tribunals combine to produce a position which rejects general principles as independent sources of international law.

In the Soviet view, Article 38 does not purport to establish general principles as a source of international law, or to empower the International Court of Justice to create law on the basis of such principles. [92]

In [Article 38] it is clearly stated that the Court decides disputes "on the basis of international law. . ." The Court does not create international law, it applies it. [93]

The majority of Soviet authors are of the view that paragraph 1(*c*) of Article 38 of the Statute of the International Court does not contemplate a special source of international law or a special method of creating norms of international law. The "general principles of law" can only be principles of international law. [94]

The requirement that the Court decide disputes "on the basis of international law" is seized upon to support the view that paragraph 1 (*c*) of Article 38 does not contemplate the application of domestic law but only international law. [95]

The International Court of Justice can in addition to international conventions and international customs apply "the general principles of law recognized by civilized nations" [Article 38(*c*), Statute of International

---

[91] J. L. Brierly, *The Law of Nations* (5th ed.: Oxford: Clarendon Press, 1955), pp. 63, 64. See also *World Peace through the Rule of Law* [Working paper for the First World Conference, June 30–July 6, 1963, Athens, Greece] (Washington, D.C.: American Bar Association, 1963), pp. 25–41.

[92] Cf. Dionisio Anzilotti, *Corso di Diritto Internazionale* [Course on International Law] (3d rev. ed.; Rome: Athenaeum, 1928), pp. 106, 107; and Gaetano Morelli, *Nozioni di Diritto Internazionale* [Theories of International Law] (3d ed., Padua: Cedam, 1951), p. 29.

[93] Tunkin, Voprosy Teorii, *op. cit., supra* note 9, pp. 147, 148. See also Professor F. Kozhevnikov, "International Court at the Crossroads," *New Times*, No. 36 (September 7, 1966), pp. 3–4; see 3.

[94] *Ibid.*, p. 152.

[95] *Ibid.*, p. 155.

Court]. Many of these principles are still of great importance for the development and affirmation of democratic rules of international law. They are realized either through the appropriate international treaties or through international custom and are in fact their generalization. Principles reflected neither in international treaties nor in international custom cannot be considered "general principles."[96]

Furthermore, the Soviets claim that general principles of domestic law do not exist, despite formal similarities in the various legal systems, for the laws of socialist and capitalist states have a different class basis and, as a consequence, substantive content.[97]

In the world there are states with two [different] social-economic systems and, as a consequence, two types of legal systems. The majority of the legal principles, despite their formal similarity, have, in some instances, different meanings in the legal systems of socialist and capitalist states. Therefore, it can be said with full justification that paragraph "c" of Article 38 of the Statute of the International Court of the U.N. was and remains for all intents and purposes a dead letter.[98]

Where domestic law influences the development of international law, it does so only because it is accepted by other states either as a treaty or customary norm.[99]

In all these cases, however, domestic legislation as well as the decisions of national courts or acts of administrative organs are not and cannot be formal sources of international law. Rather, they can be a part of the process of the formation of customary norms of international law. In some cases they can become a part of the process of establishment of conventional norms.[100]

The Western interpretation that general principles include domestic legislation is dismissed in typical Soviet polemical style as an attempt to impose the bourgeois system of law upon the socialist states and the new states of Asia and Africa.[101]

[96] *International Law, op. cit., supra* note 2, p. 12.
[97] Tunkin, Voprosy Teorii, *op. cit., supra* note 9, p. 155.
[98] Lukin, *op. cit., supra* note 3, p. 100.
[99] D. B. Levin, "Problema Sootnosheniia Mezhdunarodnovo i Vnutrigo-sudarstvennovo Prava" [The Problem of the Relationship Between International and Domestic Law], *SGIP*, No. 7 (1964), pp. 86–95; see 86, 87.
[100] *Ibid.*, pp. 90, 91.
[101] Tunkin, Voprosy Teorii, *op. cit., supra* note 9, p. 154.

Implicit in the Soviet interpretation of the general principles mentioned in Article 38 is the requirement that there be agreement upon these general principles, as it is only through agreement that formal international legal norms can be created.[102] The logical difficulty of this approach is that it tends to render surplusage, and of no effect, paragraph 1(c) of Article 38 as, under the Soviet view, all such general principles are already a part of international law as treaty or customary law.[103] An attempt to correct this difficulty and to give some meaning to paragraph 1(c) of Article 38 is reflected in Tunkin's interpretation of the word "principles" in the formulation as "the most general norms of international law."[104]

Professor V. N. Durdenevskii also considers that "general principles of law" are "by their very nature the essence of the most basic principles of international customary law." He includes in this category the well-known five principles of peaceful coexistence and several other principles of international law.[105]

Tunkin's interpretation, suggesting that these principles constitute the *jus cogens* of peaceful coexistence, does not, however, eliminate the difficulty as, in his view, the mentioned principles enter international law as treaties or customary norms. Lisovskii finesses the difficulty by dismissing the "general principles" formulation and the rest of Article 38 as merely a statement "of the sources of the norms applied by international tribunals" and "not of the sources of international law."[106]

AUXILIARY "SOURCES"

Soviet jurists recognize the existence of auxiliary "sources" of international law (e.g., resolutions of international organizations, decisions of international courts, and national legislation). These are

[102] *Ibid.*, p. 153.
[103] *Ibid.*, pp. 153 and 157. Tunkin rejects Levin's attempt to distinguish general principles (either as "normative ideas" or "basic principles of international law") from international treaties and customs as separate sources of international law. (*Ibid.*, pp. 152, 153.)
[104] *Ibid.*, p. 157.
[105] *Ibid.*
[106] V. I. Lisovskii, *Mezhdunarodnoe Pravo* [International Law] (Moscow: State Publishing House "Higher School," 1961), pp. 9, 10.

sources only in the limited sense that they represent stages in the formulation of norms through the agreement of states. They are more precisely described as auxiliary processes for the manifestation of the agreement of states (that is, other than through treaties or the acceptance of custom).[107]

There are also auxiliary processes (resolutions and decisions of international organizations, international courts and courts of arbitration; national legislation; and the decisions of domestic courts) which are a definite stage in the process of the formation of norms but do not actually result in their formation. With rare exceptions, the process of norm formation in general international law takes the form of a treaty or an international custom.[108]

As the law of peaceful coexistence is based upon the foreign policy of coexistence, it is not surprising that foreign policy is treated as an auxiliary source of international law. The Soviet position is that the foreign policy of a state, when accepted and followed by others, becomes a rule of international law, as in the case of the policy of peaceful coexistence. Not every state's foreign policy can qualify however, as only a progressive policy can produce the norms dictated by the laws of social development.[109] Under this approach, socialist foreign policy is accorded a preemptive role.

. . . [such] is the case with the Leninist idea of peaceful coexistence of states with different social systems which is not only a constitutional principle of the foreign policy of socialist states, but with the growth of the influence of the forces of socialism throughout the world has become the basic principle of international law recognized in many bilateral and multilateral declarations and in the resolutions of the General Assembly of the U.N. adopted by an overwhelming majority of the votes of its members.[110]

Lisovskii does not distinguish between types of sources of international law. He includes the sources characterized by most Soviet jurists as auxiliary, with treaties and customs as the sources of international law.[111] All of these, however, cannot contradict the fundamental principles of international law (i.e., the law of peaceful

---

[107] Tunkin, Voprosy Teorii, *op. cit.*, *supra* note 9, p. 157.
[108] *Ibid.*, p. 157, 158. See also *Mezhdunarodnoe Pravo, op. cit., supra* note 1, p. 82.
[109] *Ibid.*, pp. 216–223.
[110] Levin, Problema Sootnosheniia, *op. cit.*, *supra* note 99, p. 88.
[111] Lisovskii, *op. cit.*, *supra* note 106, p. 9.

->>><<<-

coexistence). The limitation in Lisovskii's formulation is implicit in the general Soviet view, as auxiliary sources can enter into the body of international law only by agreement of states, and the object of agreement cannot be at variance with the fundamental principles of international law.[112]

As to the resolutions of international organizations, it is said that "resolutions of the General Assembly, adopted unanimously or by a 2/3 majority where that majority includes socialist and capitalist states . . . are binding on the members of the U.N. and, therefore, have juridical force."[113] This does not conflict with the view that the agreement of states is the sole source of international law, since such a resolution constitutes, at the very least, an oral agreement.[114] The interesting aspect of this position is the apparent relaxation of the strict positivist line in that members of the United Nations not voting for a resolution are nevertheless bound by it. Having provided as a condition of the juridical effectiveness of the resolutions of international organizations the consent of the socialist states and the general requirement of compatibility with the law of peaceful coexistence, Soviet commentators appear less concerned with upholding the principle of the right of a dissenting state not to be bound. A recent (1964) Soviet commentary notes, in a half-hearted attempt to narrow the breadth of the conceptual departure from strict positivism, that the resolutions are binding only if they involve "an interpretation, clarification or further development of norms already in effect."[115]

A familiar propaganda strain is injected by Minasian in his treatment of domestic legislation as an auxiliary source:

The democratic laws of individual states (especially the socialist states) promote the development of international law and the process of international legal norm formation and, under certain conditions, serve as possible sources thereof.[116]

---

[112] Shurshalov, Review of Minasian, *op. cit.*, *supra* note 14, p. 159. See also *Mezhdunarodnoe Pravo*, *op. cit.*, *supra* note 1, pp. 80, 81; and Levin, Problema Sootnosheniia, *op. cit.*, *supra* note 99, pp. 89, 90.

[113] *Ibid.* See also *Mezhdunarodnoe Pravo*, *op. cit.*, *supra* note 1, p. 283.

[114] See O. N. Khlestov, "Razrabotka Norm Kosmicheskovo Prava" [Working Out the Norms of Space Law], *SGIP*, No. 8 (1964), pp. 67–77; see 73–76.

[115] *Mezhdunarodnoe Pravo*, *op. cit.*, *supra* note 1, p. 81.

[116] Shurshalov's concurring comment in his review of Minasian's work. (Shurshalov, Review of Minasian, *op. cit.*, *supra* note 14, p. 159.)

This formulation is especially suited to Soviet needs. In addition to the general requirement of the agreement of states, it states the condition that laws must be democratic in order to be an auxiliary source. It thereby provides the basis for a special role for socialist legislation, by definition democratic and progressive, in influencing the development of international law.[117] Other Soviet commentaries are content to treat domestic law as an auxiliary source in the context of the general view that, to become normative as "general principles" (mentioned in paragraph 1[c], Article 38 of the Statute of the International Court of Justice), domestic law must be agreed to by states.

National legislation (for example, laws regarding state monopolies of foreign trade, etc.) exerts a great influence on the formation of rules of International Law. But national legislation acquires the status of a source of International Law only when it is recognized as a rule of International Law either through international treaty or through international custom. National legislation cannot therefore be considered an independent source of International Law.[118]

It is apparent that Soviet recognition of auxiliary sources of international law is little more than a nod in the direction away from the strict positivist, self-serving approach to international law. The requirements of state consent and compatibility with the law of coexistence remain basic conditions for the effectiveness of an international legal norm.

The agreement of states is considered the key to the juridical effectiveness of international judicial decisions and legal treatises:

Absent the agreement of states, decisions of international courts, opinions of public organizations, and scientific writings cannot be sources of international law, although they may influence its application and interpretation.[119]

---

[117] N. V. Mironov, "Sootnoshenie Mezhdunarodnovo Dogovora i Vnutrigo-sudarstvennovo Zakona" [The Relationships of International Treaties and Domestic Law], *Sovetskii Ezhegodnik, 1963, op. cit., supra* note, 25, pp. 150–170; see 170, where the progressive influence of socialist legislation on international law is contrasted with the reactionary influence of the domestic law of capitalist states.

[118] *International Law, op. cit., supra* note 2, pp. 12, 13. See also *Mezhdunarodnoe Pravo, op. cit., supra* note 1, p. 81.

[119] *Mezhdunarodnoe Pravo, op. cit., supra* note 1, p. 82, citing Tunkin, Voprosy Teorii, *op. cit., supra* note 9, p. 158.

This position is said to be confirmed by paragraph 1(*d*) of Article 38 of the Statute of the International Court of Justice, which provides that "judicial decisions and the teaching of the most highly qualified publicists. . .[can be relied upon for the purposes of the particular case before the court] as subsidiary means for the determination of rules of law."[120]

Article 38(*d*) of the Statute of the International Court of Justice includes legal decisions as auxiliary means of determining rules of International Law. A court, in particular the International Court, does not make law, but applies existing law. . .the International Court's application and interpretation of a legal rule are binding only upon the parties to the given dispute and only concern the particular case in question.[121]

Nevertheless, it is conceded that decisions of the Court and treatises "have a very great importance in stating the existence or lack at a given period of rules of International Law."[122]

Central to the general Soviet approach to the sources of international law are positivist insistence upon the agreement of states as the sole means of formulating international legal norms, and the concept of the law of peaceful coexistence as *jus cogens*. This approach permits resistance to hostile international legal principles on the basis of lack of Soviet, or, in the peaceful coexistence context, socialist consent, or of conflict with the principles of peaceful coexistence. The agreement theory is principally relied upon in defending against Western views that the "general principles" referred to in paragraph 1(*c*) of Article 38 of the Statute of the International Court of Justice are sources of international law, additional to treaties and custom. The use of the agreement theory on the offense is suggested by Tunkin's view that the fundamental principles of peaceful coexistence have been accepted as "general principles" under Article 38 of the Statute of the International Court of Justice. In keeping with the general pattern followed in the statement of Soviet legal positions, propaganda is utilized to the maximum to provide position support. The main line behind the semantic front, however, remains that of consent and unilateral characterization of the progressive.

[120] Briggs, *op. cit., supra* note 79, p. 1077.
[121] *International Law, op. cit., supra* note 2, p. 13.
[122] *Ibid.*

CHAPTER FOUR

❧❧❧

SUBJECTS OF INTERNATIONAL LAW

The policy and law of peaceful coexistence require selectivity in defining subjects of international law, since only a subject can avail itself of the benefits of that law or be subordinated to it. Generally, the Soviet Union has taken a strict approach to the question of international legal personality in keeping with the basic positivist orientation of its positions on international law. Soviet jurists have been reluctant to extend the concept beyond the nation-state for fear of detracting from the prerogatives of sovereignty and encouraging world government. They have, of course, expanded international legal personality when compelled to by circumstances or when it is convenient to meet foreign policy objectives. Their belated recognition of international organizations as subjects of international law is an example of the former approach. On the other hand, their proponency of legal personality for nations struggling for liberation reflects a position of convenience. Despite relaxation of the strict view in the areas mentioned, Soviet commitment to the view that only states can create international norms presages continued emphasis upon the nation-state as the principal subject of international law.

THE NATION-STATE

The Soviets define a subject of international law as "any entity . . . which has rights and obligations under international treaties and custom."[1] This definition, basically geared to the agreement theory of norm formulation, is flexible enough to permit the

[1] *Mezhdunarodnoe Pravo* [International Law], ed. D. B. Levin and G. P. Kaliuzhnaia (Moscow: Publishing House "Legal Literature," 1964), p. 96.

inclusion of entities other than states which acquire rights and obligations under the law of coexistence. Even under the earlier view which limited international legal personality to the nation-state, provision was made for other entities because of policy needs. The 1957 textbook on international law stated the earlier position as follows:

...As a rule only a State can be such a subject under present-day International Law.

In modern bourgeois legal writings, a number of scholars (Jessup, Lauterpacht, Scelle, etc.) favour the extension of the range of subjects of International Law to include international organizations and even physical persons.

But this contradicts the very essence of International Law as interstate law, whose purpose is to regulate the relations between States on the basis of their sovereign equality.

No international organizations, still less physical persons, can be subjects of International Law.[2]

Despite this restrictive approach, premised upon the purpose of international law as regulating relations between states, the Soviet position reflected flexibility in the interest of foreign policy needs by holding, somewhat inconsistently, that "a nation, fighting for its independence and at the stage of establishing its own State, is as a rule a subject of International Law."[3] The legal support for national liberation thus provided was complemented by emphasis upon the legal equality of emerging states. "All States without exception are subjects of International Law, regardless of the level of their economic, political and cultural development."[4]

The present view reflects a broader approach to the question of international legal personality by relating it to the enjoyment of rights and obligations under treaty and customary norms, rather than the capacity to participate in interstate relations. The state, however, remains the principal subject of international law. The earlier views relating to the international legal personality of

[2] *International Law* (Moscow: Foreign Languages Publishing House, n.d.), p. 82.
[3] *Ibid.*, p. 90.
[4] *Ibid.*, p. 89.

74

nations struggling for national liberation and the equality of states
are restated. The expanded rationale of the former premises personality upon the right of self-determination.

Also included as subjects of international law are nations conducting a
struggle for national liberation which have created in the process of that
struggle organs charged with the functions of state power. Such nations are
in the process of becoming states.
. . .recognition [of a nation's international legal personality] flows from the
right of self-determination . . . one of the generally recognized principles of
contemporary international law. [5]

Special polemical treatment is given the status of emerging states as
subjects of international law:

In recent years, the number of subjects of international law has grown
considerably. As a result of the collapse of the colonial system of imperialism
there have appeared many new states which have freed themselves from the
colonial yoke and embarked upon the path of independent national development. All of these are now subjects of international law. [6]

The appeal of the Soviet position to emerging and neutralist states is
obvious and intended. The courtship of neutralist support for Soviet
policies and legal positions is readily identifiable as a feature of the
Soviet Union's approach to international law.

The general Soviet view that the state remains the principal
subject of international law[7] appears to be diluted in a 1965 commentary which emphasizes the sovereign rights of nations and

[5] *Mezhdunarodnoe Pravo, op. cit., supra* note 1, p. 96. The cease-fire agreement
relating to hostilities in Indo-China, adopted at the Geneva Conference in
1954, is cited as a precedent which supports the proposition that nations struggling for national liberation are subjects of international law, since two of the
parties to it were the resistence movements of Laos and Cambodia. (*Ibid.*, pp.
96, 97.) But cf. B. B. Ganiushkin, Review of A. N. Talalaev, *Iuridicheskaia
Priroda Mezhdunarodnovo Dogovora* [The Legal Character of International Agree-
ments] (Moscow: Publishing House of the Institute of International Relations,
1963), *SGIP*, No. 7 (1964), pp. 167–169; see 167, where it is noted that parties
to multilateral agreements can be entities which are not subjects of international
law (e.g., colonies and combatant parties) and that this neither affects the international legal character of the agreement nor bestows international legal
personality on the parties. See, generally, G. V. Ignatenko, "Mezhdunarodnaia
Pravosub'ektnost' Natsii" [International Legal Personality of Nations], *SGIP*,
No. 10 (1966), pp. 75–82.
[6] *Ibid.*, p. 98.
[7] *Ibid.*, p. 96.

peoples (e.g., to determine national destiny, select a government and social order, change foreign policies of the state and its government, decide questions of peace and war, and struggle for disarmament and arms control) and the consequent need to accord them sufficient international legal personality to realize their rights. The personality accorded is inchoate in the sense that it comes into play only if the state representing the nation or people does not reflect the national or popular will. [8]

. . . this does not mean that the people take the place of the state as a subject of international law because. . .under favorable circumstances they create their own organization of state power; and when state power expresses the will of the people, the masses do not strive for a parallel expression of their own will contrary to that of the state, which occurs wherever and whenever the state organs do not reflect the will of the people. From this it is clear that in our days the role of states in international relations must not be overestimated. [9]

The corollary to this is that in socialist states, where the interests of the people are always reflected in state policies, there is no need for the nation or people to operate as subjects of international law. On the other hand, in the exploitative societies of capitalism, state policies do not reflect the interests of the people and international legal personality is necessary as a means of struggle against the ruling circles who control the state. [10] This approach, in effect, provides support for the socialist principle of popular sovereignty (i.e., the state cannot act contrary to the real interests of the people) and for recognition, as subjects of international law, of separatist or revolutionary movements in capitalist states. The limited dilution of the primacy of the state as a subject of international law favors the cause of socialism.

[8] M. I. Lazarev, "Mezhdunarodnopravovye Voprosy Dvizheniia Narodov za Mir" [International Legal Aspects of the Peoples' Movement for Peace], *Sovetskii Ezhegodnik, 1963* (Moscow: Publishing House "Science," 1965), pp. 45–69; see 65.

[9] *Ibid.*, p. 66.

[10] *Ibid.*, pp. 63–66. See also L. A. Modzhorian, *Osnovnye Prava i Obiazannosti Gosudarstv* [The Fundamental Rights and Duties of States] (Moscow: Publishing House "Legal Literature," 1965), p. 12.

⇾⇾⟩⟨⟨⟨

Sovereignty, national, as well as state, is the key element of the Soviet approach to international legal personality.

The basic character of a subject of international law is sovereignty which is possessed by a nation [and a state], but not by a government, international organization or a person.[11]

So long as international law is a law between nation-states, the basic characteristic of its subjects will be sovereignty.[12]

This element is manipulated to accord personality to entities when it serves the Soviet interests to do so, and to attack the status of entities not favored by the policy of coexistence. As indicated above, the Soviets generously extend legal personality to nations and peoples in capitalist states in the interest of separatism or revolution; but they presume a coincidence of national (popular) and state will in socialist states which makes separate, international legal existence for the nation or people unnecessary. Furthermore, a distinction is made between nations struggling for national liberation and other types of combatants in civil conflicts.[13] The former are treated as subjects of international law because the law and policy of coexistence, structured on support for national liberation, recognize their sovereign rights; the latter remain in a legal limbo subject to ad hoc characterizations of personality, dependent upon the policy need to confer a right or impose an obligation under international law (e.g., the right to conclude an armistice agreement, or the duty to observe the laws of war). Similarly, dependent nations and colonial peoples are not treated as subjects of international law unless they are pursuing national liberation. This obvious encouragement to national liberation in the interest of the policy of coexistence is matched by the legal position that restrictions upon sovereignty resulting from neutrality and neutralism, favored statuses under that policy, do not affect international legal personality.[14] Despite the

[11] G. P. Zadorozhnyi, *Mirnoe Sosushchestvovanie i Mezhdunarodnoe Pravo* [Peaceful Coexistence and International Law] (Moscow: Publishing House "International Relations," 1965), p. 461. See also Ganiushkin, *op. cit., supra* note 5, p. 167; and Modzhorian, *op. cit., supra* note 10, p. 10.

[12] Iu. Ia. Baskin, "Institut Priznaniia v Mezhdunarodnom Prave" [Recognition in International Law], *SGIP*, No. 2 (1966), pp. 158, 159; see 159.

[13] Ganiushkin, *op. cit., supra* note 5, p. 167.

[14] *Mezhdunarodnoe Pravo, op. cit., supra* note 1, p. 100. See also *International Law, op. cit., supra* note 2, pp. 92, 93.

→>>‹‹‹-

subjectivism of Soviet criteria in identifying subjects of international law, the Soviet Union calls for the establishment of an objective criterion to prevent arbitrary characterizations.[15]

A classic example of Soviet manipulation of sovereignty as a qualification for legal personality is the difference in treatment of the component states of socialist and capitalist federations. Soviet jurists, clearly showing their political orientation, claim that restraints upon component state autonomy in capitalist federal states limit international personality to the federal entity. In contrast, they assert that a socialist federation such as the Soviet Union preserves the sovereignty of its constituent republics so that they, as well as the Union, have international personality.

A bourgeois federation, actually being one in name only, is organized without concern for the right of nations to self-determination. There is a tendency towards the strengthening of federal organs at the expense of the independence of local organs (e.g., the United States).

In international relations a bourgeois federal state has legal personality. As a rule, the individual members do not conduct international relations and are not subjects of international law.

The Soviet federation. . .is fundamentally different from a bourgeois federation. The former is based upon the voluntary union of sovereign Soviet republics and preserves their sovereignty. The U.S.S.R. is a subject of international law and in accordance with the Law of 1 February 1944, each Union Republic also is a subject of international law.[16]

---

[15] Modzhorian, *op. cit., supra* note 10, p. 10.

[16] *Mezhdunarodnoe Pravo, op. cit., supra* note 1, pp. 98, 99. See also *International Law, op. cit., supra* note 2, pp. 90, 91. Article 1 of the Statute of February 1, 1944 amended the Soviet Constitution by providing "that union republics may deal directly with foreign states and conclude agreements with them." (*Sbornik Zakonov SSSR, 1938–1961* [Collection of Laws of the U.S.S.R.] [Moscow: Publishing House "Proceedings of the Soviets of Deputies of the Working Masses of the U.S.S.R.," 1961], pp. 40, 41.) Amendment of the Soviet Constitution during the period of the formation of the United Nations provided convenient domestic law support for the Soviet bid for membership for all the constituent republics as well as the Soviet Union. This attempt was only partially successful in that the Soviet Union was given three seats in the United Nations (i.e., Ukraine, Byelorussia, and the Soviet Union). The claim is still made that the constituent republics of the Soviet Union have international legal personality, but now the purpose is to demonstrate the possibility of a state not losing its personality by incorporation into a federation such as the Soviet Union, the model for the socialist world state of the future (See V. I. Lisovskii, *Mezhdunarodnoe Pravo* [International Law] [2d ed.; Moscow: State Publishing House "Higher School," 1961], pp. 71, 72; and M. V. Ianovskii, "Sovetskie Soiuznye

The formation of the U.S.S.R. by the Soviet Republics is a supreme manifestation of their sovereignty and not a renunciation of it.[17]

In claiming the benefits of international legal personality for the constituent republics of the Soviet Union, the Soviets rely upon the formal provisions of their domestic law which appear to provide for the unhampered conduct of foreign relations. The Soviets choose this formal approach in order to ignore practical limitations on the exercise of external sovereignty by the constituent republics. In contrast, nonsocialist federations are subjected to the sterner test of the actual exercise of sovereignty in international relations. An interesting footnote to the Soviet position is the view that any action which interferes with the exercise of sovereign rights by the constituent republics of the Soviet Union violates international law.

Any action hampering the Union Republics from freely exercising their rights in international relations is a violation of international law and runs counter to the present requirement of peaceful coexistence of states with different social and political systems, because the Union Republics are acting as a progressive force in the struggle for world peace, for friendship and cooperation among the nations.[18]

This view is a specific formulation of the broader principle that interference with the actions of any progressive force (e.g., the Soviet Union, socialist and neutralist states, or nations fighting for national liberation) is a violation of contemporary international law. The blank check intended for the forces of peace and socialism—especially the Soviet Union as the vanguard of such forces —under the law of coexistence is clear and unambiguous.

Respubliki—Polnopravnye Sub'ekty Mezhdunarodnovo Prava" [The Soviet Constituent Republics—Fully Competent Subjects of International Law], *SGIP*, No. 12 [1962], pp. 55–64, for the claim that the fifteen constituent republics of the U.S.S.R. are fully qualified subjects of international law. See also Bernard A. Ramundo, *The [Soviet] Socialist Theory of International Law* [Washington, D.C.: Institute for Sino-Soviet Studies, The George Washington University, 1964], pp. 47–52).

[17] P. E. Nedbailo and V. A. Vasilenko, "Mezhdunarodnaia Pravosub'ektnost' Sovetskikh Soiuznykh Respublik" [The International Legal Personality of the Soviet Union-Republics], *Sovetskii Ezhegodnik, 1963, op. cit., supra* note 8, pp. 85–108; see 106.

[18] *Ibid.*, p. 108.

Even selective reliance upon sovereignty cannot satisfy all of the Soviet Union's needs in establishing criteria for international legal personality. A rationale based upon sovereignty provides for the state and nation, but it does not explain the reality of international organizations acting as subjects of international law.[19] A broader formulation stated in terms of the possession of rights and obligations under treaties and customary norms appears to meet the Soviet need, although it can be argued that the formulation is broad enough to include legal personality for individuals as well.[20] This troublesome exposure is finessed in the most recent Soviet textbook on international law by an enumeration of the subjects of international law palatable to the Soviet Union, without the statement of an all-embracing criterion of personality.[21]

INTERNATIONAL ORGANIZATIONS

Fearful of encouraging world government, the Soviets initially denied the legal personality of international organizations. The 1957 textbook on international law rationalizes this view as follows:

International organizations, regardless of the extent of their powers, sometimes resembling a subject of law, nevertheless cannot be equated to the States which created them, insofar as the rights of a State and the rights of international organizations have a qualitatively different foundation and nature. While the rights of a State are founded on its sovereignty, the rights of an international organization are based on agreements between States, that is, are the product of the sovereign rights of the State. International organizations act within the terms of reference laid down in their charter or other document signed by the States which set them up. The existence of a State as a subject of International Law is indivisibly linked with a particular territory and population. International organizations have none of these attributes.[22]

---

[19] Zadorozhnyi, Mirnoe Sosushchestvovanie, *op. cit., supra* note 11; and M. I. Lazarev, V. S. Vereshchetin, and L. G. Shatov, "Novaia Kniga o Pravosub'-ektnosti v Mezhdunarodnom Prave" [A New Book on Legal Personality in International Law] (Review of L. A. Modzhorian, *Osnovnye Prava i Obiazannosti Gosudarstv*" [The Fundamental Rights and Duties of States] [Moscow: Publishing House "Legal Literature," 1965], *SGIP*, No. 1 [1966], pp. 153–155; see 154.)

[20] Lazarev, Vereshchetin, and Shatov, *op. cit., supra* note 19, p. 154.

[21] *Mezhdunarodnoe Pravo* [International Law], ed. F. I. Kozhevnikov (Moscow: Publishing House "International Relations," 1964), pp. 37–39.

[22] *International Law, op. cit., supra* note 2, pp. 89, 90.

->>><<<-

Lisovskii (1961) and Modzhorian (1965) flatly state that "internathional organizations are not subjects of international law."[23] A 1964 commentary notes the lack of unanimity of views among Soviet jurists as follows:

Some authors consider that international organizations, the creature of the agreement of states, are the collective organs of these states and do not, themselves, have international legal personality. Other authors hold that the U.N. and certain other international organizations . . . have a special limited form of international personality distinguishable from that enjoyed by states.[24]

In apparently opting for the view of limited international legal personality, this commentary states that the legal personality of international organizations is strictly limited by the competence granted them under their basic constitutive charters.[25] A later commentary notes that although the matter is still in dispute, the legal personality of international organizations is widely recognized "in the Soviet science of international law."[26] Tunkin states unequivocally that international organizations "at the present time operate as subjects of international law."[27] Tunkin's view appears most compatible with Soviet efforts to utilize the United Nations as an instrument of the policy and law of coexistence, and the increased recognition of the need for international organizations to cope with the growing interdependence of states.

The agreements entered into by international organizations present a conceptual problem since, although not the agreements of states, they are said to constitute international legal norms.[28] Tunkin rejects the views advanced by some Soviet jurists that these agreements (1) are the same as agreements between states, or (2) actually represent the delegated authority of the member states (i.e., the international organization acts as "agent" for the member

[23] Lisovskii, *op. cit., supra* note 11, pp. 69, 70; and Modzhorian, *op. cit., supra* note 10, pp. 19–33.

[24] *Mezhdunarodnoe Pravo, op. cit., supra* note 1, p. 98.

[25] *Ibid.*

[26] Ganiushkin, *op. cit., supra* note 5, p. 247.

[27] G. I. Tunkin, *Voprosy Teorii Mezhdunarodnovo Prava* [Problems of the Theory of International Law] (Moscow: State Publishing House of Legal Literature, 1962), p. 80.

[28] *Ibid.*, pp. 81, 82.

states).[29] He distinguishes between the agreements of states and
those concluded by international organizations on the basis of the
constitutional limitations on the scope and competence of the latter
organizations.[30] Tunkin disposes of the conceptual problem by a
de minimis approach which discounts the importance of the norms
formulated as a result of the agreements concluded by international
organizations: "The norms created by the agreements of international organizations have an insignificant place in international
law and are secondary norms as compared to those established by
states."[31]

Tunkin's dilemma is clear. He cannot ignore the fact of international life that international organizations conclude agreements as
subjects of international law. At the same time, he wishes to maintain
the positivist status quo under which the sole formal source of international law is the agreement of states. His dismissal of the dilemma
as *de minimis* is sounder than the fictional approach embodied in the
"same as states' agreements" or "agency" theories adopted by other
Soviet jurists. The point that clearly emerges from the route around
the dilemma, be it *de minimis* or based upon a fiction, is Soviet
recognition that the agreement theory of international norm
formulation requires explanation and perhaps modification in a
world increasingly interdependent and, as a consequence, de-
creasingly, consent-oriented. The thrust of the foregoing is that, to
enhance the credibility and acceptability of their policy-oriented
legal positions, Soviet jurists are constrained to take into account
changing world conditions. This requirement substantially increases
the burden of their commitment to the realization of the foreign
policy objectives of the Soviet Union.

THE PARTY

In spite of an early flirtation with the view that the international
organization of communist parties, the Comintern (1919–1943), had

[29] The latter view has been stated as follows: "Treaties concluded between
international organisations [*sic*] express, in the ultimate analysis, the delegation
of the rights of States themselves as subjects of International Law" (*International
Law, op. cit., supra* note 2, p. 247). See also Modzhorian, *op. cit., supra* note 10,
pp. 19–33.
[30] Tunkin, Voprosy Teorii, *op. cit., supra* note 27, pp. 82–84.
[31] *Ibid.*, p. 84.

international legal personality,[32] the Soviets have never attempted to obtain recognition of the party as a subject of international law. In relations with the capitalist camp, the basic concern of the contemporary law of peaceful coexistence, party-to-party relationships are meaningless, as the communist parties in capitalist states do not formulate governmental policies. On the other hand, within the socialist commonwealth of nations, foreign policy is made by the party and relations between the party-states of the commonwealth, although cast in the form of conventional relations between states, i.e., bilateral and multilateral, "are not interstate relations in the true meaning of these words; they are instead inter-Party ties."[33] In practice, national party-dominated delegations conduct international negotiations within the socialist commonwealth.[34] A recent Soviet commentary notes the role of the parties in intra-commonwealth relations as follows:

The basic principle underlying the international relations of socialist countries. . .is the leadership and direction of the communist and workers' parties. . .The leadership of the communist and workers' parties effectively ensures unity in the foreign policy and international practice of the socialist states in developing and perfecting collaboration between socialist states as well as in formulating a common position of the socialist states in resolving the most important international problems which confront all mankind.[35]

The leading and directing role of the parties in international relations has been elevated to a basic international legal principle under

[32] See Ivo Lapenna, *Conceptions Sovietiques de Droit Internationale Public* [Soviet Conceptions of Public International Law] (Paris: A. Pedone, 1954), pp. 176–179.

[33] Ferenc A. Vali, "Soviet Satellite Status and International Law," *The JAG Journal*, XV, No. 8 (1961), pp. 169–172; see 170.

[34] See, for example, the *Pravda* accounts of negotiations between Soviet and Rumanian and Czechoslovak party leaders ("Peregovory Rukovoditelei KPSS i Sovetskovo Pravitel'stva s Partiinopravitel'stvennoi Delegatsiei Sotsialisticheskoi Respubliki Rumynii" [Negotiations between the Party and Governmental Leaders of the U.S.S.R. and Rumania] *Pravda* [September 5, 1965], p. 1; and "Peregovory Rukovoditelei KPSS i Sovetskovo Pravitel'stva s Partiino-gosudarstvennoi Delegatsiei Chekhoslovatskoi Sotsialisticheskoi Respubliki" [Negotiations Between the Party and Governmental Leaders of the U.S.S.R. and the Czechoslovak Socialist Republic], *Ibid.* [September 15, 1965], p. 1).

[35] V. M. Shurshalov, "Mezhdunarodno-pravovye Printsipy Sotrudnichestva Sotsialisticheskikh Gosudarstv" [International Legal Principles of the Collaboration of Socialist States], *SGIP*, No. 7 (1962), pp. 95–105; see 100.

socialist internationalism.[36] Furthermore, decisions and agreements reached at meetings of national party leaders approach the norm formulation produced by the agreement of states.

. . . the joint documents approved at the meetings of the representatives of the communist and workers' parties are of historical significance. . .[Although] not sources of international law in the strict legal sense, they do exert a decisive influence on the content of the treaty and other relations of socialist states.[37]

In spite of their role as international actors, however, the parties can be expected to remain in the background as the operational element behind the institutional facade of the nation-state. So long as the nonparty states of the capitalist camp continue to exist, and national statehood retains its importance in intra-commonwealth relations—the development of polycentrism within the socialist commonwealth indicates the continued importance of national identity and statehood—there is no need to confer international legal personality upon the national parties. Actually, the basic organizational principle of the communist parties (i.e., to remain separate and distinct from the institutional apparatus of the state),[38] makes necessary, at least at this stage of communist construction,[39] the nation-state as an institutional facade with the requisite international legal personality behind and through which the national parties act. This is the basic function of the nation-state, both in relations within the camp and without. It is enough for Soviet

[36] *Ibid.*

[37] *Ibid.* See also *Mezhdunarodnopravovye Formy Sotrudnichestva Sotsialisticheskikh Gosudarstv* [International Legal Forms of the Collaboration of Socialist States], ed. V. M. Shurshalov (Moscow: Publishing House of the Academy of Sciences of the U.S.S.R., 1962), pp. 35, 36, where it is stated that both the Warsaw Treaty Organization and the Council for Mutual Economic Assistance act only as implementing organs for the policy decisions made at multilateral meetings of party leaders.

[38] See, for example, Article 41(c) of the Rules of the Communist Party of the Soviet Union (1961) which provides that "Party organizations must not act in place of government. . ." (Jan F. Triska, *Soviet Communism, Programs and Rules* [San Francisco: Chandler Publishing Company, 1962], p. 179).

[39] "The need for such organizational devices (as the nation-state) is felt to be particularly great because in the current Communist thinking 'socialist' and subsequently even Communist countries will continue to exist as separate entities until a world-wide Communist society emerges." (Zbigniew K. Brzezinski, "The Organization of the Communist Camp," *World Politics*, XIII [1960–1961], pp. 175–209; see 208.)

present needs in this area to lay a legal basis for the primacy of party control within the socialist commonwealth "by imparting a legal character to the principle of the leading and directing role of the parties."[40] Moreover, it does not appear that there will be a future need for the emergence of the national parties as subjects of international law. If Soviet ideological goals are realized and a "world-wide communist society" is achieved, international law and international relations will have disappeared because of the relega- tion of the nation-state to "the museum of antiquities."[41] There will then be no international legal personality for the national communist parties to assume although they may, in fact, be the representative entities for all of the nations of the new world.

INDIVIDUALS

The Soviets oppose all attempts to extend international legal personality to physical as well as juridical persons as an infringement upon state sovereignty and a step towards world government. They fear that sovereign prerogatives and national allegiance will suffer if individuals have the right to call a state to account internationally.[42] As a consequence, the Soviet position is that neither physical nor juridical persons can be subjects of international law.[43] The con- trary views of certain Western jurists are dismissed as attempts "to depreciate the significance of state sovereignty and to provide a basis for the practice of the large imperialist states to intervene in the internal affairs of other states."[44] Given a nonsocialist world,

[40] Ramundo, *op. cit.*, *supra* note 16, pp. 36, 37.

[41] *Ibid.*, pp. 47–52. Tunkin notes the inevitability of the disappearance of international law as follows: "There has been human society without law. Mankind inevitably will come to a new organization of society which will not have any law, and hence, international law." (Tunkin, Voprosy Teorii, *op. cit.*, *supra* note 27, p. 185.) "The museum of antiquities" is part of the classic formu- lation of the withering away of the state contained in Frederick Engels, *The Origin of the Family, Private Property and the State* (New York: International Publishers, 1942), p. 158.

[42] Y. Korovin, "Peace Through Law: Two Views," *International Affairs*, No. 7 (1963), pp. 100–102; see 101. See also Zadorozhnyi, Mirnoe Sosushchestvovanie, *op. cit.*, *supra* note 11, pp. 462, 463.

[43] *Mezhdunarodnoe Pravo*, *op. cit.*, *supra* note 1, p. 97.

[44] *Ibid.*

Soviet reluctance to accept the pluralistic theory of international personality is understandable, since the orientation of the Soviet Union's approach to international law is to ensure a legal basis for the sovereign freedom of action of the nation-state.

Despite their strong opposition to the pluralistic theory of international legal personality,[45] the Soviets seem to be assisting in its development by recognizing and increasing individual rights and obligations under international law. Soviet jurists have always recognized that physical as well as juridical persons can acquire derivatively international rights and obligations, with the state interposed between the individual and the international legal order to insulate the former against international legal personality.[46] There seems to be a relaxation of this approach in recent commentaries which speak of individual rights and obligations unrelated to the state of nationality and, therefore, not derivable through it. For example, one commentary notes the "right and duty under contemporary international law of every individual to struggle for peace and the independence of his country."[47] The Soviets are also seeking to enlarge the area of personal international legal liability for aggression and other activities prohibited by the law of peaceful coexistence. In their efforts to achieve the priority objectives of peaceful coexistence, Soviet jurists appear prepared to compromise the consistency of earlier formulations concerning the international legal personality of individuals. Consistency of formulation, however, is not as essential as sensitivity to the foreign policy needs of the Soviet Union.

---

[45] "The pluralistic theory [of international legal personality] reflects the attempt of large international monopolies and cartels to acquire the rights of subjects of international law. The most avid proponents of this reactionary theory at the present time are the ruling circles of the imperialist powers." (Lisovskii, *op. cit., supra* note 16, p. 69.)

[46] *Mezhdunarodnoe Pravo, op. cit., supra* note 1, pp. 97, 98. See also *International Law, op. cit., supra* note 2, p. 90.

[47] Lazarev, *op. cit., supra* note 8, p. 46.

CHAPTER FIVE

SOVEREIGNTY

Traditionally, the Soviet Union has been a vigorous exponent of the sovereign prerogatives of the nation-state, considering state sovereignty to be "the keystone of international law."[1] Sovereignty is used both as a shield to protect the Soviet Union from interference by capitalist states, and as a weapon in its struggle with such states.[2] It is used as a shield to protect against interference in Soviet domestic affairs, and to oppose the development of nonsocialist, international organizations with supranational authority. As a weapon in the international class struggle, sovereignty—in the form of the sovereign right of peoples to national liberation, revolutionary struggle, and statehood; and noninterference with sovereign prerogatives after liberation—is a means of strengthening the socialist camp at the expense of the capitalist camp.

Sovereignty is a reliable means of defending the small States from the major imperialist Powers' attempts to subjugate them to their diktat.

The creation of aggressive blocs, the building of military bases abroad, intervention in the internal affairs of other countries and the suppression of the national liberation movement are all aggressive actions which are incompatible with the sovereignty of States and peoples.[3]

---

[1] L. B. Shapiro, "The Soviet Concept of International Law," *Yearbook of World Affairs, 1948*, II, pp. 272–310; see 273; and P. E. Nedbailo and V. A. Vasilenko, "Mezhdunarodnaia Pravosub'ektnost' Sovetskikh Soiuznykh Respublik" [The International Legal Personality of the Soviet Constituent Republics], *Sovetskii Ezhegodnik, 1963* (Moscow: Publishing House "Science," 1965), pp. 85–108; see 105, 106.

[2] Mintauts Chakste, "Soviet Concepts of the State, International Law and Sovereignty," 43 *AJIL* 21–36 (1949), p. 31. See also George C. Guins, *Soviet Law and Society* (The Hague: Martinus Nijhoff, 1953), p. 334.

[3] *International Law* (Moscow: Foreign Languages Publishing House, n.d.), p.97.

Today the struggle for sovereignty is more than ever before linked with the struggle for peace and against imperialist aggression. In this struggle the Soviet Union has the support of People's China [*sic*] and other socialist countries, and also of the friends of peace throughout the world.[4]

Soviet propaganda claims leadership for the Soviet Union in the "struggle against imperialism and colonialism and for peace, democracy, national independence and socialism."

Within the socialist camp, sovereignty is used neither as a shield nor a weapon. Rather, it is an integrating force in that socialist states are expected to exercise their sovereign rights, sacrificing national interests where necessary, in the common, higher interest of the socialist commonwealth of nations. The Soviet Union claims to be the most experienced builder of communism, therefore, in the best position to define this higher interest. This claim is being increasingly challenged—not only by the Chinese Communists in the struggle for leadership of the socialist world, but also by other socialist states as a manifestation of polycentric tendencies and increasing concentration on national rather than collective goals. Yet Soviet experience in building communism remains the cover for the bid of the Soviet Union for primacy in commonwealth affairs.

Thus, the Soviet approach to sovereignty is intended to provide flexibility in domestic and foreign policies vis-à-vis capitalist and socialist states alike. As the basic formulation of positivism, it serves minimum Soviet legal objectives by insulating the Soviet Union against the international legal order. To the extent that sovereignty is utilized to weaken the old and to create a new, international legal order, it serves maximum legal objectives. Sovereignty, a fundamental principle of the law of peaceful coexistence, is compatible with, and can serve, minimum and maximum policy objectives because it is easily manipulated in the Soviet interest.

SHIELD

In the Soviet view, "sovereignty is destined to act as a legal barrier protecting against imperialistic encroachment, and securing the existence of the most advanced social and state forms."[5] This

[4] *Ibid.*, p. 98.
[5] Chakste, *op. cit., supra* note 2, p. 31.

approach requires a championing of the sovereign prerogatives of the nation-state and the nation struggling for liberation. The Soviets employ the familiar technique of a legal campaign on behalf of sovereignty, supported by polemical propaganda attacks upon those who advocate a reduction of sovereign prerogatives, however enlightened their purpose. In these attacks, the Soviet Union and the socialist camp portray themselves as defenders of the nation-state system and the national liberation movement against those who attempt to weaken the concept of sovereignty, the stated indispensable condition of both.

. . . [imperialist powers] hold that international law, if it does not already do so, at least is approaching a negation of state sovereignty, the recognition of individuals as subjects of international law, the conversion of international organization into something like a superstate, and the condoning of extensive interference in the internal affairs of states . . . as part of their struggle against the socialist countries and the national liberation movements in the colonies.[6]

Such developments as the formation of the world socialist system and its increasingly decisive influence in international affairs, the collapse of the colonial system, and the emergence of many new states are said to have upset imperialist plans to undermine state sovereignty, and to have resulted in the strengthening of the principles of respect for sovereignty, noninterference in internal affairs, and other progressive principles directed against aggression and colonialism as part of the new law of peaceful coexistence.[7] The Soviets claim that these results have been achieved because "the Soviet Union consistently combines the struggle for its own independence, sovereignty and security with the struggle for the independence and sovereignty of all peoples."[8] The magnitude of the "victory" over the forces of imperialism is measured by the

[6] G. I. Tunkin, *Voprosy Teorii Mezdunarodnovo Prava* [Problems of the Theory of International Law] (Moscow: State Publishing House of Legal Literature, 1962), pp. 203, 204.

[7] *Ibid.*, p. 204.

[8] *International Law, op. cit., supra* note 3, p. 96. See also Victor Maevskii, "Pokonchit' s Vmeshatel'stvom Imperialistov vo Vnutrennie Dela Narodov" [End the Interference of Imperialists in the Internal Affairs of Nations], *Pravda* (October 9, 1965), p. 3.

incorporation into the Charter of the United Nations of the basic organizational principle of "the sovereign equality of all its Members." [9]

Soviet jurists define sovereignty in the traditional terms of "the supremacy of a state in its own territory and independence in international relations." [10] Their apparent concern over world government, in the form of supranational international organizations or some other, is clearly evident from the cautionary comment that "In the interest of greater accuracy, it would be well to add that independence [in international relations] is expressed in the absence of subordination of a state to the power of other states, directly as well as through international organizations." [11] Yet the Soviets do recognize the efficacy of voluntary restrictions upon sovereignty in the interests of international cooperation. They emphasize that these restrictions, either in the form of entry into an international organization or the conclusion of a treaty, must be freely accepted by the state concerned. [12] Restrictions which are contained in agreements with socialist states are *ipso facto* truly voluntary, and therefore above question; those arising in the practice of capitalist states are presumptively exploitative and an infringement upon the sovereignty of the state concerned. Reverse discrimination against capitalist states is provided for in the proposition that a defeated aggressor state can be involuntarily subjected to restrictions upon its sovereignty. The discrimination results from the concept of aggression which is associated only with the acts of capitalist states in Soviet legal characterizations. This view, clearly showing its polemics, is formulated as follows:

> The forcible restriction of the sovereignty of States which are members of the international community is impermissible, except following aggression. The subjection of small States to the will of large States, or the subordination of the former by the latter is also impermissible. This is often cloaked by

---

[9] *Ibid.*, quoting Article 2(*1*) of the Charter of the United Nations.

[10] V. K. Sobakin, Review of N. A. Ushakov, *Suvernitet v Sovemennom Mezhdunarodnom Prave* [Sovereignty in Contemporary International Law] (Moscow: Publishing House of the Institute of International Relations, 1963), *SGIP*, No. 3 (1964), pp. 153–154; see 153.

[11] *Ibid.*

[12] *International Law, op. cit., supra* note 3, p. 97. See also *Ibid.*, p. 245.

hypocritical reference to the weak states' "voluntary restriction of sovereignty." The utter untenability of such references is particularly manifest in the relations between the colonial Powers and the so-called non-self-governing territories—relations which are tantamount to annexation.[13]

In effect, the Soviet position provides a double standard for judging infringements upon sovereignty, with restrictions in the interest of socialism presumed to be acceptable to the state concerned or provided for "as a matter of law."

In addition to voluntary restrictions upon their independence in external affairs, states must also observe the requirements of international law.

> Sovereignty is supremacy of a state within its own territory and independence in international affairs without, however, violation of the rights of other states and the generally accepted principles of international law. Sovereignty does not mean arbitrary rule or freedom to violate the principles of international law and international obligations. A violation or arbitrary unilateral denunciation of obligations undertaken cannot be justified by the invocation of sovereignty.[14]

Lisovskii takes a stricter view, reflecting earlier Soviet defensism vis-à-vis the international legal order, in defining sovereignty as "state power independent of every other power in domestic and foreign affairs."[15] Soviet proponency of the new international law of peaceful coexistence and the call for greater deference to that law, however, require a departure from earlier highly "individualistic" approaches (such as Lisovskii's) which negated the existence of a *jus cogens* to which state sovereignty is subordinate.[16] The attempt to create a new international legal order, of necessity, calls for a modification of conceptual predispositions towards absolute sovereignty. The Soviets now say that:

> ...the concept of absolute sovereignty ... is incompatible with ... contemporary international law [i.e., the law of peaceful coexistence].

---

[13] *Ibid.*

[14] *Mezhdunarodnoe Pravo* [International Law], ed. D. B. Levin and G. P. Kaluizhnaia (Moscow: Publishing House "Legal Literature," 1964), p. 100. See also *International Law, op. cit., supra* note 3, pp. 93, 96, and 97.

[15] V. I. Lisovskii, *Mezhdunarodnoe Pravo* [International Law] (2d ed.; Moscow: State Publishing House "Higher School," 1961), p. 64.

[16] T. A. Taracouzio, *The Soviet Union and International Law* (New York: Macmillan Company, 1935), pp. 26, 27.

➤➤❬❬

Proclaiming unlimited sovereignty of one state and thereby rejecting the sovereignty of all other states is in effect a rejection of sovereignty as a principle of international law.[17]

This departure from the extreme positivism of earlier positions is more apparent than real. The subordination of Soviet sovereign prerogatives to a new legal order based upon peaceful coexistence costs little in terms of loss of freedom of action, since the Soviet Union is structuring the new order to meet its foreign policy needs, and, as a fallback, maintaining the primacy of state sovereignty as the fundamental, underlying principle of coexistence.[18]

Soviet jurists preserve the efficacy of sovereignty as a fallback by taking the position that respect for sovereignty is indispensable to the peaceful coexistence of states.[19] ". . . the principle of sovereignty is inextricably connected under contemporary conditions with the necessity for ensuring peaceful coexistence. . ."[20] The five basic principles of peaceful coexistence, the Pancha Shila, for the most part, are related to the concept of sovereignty. In the principles of respect for territorial integrity and sovereignty and of noninterference in internal affairs the primacy accorded sovereignty is clear. The Soviets interpret the principle of equality and mutual benefit in international relations to flow from the sovereign equality of states, with arrangements which favor one party over the other considered a violation of the sovereignty of the disadvantaged party.[21] The principle of nonaggression, a limitation upon absolute sovereignty (i.e., the right to resort to war), is treated as "a legal guarantee of the sovereignty of all states."[22] Peaceful coexistence, as the principle embodying all that is progressive in international law, is premised upon respect for state sovereignty, the stated basis for the further progressive development of international law. The Soviet view is that sovereignty, the key element in the international legal order, is

[17] *Mezhdunarodnoe Pravo* [International Law], ed. F. I. Kozhevnikov (Moscow: Publishing House "International Relations," 1964), pp. 166, 167.

[18] See G. P. Zadorozhny, *Mirnoe Sosushchestvovanie i Mezhdunarodnoe Pravo* [Peaceful Coexistence and International Law] (Moscow: International Relations Publishing House, 1964), pp. 122–156.

[19] *Mezhdunarodnoe Pravo, op. cit., supra* note 14, p. 104.

[20] Sobakin, *op. cit., supra* note 10, p. 154.

[21] *Ibid.*

[22] *Ibid.*

"in one way or another related to all legal principles, institutions and norms."[23] The centrality of sovereignty is reflected in the following:

...international relations of sovereign states constitute the basic premise of international law, and international law serves as one of the means of asserting state sovereignty in international relations.[24]

The Soviet approach to sovereignty cannot be unequivocal lest unqualified positivism serve the maintenance of the status quo rather than the building of communism (i.e., the dynamism of foreign policy). Flexibility for foreign policy needs dictates a variable concept of sovereignty invokable at will in the interest of socialism which is to say, the Soviet Union. For example, the principle of the inviolability of a state's territory is described as "one of the most important generally recognized and generally binding principles of contemporary international law. . . [which] means the impermissibility and illegality of any violation against the territory of any state and of any measure directed against the territorial integrity of states."[25] Further, it is said that:

Territorial supremacy of a State constitutes an organic part of state sovereignty, and its infringement is impermissible.
The inviolability of state territory is one of the most important principles of present-day International Law.[26]

The principle is invoked in its most positivist form to protect socialist (1) systems from outside interference[27] and (2) boundaries against hostile claims, e.g., "The boundaries now effective in Europe are inviolable. Their maintenance is in the interest of all peoples."[28] The concept of territorial inviolability, however, is not so restrictively interpreted as to rule out socialist change.

[23] *Ibid.*, p. 153.
[24] Sobakin quoting Ushakov with approval in *Ibid.*, p. 154.
[25] N. A. Ushakov, "Poslanie N. S. Khrushcheva i Mirnoe Uregulirovanie Territorial'nykh Sporov mezhdu Gosudarstvami" [N. S. Khrushchev's Letter and the Peaceful Settlement of Territorial Disputes Between States], *SGIP*, No. 5 (1964), pp. 3–10; see 5.
[26] *International Law, op. cit., supra* note 3, pp. 176, 177.
[27] Zadorozhny, Mirnoe Sosushchestvovanie, *op. cit., supra* note 18, p. 399.
[28] "Ensure Security in Europe," trans. from *Pravda* (October 11, 1965), in *CDSP*, XVII, No. 41, p. 21.

The requirement for unconditional respect for territorial supremacy and territorial inviolability of any state. . .does not mean and cannot mean recognition and preservation of the status quo. It. . .does not rule out peaceful change.[29]

The peaceful change contemplated is socialist in character because it is specifically related to the right of self-determination which is the stated legal basis for progressive revolutionary change.

Contemporary international law accepts the possibility and necessity of territorial changes as part of the confirmation of the right of peoples and nations to self-determination as a basic principle.[30]
. . .present-day International Law and order . . . affirms that any nation has the right fully to determine its destiny and the destiny of its territory.[31]

The proposition that territory belongs to nations and peoples (not only the sovereign state) provides another manipulative basis for weakening the traditional principle of territorial sovereignty in the interest of socialism by application of the principle of popular sovereignty which would seem to require the use of territory in accordance with the real interests of the masses. Thus, it is possible to attack military base agreements as a use of territory by the state contrary to the real interest of the people of the nation in peace and neutralism.[32] The thrust of the foregoing is that if the concept of sovereignty is to assist in the realization of foreign policy objectives, it must be capable of manipulation in the Soviet interest.

Soviet insistence upon sovereign prerogatives (initially the reaction of the isolated Bolshevik regime to an international environment deemed hostile to it) still serves a protective function. The protective umbrella, however, has been expanded to include the members of the socialist commonwealth of nations, other socialist states, and the newly emerging states of Africa, Asia, and Latin America. It also takes into account the possibility of interference in

[29] Ushakov, *op. cit.*, *supra* note 25, p. 6.

[30] *Ibid.*, p. 7. See also *Mezhdunarodnoe Pravo, op. cit.*, *supra* note 14, p. 179.

[31] *International Law, op. cit.*, *supra* note 3, p. 180.

[32] See *Ibid.*, p. 245. See also, G. I. Tunkin and B. I. Nechaev, "Pravo Dogovo-rov na XV Sessii Komissii Mezhdunarodnovo Prava OON" [The Law of Treaties at the Fifteenth Session of the International Law Commission of the U.N.], *SGIP*, No. 2 (1964), pp. 84–92; see 85.

internal affairs by international organizations.[33] For example, efforts of the United Nations to delve into the events in Hungary in 1956 have been resisted on the basis of the sovereign principle of noninterference in domestic affairs reflected in Article 2(7) of the Charter of the United Nations. Similarly, despite the continuing, bitter split between the Soviet and Chinese Communist Parties, the Soviet delegate opposed consideration of the Tibet question at the Twentieth Session of the General Assembly of the United Nations as an invasion of the sovereignty of the Chinese People's Republic.[34] At the same session, the Soviet Union tabled a Draft Declaration on Non-Interference in the Internal Affairs of States and on Upholding their Independence and Sovereignty which was intended to strengthen the sovereignty umbrella through codification, and in the process, to demonstrate Soviet support for the sovereign prerogatives of the emerging states and the principles of the Charter of the United Nations.[35] Proponency of the Declaration is part of the portrayal of the Soviet Union as the principal defender of the prerogatives of

[33] Nikolai Ushakov, "Non-interference into the Affairs of Other States Must Be Observed," *Moscow News*, No. 28 (July 9, 1966), p. 6.

[34] "XX Sessiia General'noi Assamblei OON" [The Twentieth Session of the General Assembly of the United Nations], *Pravda* (September 24, 1965), p. 5.

[35] See the lead article, "The General Assembly" in *New Times*, No. 40 (October 6, 1965), pp. 1, 2. The operative portion of the Declaration provides pertinently:

The General Assembly

. . . .

Further points out that the U.N. Charter proclaims the principle of the sovereign equality of all U.N. members and does not tolerate any interference in the internal affairs of states, and that this generally accepted principle of international law was also emphasized repeatedly in the decisions and declarations of the Bandung, Belgrade, and Cairo conferences, which were attended by many U.N. member states.

Therefore, the General Assembly considers it its duty:

(1) To reaffirm that every sovereign state, every people has an inalienable right to freedom, independence and the defense of its sovereignty, and that this right must be fully upheld;

(2) To call insistently on all U.N. member states for unfailing compliance with their obligations under the United Nations Charter;

(3) To firmly demand the immediate cessation and non-commission in future of actions which constitute armed or any other interference in the internal affairs of states, and of all actions directed against the just struggle of people for national independence and freedom;

state sovereignty and opponent of the imperialist "law of the jungle."[36]

The Soviet initiative opposing intervention is meaningful only in the context of the double standard used to determine the legality of intervention—a prime example of unilateral characterization in the Soviet interest. The legality of intervention depends upon the type of state involved as, by definition, only capitalist states "intervene" in the internal affairs of other states.

Intervention [is] the armed invasion or interference of one or several capitalist states in the internal affairs of another state aimed at the suppression of a revolution, seizure of territory, acquisition of special privileges, establishing domination, etc.[37]

The familiar tactic of the common plight is used to demonstrate the community of interest of socialist and neutralist states in resisting capitalist interference.

The imperialist states have made repeated attempts to interfere in the internal affairs of the Soviet state and other socialist countries, and also in the internal affairs of countries which have freed themselves from the yoke of colonialism (Indonesia, the countries of the Near and Middle East and others).[38]

The United States in its "shameful role as gendarme of the World" is said to have a long tradition of intervention under the doctrines of Monroe and succeeding presidents.[39] In contrast, the socialist states are portrayed as opposed in principle to intervention because it negates the peaceful coexistence of states.

---

(4) To call on all states to adhere in their international relations to the principle of mutual respect and non-interference in internal affairs, on whatever grounds—economic, political or ideological.

The General Assembly warns all states which in defiance of the United Nations Charter are interfering in the internal affairs of other states that they are thereby incurring severe responsibility in the eyes of all peoples." ("Documents" in *Ibid.*, p. 31.)

[36] Maevskii, *op. cit., supra* note 8.

[37] *Politicheskii Slovar'* [Dictionary of Political Terms], ed. B. N. Ponomarev (2d ed.; Moscow: State Publishing House of Political Literature, 1958), p. 211.

[38] *Mezhdunarodnoe Pravo, op. cit., supra* note 14, p. 106.

[39] L. A. Modzhorian, "Amerikanskie Doktriny Grabezha i Razboia: ot Monro do Zhonsona" [American Doctrines of Plunder and Brigandage from Monroe to Johnson], *SGIP*, No. 9 (1965), pp. 57–64.

The Soviet Union and all peace-loving states consider the principle of noninterference the most important means of realizing the principle of the peaceful coexistence of states with different social systems and an effective means of developing collaboration between states.[40]

When action comparable to intervention is taken by socialist countries, it can be characterized as fraternal assistance because, in the Soviet lexicon, intervention is defined as the exclusive sin of capitalist states. It can also be justified on the basis of the purpose served by the intervention. For example, assistance in the crushing of a popular uprising in a socialist country is not intervention since such an uprising, being nonsocialist in character, is not sanctioned by the principle of self-determination, the violation of which constitutes the principal Soviet criterion of the intervention barred by international law. Similarly, the current anti-racist campaign has produced the Soviet position that action in opposition to racism does not constitute intervention under international law.

Racism has been branded as a crime against peace and humanity. It has ceased to be a private affair of individual countries and nations. Responsibility for racist crimes has also ceased to be a question of domestic, national jurisdiction and has acquired international significance.[41]

The Soviet doctrine of intervention has been described by a competent Western observer as opposed "in principle . . . [to] all forms of intervention with the exception of those which answer the aims of Soviet policy and which may be characterized in a different way."[42]

Soviet initiatives in this area reflect a residual defensism vis-à-vis the existing legal order, and the ever-present courtship of neutralist states in a bid for extra-camp support for the policy and law of peaceful coexistence. At the very least, these initiatives are part of a continuing propaganda-diplomatic effort to maintain the integrity of the shield of sovereignty—in the United Nations context, the domestic jurisdiction limitation on its right of intervention (Article 2[7] of the Charter)—and to neutralize or counter Western influence among neutralist states. More importantly, they reflect

[40] *Mezhdunarodnoe Pravo, op. cit., supra* note 14, p. 106.
[41] V. Chkhikvadze, "The Nations Repudiate Racism," *International Affairs*, No. 5 (1966), pp. 49–54; see 54.
[42] Ivo Lapenna, *Conceptions Soviétiques de Droit Internationale Public* [Soviet Conceptions of Public International Law] (Paris: A. Pedone, 1954), p. 242.

recognition that, if foreign policy objectives are to be realized, sovereignty, the key element in the law which is to assist in their realization, cannot be used principally in a defensive role.

SWORD

Just as they attribute international personality to nations struggling for national liberation as a means of lending legal support to the struggle against imperialism and colonialism, Soviet jurists include in the concept of sovereignty the sovereign right of nations to independence and statehood. To accommodate this view conceptually, they divide sovereignty into state and national sovereignty. The latter, the right of every nation to self-determination, is said to be closely tied in with, if not identical to, state sovereignty under contemporary conditions.[43]

The question of the relationship between state and national sovereignty is of great theoretical importance. By national sovereignty we understand the right of each nation to self-determination and independent development. Each nation has this right, regardless of whether or not it has its own statehood. National sovereignty merges with state sovereignty if the nation has achieved independence and formed its own State. When the nation has not yet been able to form its own independent State, its sovereign right to self-determination constitutes the basis for its just struggle to establish such a State.[44]

The close identification of state and national sovereignty is described as "an approach peculiar to socialism which is not supported by the forces of imperialism."[45]

[43] Sobakin, *op. cit., supra* note 10, p. 153. See also G. V. Ignatenko, "Mezhdunarodnaia Provosub'ektnost' Natsii" [International Legal Personality of Nations], *SGIP*, No. 10 (1966), pp. 75–82; see 79–81.

[44] *International Law, op. cit., supra* note 3, p. 98. See also Sobakin, *op. cit., supra* note 10, p. 154, for criticism of the view that national sovereignty is only an anticolonial principle giving each nation a right to form independent states. Sobakin notes that under contemporary international law, the principle also includes the right of nations within the independent state to freely select and change the social order. This broader approach effectively provides the legal basis for revolution.

[45] Sobakin, *op. cit., supra* note 10, p. 153.

Socialist initiative in this area is used as the point of departure for a virulent propaganda campaign in support of the Soviet position:

> The Soviet state, arising from the fire of a liberation, socialist revolution and a struggle against imperialist occupation forces, unalterably supports the freedom and independence of nations and their inalienable right to the defense of their sovereignty.

. . . .

> In the armed struggle against sovereign states and against the freedom and independence of nations, the imperialist powers join forces. Thus the U.S.A. supports the provocations of England in South East Asia and the efforts of British imperialism to suppress the national liberation struggles of the nations of the Arabian peninsula.[46]

Of particular interest in the propaganda line is the new, special emphasis upon "liberation" in describing the October Revolution which had been described previously as socialist. This change reflects, as does the emphasis upon peace as the principal purpose to be served by international law, the effort to identify Soviet experience and goals with those of the emerging states to gain their support in the international class struggle. Another aspect of this attempt at identification is the position taken on the right of a new state to select the obligations which bind it and to be accorded recognition by other states—difficult questions for today's emerging states as well as the Soviet state of 1917. In the Soviet view, a new state (i.e., one which did not exist before or did exist in nonsocialist form) resulting from the struggle for national liberation or socialist revolution is bound only by those obligations which are compatible with the law of peaceful coexistence:

> . . .state succession does not mean the automatic applicability of all rights and obligations. State succession may be partial, i.e., only a part of the rights and obligations may be applicable . . . The criterion for the resolution of this question is the following: Do the rights and obligations of the succeeding state correspond to the generally recognized democratic principles of international law. . . . Only those which contribute to the preservation of peace and elimination of the danger of war are applicable [to the succeeding state].[47]

---

[46] Maevskii, *op. cit.*, *supra* note 8.

[47] M. M. Abakov and B. A. Mel'tser, Review of J. Kirsten, *Einige Probleme der Staatennachfolge* [Some Problems of State Succession] (Berlin: Deutscher Zentralverlag, 1962), *SGIP*, No. 6 (1964), pp. 144–146; see 146.

Further, such a new state is entitled to *de jure*, official recognition, as *de facto* and other lesser forms of recognition are incompatible with the principle of the sovereign equality of states. Selective recognition, although actually practiced by the Soviet Union (e.g., its recognition of the Union of Zanzibar and Tanganyika in 1964 was motivated by the Union's recognition of the German Democratic Republic), is said to reflect the practice of capitalist states under "the old international law" as a means of suppressing revolutionary change.

A new state regardless of its location, size of territory and population, nature of social system, form of government and state structure, has a right to complete and final recognition. . . .There are no legal arguments to justify the granting of some new states incomplete, even though official, recognition.[48]

The nonrecognition of a new state resulting from a socialist or national liberation revolution is said to constitute a form of intervention which violates the law of peaceful coexistence, specifically the principle of self-determination.[49] As a hedge against the failure to obtain general acceptance of the existence of a legal obligation to accord recognition, the Soviets reject the constitutive theory of recognition. They hold that viable states resulting from national liberation, or viable governments resulting from a social revolution exist notwithstanding nonrecognition. Recognition, having only a declarative character, merely normalizes relations between states, and thereby strengthens peace and security.[50]

[48] D. I. Fel'dman, "O Nekotorykh Formakh i Sposobakh Mezhdunarodno-pravovo Priznaniia Novykh Gosudarstv" [Some Forms and Methods of International Legal Recognition of New States], *Sovetskii Ezhegodnik, 1963, op. cit., supra* note 1, pp. 129–149; see 147–149. Modzhorian condemns the recognition practice of colonial powers in the following terms:

"The rights and international legal personality [of nations and peoples struggling for national independence] are negated by colonial powers through nonrecognition of new states or the recognition of puppet regimes forcibly imposed upon nations seeking independence." (L. A. Modzhorian, *Osnovnye Prava i Obiazannosti Gosudarstv* [The Fundamental Rights and Duties of States] [Moscow: Publishing House "Legal Literature," 1965], p. 6.)

[49] D. I. Fel'dman, *Priznanie Gosudarstv v Sovremennom Mezhdunarodnom Prave* [The Recognition of States in Contemporary International Law] (Kazan': Publishing House of Kazan' University, 1965), pp. 225 and 241, 242.

[50] Modzhorian, *op. cit., supra* note 48, pp. 82–84. Modzhorian describes the constitutive theory as follows: ". . .recognition creates subjects of international

The significance of the Soviet formulations in this area is best appreciated in the context of the type of state in whose favor the rights are proclaimed. As only socialist or neutralist (i.e., friendly to socialism) states benefit from these formulations, Soviet interests are furthered both in the attempt to develop law along these "progressive" lines as well as in the good will and support generated among the states benefited.

Another use of sovereignty on the offense is the expansion of the concept of the sovereign equality of states to include the equality of the capitalist and socialist systems.[51] The expanded concept is intended to provide the legal basis for recognition of the existence of a world socialist system and, as a corollary, its equal voice in shaping the international legal order.

In international organizations and at conferences there is increasing recognition that any attempt to decide international questions in a manner unacceptable to socialist states is pointless and harmful for the cause of peace and that the only way to decide these questions is the agreement of the states of the two systems.[52]

The principle of the equality of the two systems is intended as a long step in the direction of acceptance of the law of peaceful coexistence as the underlying premise of that law is the simultaneous existence of two world systems whose struggle for supremacy must be controlled in the interest of the survival of mankind.[53]

The Soviets are attempting to hone another edge to the sword of sovereignty through the concept of popular sovereignty. Although they admit that, in the context of general international law, popular

---

law and permits governments to act in their name in the international arena." (p. 82.)

[51] Tunkin, Voprosy Teorii, *op. cit.*, *supra* note 6, p. 209.

A recent commentary derives from the concept of the sovereign equality of states the equality of all subjects of international law to expand the rights of nations struggling for national liberation to include the right to resort to force, to be protected against interference in its internal affairs, to maintain relations with states and other nations, to participate in international organizations and conferences, and to assist in the formulation of international legal norms. (Ignatenko, *op. cit.*, *supra* note 43, pp. 80,81.)

[52] *Ibid.*

[53] See *Ibid.*, p. 210 and Zadorozhnyi, Mirnoe Sosushchestvovanie, *op. cit.*, *supra* note 18, pp. 212–218.

sovereignty is still a domestic law concept,[54] they claim that world public opinion, a form of such sovereignty, is influencing the development of contemporary international law.

World public opinion is one of the most important forces influencing contemporary international [legal] science. . .both in the formulation of new norms and principles of international law and in the observance of international law already in effect.[55]

In the higher type relations within the socialist commonwealth of nations, popular sovereignty already has normative force as one of the fundamental international legal principles of socialist internationalism. Popular sovereignty in the formulation of legal norms is, therefore, a progressive legal principle of the future. Its substantive content is that state agreement to international legal norms must coincide with, and reflect, the "true" interests of the people (presumptively, peaceful coexistence). The implication is that norms which do not satisfy this requirement cannot have legal effect.[56]

International agreements and treaties of capitalist states formally concluded in the name of the people, in fact, deeply contradict the vital interests of the working masses. The treaties establishing the NATO, SEATO, CENTO and other aggressive alliances of imperialist states are examples of this.[57]

In contrast,

. . .all international legal acts [mezhdunarodno-pravovye akty] to which the signature of the U.S.S.R. or any other country of the socialist camp is affixed, correspond to the interests of all people and promote the cause of peace, although in a number of cases, due to the opposition of the capitalist parties to these acts, they cannot fully and completely reflect these noble aims.

---

[54] Sobakin, *op. cit.*, *supra* note 10, p. 153.

[55] B. I. Melekhin, "Rol' Mirovovo Obshchestvennovo Mneniia v Formirovanii i Obespechenii Mezhdunarodnovo Prava" [The Role of World Public Opinion in the Formulating and Ensuring of International Legality], *Sovetskii Ezhegodnik*, 1963, *op. cit.*, *supra* note 1, pp. 498, 499; see 499.

[56] See Bernard A. Ramundo, *The (Soviet) Socialist Theory of International Law* (Washington, D.C.: Institute for Sino-Soviet Studies, The George Washington University, 1965), pp. 35, 36.

[57] V. M. Shurshalov, "Mezhdunarodno-pravovye Printsipy Sotrudnichestva Sotsialisticheskikh Gosudarstv" [International Legal Principles of the Collaboration of Socialist States], *SGIP*, No. 7 (1962), pp. 95–105; see 100.

In all cases where the Soviet Union or some other socialist state is a party to an agreement, the agreement by its very nature cannot be contrary to the popular will or aggressive. [58]

The principle of popular sovereignty and the presumption of the legality of socialist treaties under that principle provide a convenient basis for attacking the legality of agreements entered into by nonsocialist states. In effect, the principle reinforces peaceful coexistence and socialist internationalism by making available a still less definite principle under which characterizations in the Soviet interest could be invoked as the criterion of the validity of international agreements.

The fertile imagination of Soviet jurists can be expected to produce other uses of sovereignty in clearing a path for the law of peaceful coexistence. Greater demands are made on their ingenuity in the area of capitalist-socialist state relationships, because the elements of power equality and conflict tend to require a higher degree of salability for each attempt to seek advantage through manipulation of the sovereignty concept. In the socialist commonwealth, on the other hand, the primacy of the Soviet Union tends to enhance as well as to accelerate the acceptability of new formulations which cast sovereignty in the role of integrating force.

INTEGRATING FORCE

Respect for sovereignty, regarded as the indispensable condition for the peaceful coexistence of states with different social systems, is also a fundamental principle of socialist internationalism. It is claimed that socialist states base their relationships "on the immutable observance of the full sovereignty of each socialist state."[59] In the context of the progressive relations within the socialist commonwealth of nations, however, sovereignty has acquired a new, euphemistically formulated, substantive content:

[58] *Mezhdunarodnopravovye Formy Sotrudnichestva Sotsialisticheskikh Gosudarstv* [International Legal Forms of the Collaboration of Socialist States], ed. V. M. Shurshalov (Moscow: Publishing House of the Academy of Sciences of the U.S.S.R., 1962), p. 26.

[59] E. T. Usenko, "Osnovnye Mezhdunarodnopravovye Printsipy Sotrudnichestva Sotsialisticheskikh Gosudarstv" [The Basic International Legal Principles of the Collaboration of Socialist States], *SGIP*, No. 3 (1961), pp. 16–29; see 23.

...the people's sovereignty of the socialist countries does not know that isolation and ethnic exclusivity of individual countries, because it permits, in necessary circumstances, the subordination of the interests of an individual country to the more important international interests of the entire socialist commonwealth.[60]

It is also said that "state sovereignty must be exercised with consideration of the general interests of the entire socialist camp as well as the national interest."[61] The concept of sovereignty within the socialist commonwealth, therefore, is intended to serve as an integrating force with a positive role in support of the new social order and, until its realization, all that is claimed to be necessary in the building of communism.

The principle of nonintervention, a corollary of sovereignty, is similarly influenced by socialist internationalism.

...the principle of nonintervention is harmoniously combined with the requirements of socialist internationalism. The independence of states and nations in the socialist commonwealth is dialectically connected with fraternal mutual assistance, socialist international division of labor, broad exchange of experience in economic and state organization, the coordination of national economic plans and specialization in production.[62]

[The impact of socialist internationalism is] a correct combination of the national interests of the individual countries with the international interests of the entire socialist camp and the observance of the strict independence of individual countries coupled with the preservation of the indissoluble unity and monolithic nature of the commonwealth of socialist states.[63]

The essence of the new content provides the legal basis for interference in internal affairs in the greater interest of the socialist commonwealth. The basis for Soviet license under this formulation is provided by the complementary position that the foreign policy of the Soviet state always coincides with the needs of socialist internationalism and the interests of the proletariat of all countries.[64]

[60] Shurshalov, Mezhdunarodno-pravovye Printsipy, *op. cit.*, *supra* note 57, p. 103.

[61] *Ibid.*

[62] *Ibid.*, pp. 104, 105.

[63] *Mezhdunarodnopravovye Formy Sotrudnichestva Sotsialisticheskikh Gosudarstv*, *op. cit.*, *supra* note 58, pp. 56, 57.

[64] Tunkin, Voprosy Teorii, *op. cit.*, *supra* note 6, p. 311.

Thus, the socialist, more progressive content of the principle of nonintervention is essentially a rationalization for the relationship of subordination by a large, powerful state of its smaller neighbors who have been sentenced by history and geography to a client-state status.

It should be noted that the limitations upon the sovereignty of the socialist states are oriented toward a regional rather than world order. The Moscow Declarations of 1957 and 1960 (said to be equally valid today)[65] proclaim fraternal collaboration under socialist internationalism the "inviolable law of the mutual relations between socialist countries."[66] This "law" contemplates *"all-round economic, political and cultural cooperation, which meets both the interests of each socialist country and that of the socialist camp as a whole."*[67] The concepts of "international socialist division of labor," "socialist solidarity," and "socialist unity" have been developed as slogan-like formulations which connote service to an interest higher than that of the nation-state. The Moscow Declarations expressly endorse "the solidarity and close unity of the Socialist countries"[68] as the indispensable "condition. . .for the successful accomplishment of the tasks of the socialist revolution and of the building of socialism and communism."[69] The Declarations also expressly recognize the leading role of the Soviet Union in camp affairs, thereby confirming the Soviet presumption that the foreign policies of the Soviet Union

[65] Observer Article, "A Compass to Steer By," *New Times*, No. 50 (December 15, 1965), pp. 2, 3; see 2.

[66] See, for example, Declaration of Representatives of the Eighty-one Communist Parties (November-December 1961) in *The New Communist Manifesto*, ed. Dan N. Jacobs (2d ed.; Evanston, Illinois and Elmsford, New York: Row, Peterson and Company, 1962), pp. 11–47; see 21.

[67] *Ibid.*

[68] Declaration of the Twelve Communist Parties in Power in *The New Communist Manifesto*, *op. cit.*, *supra* note 66, pp. 169–182; see 175. See also, "Declaration of Representatives of the Eighty-one Communist Parties," *op. cit.*, *supra* note 66, p. 45. See also "Za Edinstvo Kommunisticheskikh Riadov, za Internatsional'nuiu Splochennost' " [For The Unity of Communist Ranks, For International Solidarity], *Pravda* (October 23, 1965), p. 4; and "Druzhba i Bratstvo" [Friendship and Brotherhood], *Ibid.* (January 8, 1966), p. 1.

[69] Declaration of Representatives of the Eighty-one Communist Parties, *op. cit.*, *supra* note, 66, p. 45.

are in the best interests of the socialist world.[70] Implicit in these formulations is the requirement for concerted action in following the Soviet lead in ordering the affairs of the socialist commonwealth.

The requirement of solidarity and unity is equally significant in relations outside the commonwealth, i.e., the international class struggle.[71] Socialist states are expected to close ranks and present a united front in the struggle against capitalism. In these relations, the socialist states attempt to blunt the "exploitative and reactionary policies" of the enemy capitalist states, and to seek the support of neutralist states by insistence upon "respect for state sovereignty" as one of the basic elements of the policy and law of peaceful coexistence.[72] The concept of the international class struggle with its requirement for a united front against capitalist states requires socialist states to resist as a group any limitations on their sovereignty which would strengthen the forces of imperialism. At the same time, they must acquiesce in the limitations on national freedom of action which are implicit in the concept of socialist unity in waging the struggle against imperialism and for communism. Thus, the sovereign prerogatives of members of the socialist commonwealth of nations can be limited by Soviet insistence upon the overriding importance of the socialist collective interest in communist construction which, in the totality of its sweep, touches every aspect of state power, domestic and foreign.

[70] For example, "the invincible camp of socialist countries headed by the Soviet Union" (Declaration of the Twelve Communist Parties in Power, op. cit., supra note 66, p. 173) and "the Communist and workers' parties unanimously declare that the Communist Party of the Soviet Union has been, and remains, the universally recognized vanguard of the world Communist movement." (Declaration of Representatives of the Eighty-one Communist Parties, op. cit., supra note 66, p. 46).

[71] Declaration of Representatives of the Eighty-one Communist Parties, op. cit., supra note 66, pp. 27–29.

[72] R. L. Bobrov, Review of G. I. Tunkin, Voprosy Teorii Mezhdunarodnovo Prava [Problems of the Theory of International Law] (Moscow: State Publishing House of Legal Literature, 1962), SGIP, No. 5 (1963), pp. 167–170; see 168. See also "Internationalist Duty of Communists of All Countries," trans. from Pravda (November 28, 1965), in Moscow News, Supplement to No. 49 (December 4, 1965), pp. 9–18.

The result of this approach is a legal basis for significant restraints, in the Soviet interest, upon state action within the socialist commonwealth. Although these restraints are order-oriented, they do not contribute to world order. The order-orientation to regionalism deemed to be engaged in an international class struggle with the forces of capitalism is hardly a step in the direction of world order; especially when the outer face of this regionalism champions positivism as a counter to nonsocialist world order. The socialist brand of regionalism is not an encouraging development for those advocates of greater order who usually are heartened by manifestations of regional cooperation and collaboration.

PART II

SOVIET POSITIONS ON BASIC INTERNATIONAL LEGAL RELATIONSHIPS

CHAPTER SIX

PEACE AND WAR

THE POLICY

Influenced by the Marxist concept of class struggle, the Soviet leadership has always tended to view international relations as a continuation of that struggle in the relations of states. During the pre-World War II period, Stalin coined the expression "capitalist encirclement" to describe the position of the Soviet Union in a hostile world of capitalist states. After World War II, the emergence of other socialist regimes, primarily in Eastern Europe, resulted in emphasis upon the two-camp theory of struggle for world supremacy between the forces of capitalism and socialism. Stalin proclaimed as part of this theory that an armed conflict between the camps of socialism and capitalism was inevitable. After Stalin's death, this position was discarded in favor of a new policy of peaceful coexistence which was announced at the Twentieth Party Congress of the Communist Party of the Soviet Union (1956).[1] The change in policy was attributed to the emergence of a world socialist system and the ever growing strength of the forces of peace and socialism.

The transformation of socialism into a world system and its steady consolidation, the establishment of an extensive "Zone of Peace" embracing more than half the population of the world and the growth of the worldwide peace movement and of the labour movement in the capitalist

---

[1] S. Viskov, *Za Mir bez Oruzhiia, za Mir bez Voin* [For a World without Arms and War] (Moscow: The Publishing House of Social-Economic Literature, "Thought," 1964), pp. 8–39. See also Bernard A. Ramundo, *The (Soviet) Socialist Theory of International Law* (Washington, D.C.: Institute for Sino-Soviet Studies, The George Washington University, 1964), pp. 43–48.

countries enabled the Twentieth Congress of the Communist Party of the Soviet Union to conclude that war was not a fatal inevitability.[2]

As formulated by Soviet writers, the policy of peaceful coexistence encompasses a struggle to preserve peace in the interest of averting a nuclear world war, the peaceful settlement of international disputes, an end to the arms race through general and complete disarmament, support for national liberation movements against colonialism and imperialism, and achievement of the world victory of socialism through peaceful competition.[3]

[The policy is] . . . directed towards ensuring peaceful conditions for the building of socialism and communism, strengthening the world socialist system, supporting in all ways the struggle of peoples for freedom and independence, preventing a new world war, realizing the principles of the peaceful coexistence of states with different social-political orders, strengthening peace and international security, . . . and developing fraternal relations and all-around collaboration with socialist countries [in the interest] of further solidarity of the world socialist commonwealth.[4]

---

[2] *International Law* (Moscow: Foreign Languages Publishing House, n.d.), p. 402. See also *Mezhdunardnoe Pravo* [International Law], ed. D. B. Levin and G. P. Kaliuzhnaia (Moscow: Publishing House "Legal Literature," 1964), p. 414. The Resolution of the Twenty-third Party Congress (1966) notes that "the balance of strength in the world keeps changing in favor of socialism, the working-class and the national liberation movement." ("Resolution of the Twenty-third Congress of the Communist Party of the Soviet Union on the Report of the Central Committee of the CPSU," trans. from *Pravda* [April 9, 1966], in *Moscow News*, Supplement to No. 16 [April 16, 1966], pp. 2–10; see 4.)

[3] See for example, V. A. Zorin, "Disarmament Problems and Peking's Maneuvers," trans. from *Izvestiia* (June 30, 1964), in *CDSP*, XVI, No. 26, pp. 11–13; see 11; "Peaceful Coexistence and Revolutionary Struggle," trans. from *Kommunist* (March 1963) in *The Daily Review* (Moscow), IX, No. 22 (March 26, 1963); and "Pravda Editorial Article on Soviet Goals and Policies," trans. from *Pravda* (November 1, 1964), in *CDSP*, XVI, No. 44, pp. 6–8; see 7. See also "Uprochit' Mir na Zemle" [Strengthen Peace on Earth], *Pravda* (December 14, 1964), p. 1; and "The Noble Aims of Soviet Foreign Policy," trans. from *Pravda* (August 8, 1965), in *Moscow News*, Supplement to No. 33 (August 14, 1965), pp. 16–29.

[4] "V Interesakh Mira i Druzhby mezhdu Narodami" [In the Interests of Peace and Friendship between Nations], *Pravda* (January 15, 1966), p. 1. See also L. I. Brezhnev, "Report of the Central Committee of the Communist Party of the Soviet Union to the Twenty-third Congress of the CPSU," trans. from *Pravda* (April 30, 1966), in *Moscow News*, Supplement to No. 14 (April 2, 1966), pp. 13–15; and Resolution of the Twenty-third Party Congress, *op. cit.*, *supra* note 2, pp. 4, 5.

The essential element, however, is the peaceful settlement of international disputes between the socialist and capitalist camps as a
means of avoiding a thermonuclear world war.

In our time, war cannot and must not serve as a method for resolving
international disputes. We must not permit the unleashing of a thermonuclear world war, in the course of which hundreds of millions of people
would be destroyed and irreparable harm would be done to the development of the productive forces of society and to the world revolutionary
process.[5]

In an effort to preserve the concept of revolutionary international
class struggle, implicitly negated by the call for peaceful settlement of
disputes with capitalist states, the Soviets claim that peaceful
coexistence does not mean abandonment of the class struggle;
rather, it is "an integral part of the revolutionary struggle against
imperialism."[6]

Peaceful coexistence does not mean that the struggle of the two systems,
particularly the ideological struggle, is to cease. As noted in the Party
Program it constitutes a specific form of class struggle between socialism
and capitalism on an international level. Competition between the two
systems, like their coexistence, is an objective reality. . .peaceful coexistence
implies that. . .the historical debate as to which system is better is to be
settled through their peaceful. coexistence.[7]

The struggle of the two systems by peaceful means—economic, political,
social, ideological, technical and cultural competition—continues and
must continue. Nothing can stop the class struggle.[8]

---

[5] "Pravda Editorial Article on Soviet Goals and Policies," op. cit., supra
note 3, p. 7.

[6] "Otkrytoe Pis'mo, Tsentral'novo Komiteta Kommunisticheskoi Partii
Sovetskovo Soiuza, Partiinym Organizatisiiam, Vsem Kommunistam Sovetskovo Soiuza" [Open Letter of the Central Committee of the Communist Party
of the Soviet Union to All Party Organizations and All Communists of the
Soviet Union], Pravda (July 14, 1963), p. 2. See also "Pravda Editorial Article
on Soviet Goals and Policies," op. cit., supra note 3, p. 7.

[7] G. I. Tunkin, "XXII S'ezd KPSS i Mezhdunarodnoe Pravo" [The
Twenty-second Congress of the CPSU and International Law], Sovetskii
Ezhegodnik, 1961 (Moscow; Publishing House of the Academy of Sciences, 1962),
pp. 15–35; see 29. See also G. I. Tunkin, Voprosy Teorii Mezhdunarodnovo Prava
[Problems of the Theory of International Law] (Moscow: State Publishing
House of Legal Literature, 1962), p. 9.

[8] From Wladislaw Gomulka's Speech at the Thirteenth Plenum of the
Central Committee of the Polish Communist Party reported in Pravda (July 21,
1963), p. 3.

Behind this lip service to ideological pronouncements concerning the international class struggle is a realistic awareness of the existence of a new imperative of interdependence—the need to avoid the consequences of the destruction made possible by technological advances in weaponry. The Soviets realize that the only alternative to peaceful coexistence is the most destructive war in history[9]—a war which "would deal a severe blow to the cause of communism."[10]

Peaceful coexistence is principally motivated by Soviet domestic and foreign policy needs in building communism.

The principal task of the domestic policy of the U.S.S.R.—the intensive building of a communist society and creation of the material and technical bases of communism—has shaped the basic tasks of the foreign policy of the country. The principal task of the foreign policy of the U.S.S.R. for the coming historical period is to ensure peaceful conditions for the building of communism in the U.S.S.R., for the development and strengthening of the world socialist system, and together with all peace-loving peoples to deliver humanity from the threat of a destructive world war.[11]

The Soviets recognize that their new society cannot be built upon the ashes of a thermonuclear war.

War always means a terribly wasteful destruction of resources, human and material, a deterioration of living standards. Modern war, with its incalculably destructive weapons, threatens suffering and death on a scale mankind has never experienced.

In the light of this, how can Communists worth the name possibly want war, link their hopes for the victory of the new social system with war?

---

[9] Viskov, *op. cit., supra* note 1, pp. 30, 31.

[10] M. A. Suslov, "O Bor'be KPSS za Splochennost' Mezhdunarodnovo Kommunisticheskovo Dvizheniia" [On the Struggle of the CPSU for the Solidarity of the International Communist Movement], a speech delivered to the Plenum of the Central Committee of the CPSU on February 14, 1964, *Pravda* (April 3, 1964), pp. 1–8; see 3. In contrast, and a basic element in the Sino-Soviet split, is the Chinese view that (*a*) the advent of nuclear weapons has not changed the character of the international class struggle and (*b*) creation of the bright world of the future would be assisted by a thermonuclear war (*Ibid.* See also Ramundo, *op. cit., supra* note 1, pp. 13–16). The Soviet line is that the Chinese desire to have nuclear weapons in opposition to the Soviet Union's policy against proliferation and in view of the ready availability of Soviet weapons to protect the socialist camp is sinister as it can only be explained by the "special" goals (i.e., unrelated to the world struggle for socialism) of the Chinese leadership (Zorin, *op. cit., supra* note 3, p. 11).

[11] Viskov, *op. cit., supra* note 1, p. 3. See also "Marshal Sokolovsky on Art of War in Nuclear Age," trans. from *Krasnaia Zvezda* [Red Star], in *CDSP*, XVI, No. 38, pp. 14–18; see 14.

The Soviet people are not building houses, industrial plants, palaces of culture, colleges, great dams and canals to see them serve as targets for nuclear bombs.

. . . .

. . . that is why the true Marxist-Leninist bends every effort to prevent war and never tires of stressing that wars between countries are not essential for the victory of Communism. If communist civilization is to serve the welfare of mankind and to reach new heights of progress, it cannot be built on the ashes left by war, or the ruins of civilization.

. . . the very aims they have set themselves make real Communists convinced advocates of normal international relations, of ending the cold war, of complete and general disarmament.

. . . .

Whether we think of the immediate or the more distant interests of Communism, peace and the peaceful coexistence of the two systems is the most desirable state of international relations. Lasting peace is a vital necessity for building Communism. It is on the strength of this that the program of the Communist Party of the Soviet Union declares peaceful coexistence to be the cornerstone of Soviet foreign policy.[12]

Thus, to the extent that it seeks to avoid nuclear world war, the Soviet policy of peaceful coexistence is a peace policy.

Peaceful coexistence does not, however, mean peace in the sense of no war. Soviet commentaries distinguish between peace under peaceful coexistence, and peace in the sense of "general, everlasting peace,"[13] the condition in the socialist commonwealth of nations.

. . . the Soviet Union builds its relations with imperialist states not on the platform of pacifism, but on the principles of peaceful coexistence. . . .The outstanding feature of the relations between these states, irreconcilable because of their class nature, is not that there is no war between them, but that class struggle and competition between them continues in nonmilitary form.[14]

---

[12] *U.S.S.R.*, *Soviet Life Today*, No. 12 (1964), pp. 37 and 44, the answer to the question "What are Communists Really Interested In—International Tension and Wars, or a Stable International Situation and Peace?" See also *Ibid.*, p. 60, the answer to the question, "What is the Goal of Communism?"

[13] M. I. Lazarev, "Mezhdunarodnopravovye Voprosy Dvizheniia Narodov za Mir" [International Legal Aspects of the Peoples' Movement for Peace], *Sovetskii Ezhegodnik, 1963* (Moscow: Publishing House "Science," 1965), pp. 45–69; see 51. Also, p. 67: "The concept of 'peace' as such, in the broad sense of the word, can be defined as relations between countries in which the basic principles of peaceful co-existence are observed."

[14] Gleb Starushenko, "Internationalism—Steadfast Principle of Soviet Foreign Policy," *Moscow News*, No. 6 (February 5, 1966), p. 3.

≫≫⟫⟪⟪⟪

In the Soviet view peaceful coexistence means only that the struggle between the capitalist and socialist camps is to be waged in a lower, nonnuclear key. Only nuclear and unjust wars—in the Soviet lexicon, wars of aggression or wars serving the interests of the forces of imperialism—are barred. Consistent with the support for national liberation implicit in the policy of peaceful coexistence, wars of national liberation and defensive wars are characterized as "just" and, therefore, permissible.

> Revolutionary national-liberation wars, like class struggle in any capitalist country, do not clash with coexistence and can be brought to success only under peaceful coexistence.[15]
> Our attitude towards civil wars of liberation, popular uprisings is, in principle, different. People who take up arms in the struggle for freedom and independence, and for socialism, wage just war. We have always supported, and will support, such people.[16]
> Peaceful coexistence means abstention from any armed force in relations between states so long as wars of national liberation and the struggle against aggression and colonialism are not involved.[17]

At the Twenty-third Party Congress of the Communist Party of the Soviet Union (1966) Brezhnev emphasized that peaceful coexistence does not mean the end of revolutionary warfare.

> ...there can be no peaceful coexistence where matters concern the internal processes of the class and national liberation struggle in the capitalist countries or in colonies. Peaceful coexistence is not applicable to the relations between oppressors and oppressed, between colonialists and the victims of colonial oppression.[18]

The Soviet approach, in effect, preserves the use of force in the interest of socialism but bars its use by capitalist states. "This [peaceful coexistence] means that international relations based on

[15] "Lenin's Behest: Peaceful Coexistence," *International Affairs*, No. 4 (1962), pp. 7–11; see 11.

[16] "Zaiavlenie Sovetskovo Pravitel'stva" [Declaration of the Soviet Government], *Pravda* (September 21, 1963), pp. 1, 2 (Part I) and (September 22, 1963), pp. 1, 2 (Part II); see Part II, p. 1. See also "A. N. Kosygin's Interview to James Reston" in Documents Section, *New Times* No. 51 (December 22, 1965), pp. 30–33; see 32.

[17] *Mezhdunarodnoe Pravo* [International Law], ed. F. I. Kozhevnikov (Moscow: Publishing House "International Relations," 1964), p. 71.

[18] Brezhnev, *op. cit., supra* note 4, p. 15. See also "The Party Reports to the People," *Moscow News*, No. 14 (April 2, 1966), p. 3.

the 'balance of terror,' the threat of force or the race in nuclear and other armaments cannot be regarded as genuine peace."[19]

The Soviet formulations "peace," "general, everlasting peace" and "genuine peace," are intended to provide a basis for characterizations, favorable to the Soviet Union, which readily lend themselves to policy and propaganda exploitation. Peaceful coexistence, therefore, is in fact only a partial peace policy, falling far short of such sweeping Soviet formulations as "universal peace," "peaceful competition with the capitalist camp," and "the easing of world tension."[20]

The dispute with the Chinese leadership over the possibility of achieving the victory of socialism through "peaceful competition" has revealed still another aspect of the policy of peaceful coexistence. In demonstrating the revolutionary nature of peaceful coexistence in the struggle with capitalism, the Soviets have indicated the expediency of their policy. In addition to seeking avoidance of nuclear warfare as a necessary condition of internal development, the Soviets use peaceful coexistence (with its support for national liberation and the prerogatives of sovereignty) as a means of enlisting the neutralist states (i.e., those neither socialist nor capitalist) as allies in the struggle against the capitalist camp.[21] Although the neutralist states have no class stake in the international class struggle between capitalism and socialism, their support for socialism is considered attainable through use of the cover of the general appeal of peace and national liberation.[22]

The Soviet Union and the countries of socialism are taking concrete steps to defend the peace. . . .The firm and consistent struggle of the Soviet Union for peace, for general and complete disarmament, for the prohibition

---

[19] Lazarev, *op. cit.*, *supra* note 13, p. 67.

[20] Zorin, *op, cit.*, *supra* note 3, pp. 11–13.

[21] Ramundo, *op. cit.*, *supra* note 1, pp. 43–45. It is said that the socialist camp and these neutral states have joined in the establishment of a "peace zone" (*Ibid.*, p. 44).

[22] Interestingly—and perhaps the measure of the correctness of this observation—the Soviets countercharge that imperialist states use peace to mask their policies of aggression, colonialism, and neocolonialism. (Lazarev, *op. cit.*, *supra* note 13, p. 49.) The Soviets frequently betray their own intentions by the charges levelled against capitalist states (e.g., imperialist states are seeking to capture the international legal order and the United Nations for their sinister purposes).

of nuclear weapons tests, for the implementation of practical measures aimed at clearing international relations of the remnants of World War II enhance the prestige of socialism, of the communist movement, in the eyes of the peoples. The banner of peace help [*sic*] the Marxist-Leninist parties rally the masses to speed up the transition from capitalism—which is of the source of bloody wars—to socialism which stands for eternal peace on earth, for friendship and cooperation of people. *The policy of peaceful coexistence is aimed at mobilizing the masses against the enemies of peace.*[23]

Being a form of class struggle on a world scale, the struggle for victory and acceptance of the principle of peaceful coexistence and for the liquidation of wars transcends the struggle of the two systems . . . All peace-loving forces are united in the struggle for the prevention of war. Although different in their class composition and orientation they can be united in the struggle for peace, for prevention of war, because the atom bomb recognizes no class distinction—it destroys all in its wake of destruction.[24]

. . . observ[ance of] the principle of peaceful coexistence with the capitalist states [respect for sovereignty of other states, denunciation of the "export of revolution," acceptance of the will of the peoples, etc.] . . . enables the countries of socialism to successfully combine the struggle for the national and social liberation of the world with the implementation of another international duty—the struggle to prevent world thermonuclear war.[25]

In effect, the policy of peaceful coexistence constitutes an adjustment of Soviet strategy to the new reality of the national liberation movement being the most significant contemporary revolutionary force, and the near-universal appeal of the principle of the impermissibility of nuclear world war.[26]

"LAW IN THE SERVICE OF PEACE"

The new law of peaceful coexistence is extolled as "law in the service of peace."[27] Based upon the Marxist-Leninist teaching which "condemns war as a means of settling international disputes and differences,"[28] the Soviets have proclaimed the "right of nations to

[23] "Peaceful Coexistence and Revolutionary Struggle," *op. cit., supra* note 3, p. 14.

[24] Viskov, *op. cit., supra* note 1, p. 33.

[25] Starushenko, *op. cit., supra* note 14.

[26] "Peaceful Coexistence and Revolutionary Struggle," *op. cit., supra* note 3, p. 17.

[27] See section entitled "Pravo na Sluzhbe Mira" [Law in the Service of Peace], *SGIP*, No. 6 (1965), p. 134.

[28] *International Law, op. cit., supra* note 2, p. 401.

peace" to be the fundamental proposition served by all of the principles of the law of peaceful coexistence.[29]

Contemporary international law prohibits resort to war, forbids the use or threat of force against the territorial and political independence of any state or in any manner incompatible with the goals of the United Nations. States are bound to decide their disputes only by peaceful means.[30]

Proponency of the legal principles of nonaggression, peaceful settlement of disputes, prohibition of propaganda for war, peaceful coexistence, and disarmament is said to be an integral part of the tireless struggle of the Soviet Union to eliminate the so-called "right of states to wage war."[31]

It is said that before the October Revolution, the right to wage war was considered a prerogative of sovereignty; however, commencing with the very first international act of the new Soviet state (i.e., the 1917 Decree on Peace), Soviet initiative has resulted in the outlawing of aggressive war.[32]

Old international law recognized two types of permissible relations between states: peace and war.

At the present time, the unleashing of war is the most flagrant violation of international law, involving heavy responsibility for the aggressor state and personal criminal liability for the guilty parties. The condition of war has ceased being a normal legal relationship between states.[33]

---

[29] F. I. Kalinychev, "Pravo Narodov na Mir" [The Right of Nations to Peace], *SGIP*, No. 3 (1961), pp. 3–15. See also Tunkin, Voprosy Teorii, *op. cit.*, *supra* note 7, p. 54.

[30] Tunkin, Voprosy Teorii, *op. cit.*, *supra* note 7, p. 206.

[31] G. V. Sharmazanashvili, "Dogovory (Pakty) O Nenapadenii—Vazhnoe Sredstvo Ukrepleniia Mezhdunarodnovo Mira i Bezopasnosti" [Nonaggression Pacts—An Important Means of Strengthening International Peace and Security], *SGIP*, No. 4 (1964), pp. 108–112; see 108.

[32] N. A. Ushakov, "Poslanie N. S. Khrushcheva i Mirnoe Uregulirovanie Territorial'nykh Sporov mezhdu Gosudarstvami" [N. S. Khrushchev's Message and the Peaceful Settlement of Territorial Disputes between States], *SGIP*, No. 5 (1964), pp. 3–10; see 4, 5.

[33] Tunkin, Voprosy Teorii, *op. cit.*, *supra* note 7, p. 207. "Loss of the 'right of a state to wage war' and appearance of the international legal principle of nonaggression led to liquidation of the 'rights of the conqueror' and the institution of conquest and extension of the principle of state responsibility for war and its consequences." (*Ibid.*, p. 208.)

119

Soviet legal writing continually points up differences in the "old" and "new" international laws as part of the standard presentation that the content of international law has changed since the appearance of the first socialist state. This change, expressing "the new socialist essence and purpose of international law," is said to have produced new socialist principles and to have filled traditional principles of general international law with a new socialist content.[34] The preoccupation of Soviet jurists with the dichotomy of form and content is a device of convenience which permits manipulation of traditional principles and concepts to serve the foreign policy needs of the Soviet Union.

The legal campaign in support of coexistence actually supports and complements, and is supported and complemented by, Soviet propaganda-diplomatic initiatives which are intended to demonstrate peaceful coexistence in action. Examples of initiatives exploited for this purpose are the so-called "Kosygin proposal," modifying the Soviet draft nonproliferation treaty, and the Soviet Union's role in bringing about the discussions at Tashkent which produced the Tashkent Declaration.[35] The Soviet aim is to demonstrate that (1) the Soviet Union, as part of the world system of socialism, is "a reliable bulwark and a shield of peace"[36], and (2) "communism and peace on earth are indivisible and interdependent."[37] The over-all concept of indivisibility and interdependence, in turn, is relied upon to justify the need for the law of peaceful coexistence as international law interpreted and developed to serve

[34] *Mezhdunarodnoe Pravo* (Kozhevnikov), *op. cit., supra* note 17, pp. 26 and 112.

[35] "Poslanie Predsedatelia Soveta Ministrov SSSR Uchastnikam Komiteta 18 Gosudarstv po Razoruzheniiu v Zheneve" [Communication of the Chairman of the Council of Ministers of the U.S.S.R. to the Participants in the Eighteen-Nation Disarmament Committee at Geneva), *Pravda* (February 3, 1966), pp. 1, 2; and "Tashkent," *New Times*, No. 3 (January 19, 1966), pp. 1, 2. See also "Uspeshnoe Zavershenie Vstrechi v Tashkente" [Successful Conclusion of the Tashkent Meeting], *Pravda* (January 11, 1966), p. 1.

[36] Fyodor Konstantinov, "Communism and Peace on Earth Are Indivisible," *Moscow News*, No. 25 (June 19, 1965), p. 3.

[37] *Ibid.* ". . .we communists are proud that we are in the vanguard of the anti-imperialist progressive forces, and that we are by right regarded [as] staunch and convinced [sic] champions of peace. That is why we say that communism and peace on earth are indivisible."

120

"the interests of peace and socialism."[38] Thus, law, propaganda, and diplomacy are skillfully orchestrated to fashion a legal lever for use in the Soviet interest.

While war is still a problem giving rise to the need for the legal restraints of peaceful coexistence in general international law, it has ceased to be one in the enlightened relationships within the socialist commonwealth. The legal principle governing such relationships, socialist internationalism, is said to include as one of its basic components the principle of everlasting, permanent peace.[39] The possibility of realizing the Marxist ideal of permanent peace in the commonwealth is attributed to the absence of contradictions because of an identity of interests in the building of socialism and communism (i.e., the absence of international class conflict). "The principle of permanent peace has full and complete sway in the relations of all countries of the world socialist system, where the economic and social causes of the antagonistic contradictions giving rise to wars have been abolished."[40] Its realization world-wide, however, must await the victory of socialism in the international class struggle.

There emerges from the Soviet approach to peace and war the like-sounding, but different, formulations of "peaceful coexistence" in relationships outside the socialist commonwealth and "peace" within the commonwealth. The key to the difference in formulation lies in the qualified prohibition of war by the law of peaceful co-existence.

LAWFUL WAR

The Soviets do not condemn the waging of war in any form. To do so would conflict with the Soviet Union's policy of full support

---

[38] G. I. Tunkin, "The Twenty-second Congress of the CPSU and the Tasks of the Soviet Science of International Law," *Soviet Law and Government* (New York: International Arts and Sciences Press, Winter 1962/63), I, No. 2, pp. 18–27; see 25.

[39] Ramundo, *op. cit., supra* note 1, pp. 34, 35.

[40] *Mezhdunarodnopravovye Formy Sotrudnichestva Sotsialisticheskikh Gosudarstv* [International Legal Forms of the Collaboration of Socialist States], ed. V. M. Shurshalov (Moscow: Publishing House of the Academy of Sciences of the U.S.S.R., 1962), p. 19.

for the forces of national liberation. As a means of accommodating this policy and the desire to avoid a thermonuclear war, Soviet jurists have proclaimed that only aggressive, unjust, and nuclear wars are prohibited by international law.[41]

The Soviets claim that aggressive war is regarded in international law as "the most heinous crime against peace and mankind."[42] It is defined as "unjust . . . predatory, imperialist and interventionist" war.[43] The prohibition is broadly stated to protect (1) the Soviet Union against future world, or preventive wars which have become more dangerous to it because of rocket technology and thermonuclear weaponry,[44] and (2) the cause of national liberation against imperialist export of counterrevolution. The prohibition extends also to the planning and preparation of wars of aggression,[45] a concept which can be expanded in the Soviet interest to undermine the legality of foreign military bases, the deployment of military forces abroad, hostile collective security arrangements, and budget expenditures for armaments. The availability of force to meet Soviet needs is ensured by recognition of the legality of defensive wars, and of the monopoly of the Security Council on the collective use of force (other than in self-defense).[46] Given the pliability of Soviet characterizations and the availability of the veto in the Security Council, the Soviet Union can rationalize unilateral resort to force as well as influence the organizational use of it.

In support of national liberation, aggression is broadly defined to include direct military action as well as indirect interference in the internal affairs of another state. The latter includes economic (e.g., economic blockade, subjecting another state to economic

[41] *International Law, op. cit., supra* note 2, p. 403. See also *Mezhdunarodnoe Pravo, op. cit., supra* note 2, pp. 388–392.

[42] P. S. Romashkin, "Agressiia—Tiagchaishee Prestuplenie protiv Mira i Chelovechestva" [Aggression—The Most Heinous Crime Against Peace and Mankind], *SGIP*, No. 1 (1963), pp. 55–67; see 55.

[43] *Mezhdunarodnoe Pravo, op. cit., supra* note 2, p. 391.

[44] V. K. Sobakin, *Kollektivnaia Bezopasnost'—Garantiia Mirnovo Sosushchestvovaniia* [Collective Security—Guarantee of Peaceful Coexistence] (Moscow: Publishing House of the Institute of International Relations, 1962), pp. 27 and 62.

[45] *Mezhdunarodnoe Pravo, op. cit., supra* note 2, p. 392.

[46] L. A. Modzhorian, "Amerikanskie Doktriny Grabezha i Razboia: ot Monro do Zhonsona" [American Doctrines of Plunder and Brigandage from Monroe to Johnson], *SGIP*, No. 9 (1965), pp. 57–64; see 63.

pressures, or interfering with exploitation of natural resources or their nationalization) as well as ideological (e.g., propaganda for war, racism or intolerance towards other states) encroachments upon state sovereignty.[47] Specifically, colonial wars are characterized as direct aggression[48] and "wars of national liberation. . .[as] defense against aggression with all of the consequences which flow from it."[49] The basis for this position is the view that ". . . forcible retention of nations seeking independence in all cases constitutes annexation (i.e., direct aggression) no matter how long ago it was done."[50] "Nations under the colonial yoke strive for freedom and independence by peaceful means. However, frequently colonial powers resist with force the just striving for liquidation of the colonial regime. In such cases, the captive nations can only resort to the use of arms—this is their sacred right."[51] Any form of struggle, including armed conflict for national liberation or independence or for the return of national territory, is considered "completely legal."[52]

The legitimacy of wars of liberation is also confirmed in the Declaration of the Rights of Man adopted by the U.N. ("as the last means . . . against tyranny and aggression . . .") and in the decisions of the 1954 Geneva conference on Indochina and in many other generally accepted international documents. The Cairo conference of nonaligned countries was particularly firm in pointing out the legality of national liberation wars.

The absolute majority of the states of the world and all of world public opinion unconditionally recognize the just, progressive character of wars of liberation.[53]

---

[47] *Mezhdunarodnoe Pravo, op. cit., supra* note 2, pp. 391, 392. See also *International Law, op. cit., supra* note 2, p. 405.

[48] R. A. Tuzmukhamedov, "Mirnoe Sosushchestvovanie i Natsional'no-osvoboditel'naia Voina" [Peaceful Coexistence and Wars of National Liberation], *SGIP*, No. 3 (1963), pp. 87–94; see 88.

[49] R. L. Bobrov, "Mezhdunarodnoe Pravo i Istoricheskii Progress" [International Law and Historical Progress], *SGIP*, No. 12 (1963), pp. 3–11; see 8.

[50] Ushakov, Poslanie N. S. Khrushcheva, *op. cit., supra* note 32, p. 8.

[51] *Ibid.*

[52] Tuzmukhamedov, *op. cit., supra* note 48, pp. 91–94. It is said that the "moral correctness and juridical propriety of wars of national liberation reflect the fact that in these wars imperialism is at fault." (*Ibid.*, p. 94.) See also "Wars of National Liberation—The Soviet Thesis" in *Soviet Impact on International Law* (External Research Paper 156) (Washington, D.C.: U.S. Department of State, Bureau of Intelligence and Research, [May 1964), p. 5.

[53] G. Starushenko, "Fiction and Truth About Wars of Liberation" translated from *Kommunist* (August 1965), in *CDSP*, XVII, No. 34, pp. 5, 6; see 5.

Only legal are wars which states are forced to wage in self-defense against aggression, national liberation wars against foreign domination, or national revolutionary wars, uprisings against exploiters, reactionary regimes and tyrants. In these wars the people are struggling for self-determination, social and independent national development.

In waging national liberation wars and rising against the exploiters, the people do not breach world peace or disrupt peaceful coexistence. Rather, the war of foreign states against a nation struggling for its national or class freedom constitutes aggression, a violation of international peace incompatible with peaceful coexistence. [54]

Further, it is said that only a state can commit aggression, thereby "excluding the possibility of characterizing internal armed conflicts (i.e., insurgency incident to civil wars or wars of national liberation) as aggression." [55]

The Soviets' desire to avoid thermonuclear warfare is given legal expression in their position that the use of nuclear weapons in warfare is illegal:

...even in the absence of any special international agreement banning nuclear weapons, their use clashes with all the rules regulating the conduct of belligerents which have evolved over the years (the so-called laws and customs of war), that is, the Hague Conventions of 1899 and 1907, and 1925 Geneva Protocol, and all the unanimous demands of international democratic opinion. [56]

Related to the laws of war in prohibiting nuclear warfare is international medical law, a branch of general international law (i.e., peaceful coexistence) which the Soviets increasingly invoke for this purpose. ". . .[Nuclear] war is the greatest calamity for mankind . . . That is why one of the cardinal tasks facing international medical

---

[54] G. P. Zadorozhnyi, *Mirnoe Sosushchestvovanie i Mezhdunarodnoe Pravo* [Peaceful Coexistence and International Law] (Moscow: Publishing House "International Relations," 1964), pp. 110, 111.

[55] *Mezhdunarodnoe Pravo, op. cit., supra* note 2, p. 391.

[56] Y. Korovin, "The Way to Peace" *International Affairs*, No. 11 (1964), pp. 73–75; see 73. See also A. N. Talalaev, Review of O. V. Bogdanov, *Iadernoe Razoruzhenie* [Nuclear Disarmament] (Moscow: Publishing House of the Institute of International Relations, 1961), *Sovetskii Ezhegodnik, 1962* (Moscow: Publishing House of the Academy of Sciences of the U.S.S.R., 1963), pp. 308–310; see 308.

law is work for the banishment of war forever."[57] The prohibition against nuclear wars extends to "local" and "limited" wars because of their potential for escalation[58] and serves as a basis, in addition to the "aggression" and "unjust" characterizations, to attack the legality of such wars. Propaganda support for the legal position against aggression and nuclear war usually takes the form of (*1*) condemnation of warmongering capitalist policies, (2) repeated praise for "the struggle against aggressive and unjust wars . . . [the] deep and durable tradition of the entire international workers' movement," and (*3*) emphasis upon the awesome destruction potential of nuclear warfare.[59]

"*Just*" *Wars.* Just wars are those which "defend oppressed classes against capitalists, oppressed nations against their oppressors, the socialist revolution against foreign invasions," whereas, unjust wars are "reactionary. . .imperialist wars. . .for the sake of capitalist wealth and suppression of small and weak nations."[60]

A just war is a non–predatory, liberatory [*sic*] war. Its aim is the defense of a people against external attacks and attempts to enslave it. Just wars include defensive wars and wars of national liberation. All progressive mankind sympathises [*sic*] with such wars, and supports those fighting for freedom and independence.

. . . .

An unjust war is a predatory war. It aims at the seizure and enslavement of foreign lands and peoples. Unjust wars include aggressive, imperialist wars.[61]

---

[57] V. S. Mikhailov, "K Voprosu o Mezhdunarodnom Meditsinskom Prave" [Concerning International Medical Law], *Sovetskii Ezhegodnik, 1963, op. cit., supra* note 13, pp. 308–322; see 322. See also O. S. Padbil', "Nekotorye Problemy Mezhdunarodnovo Meditsinskovo Prava" [Some Problems of International Medical Law], *Ibid.*, pp. 303–307.

[58] I. Grishanko, "The Weapons Revolution and World Security," *New Times*, No. 42 (October 20, 1965), pp. 3–5; see 4, 5.

[59] A. Veber and A. Chernyayev, "Policy of Aggression and the Social Democrats," trans. from *Pravda* (July 30, 1965), in *CDSP*, XVII, No. 30, pp. 20, 21; see 20; Konstantinov, *op. cit., supra* note 36; and Grishanko, *op. cit., supra* note 58.

[60] *Mezhdunarodnoe Pravo, op. cit., supra* note 2, p. 389, citing examples of just and unjust wars, the principal criterion for distinguishing between them being the effect on the Soviet Union.

[61] *International Law, op. cit., supra* note 2, p. 402.

It would appear that the principal distinction is between just and unjust wars, with "wars of aggression," although included under the latter, serving the important function of providing a more traditional, substantive content for an international legal principle. (Soviet commentaries have switched recently to the more expressive term, "dirty war," as a substitute for unjust war, in describing the United States military effort in Vietnam.)[62] The basic qualitative difference between just and unjust wars is said to be reflected in the nature of the peace treaties which follow such wars.

> The character of a peace treaty. . .[is related] to the character of the war. Wars of aggression and unjust wars lead, in the event of victory of the aggressor, to unequal, harsh international agreements.
>
> Entirely different should be the evaluation of treaties resulting from a just war. In the conclusion of these treaties the will of the people of the conquered country is considered, its interests and democratic rights. It is clear that those treaties are legal.[63]

The Soviet position, therefore, is that unjust wars, as well as their results, are illegal.

Despite the absence of the concept of just wars in the Charter of the United Nations, it is said that, in effect, the general prohibition against the threat or use of force and recognition of the right of individual or collective self-defense provide, in combination, the

---

[62] See, for example, M. Nersisyan, "Genocide Is Gravest Crime Against Humanity," translated from *Pravda* (April 24, 1965), in *CDSP*, XVII, No. 17, pp. 24, 25; see 25; and "The Debate Continues," *New Times*, No. 41 (October 13, 1965), pp. 6–8; see 6. The origin of the term "dirty war" is interesting. It was used by the Vietnamese communist, Truong Chink in 1947 to describe the national liberation struggle against the French. See "The August Revolution" and "The Resistance Will Win" in *Primer for Revolt* (The Communist Takeover in Vietnam), ed. Bernard B. Fall (New York and London: Praeger, 1963). See also Y. Oleshchuk: " 'Small Wars' and the Aggression in Viet-nam," *International Affairs*, No. 5 (1966), pp. 35–39. The formal statement concerning the United States military effort in Vietnam adopted at the Twenty-third Party Congress characterizes it as "disgraceful," "brutal," and "criminal war against the South Vietnamese patriots." ("Statement of the Twenty-third Congress of the C.P.S.U. Concerning U.S. Aggression in Vietnam," trans. from *Pravda* [April 9, 1966], in *Moscow News*, Supplement to No. 16 (April 16, 1966), pp. 11, 12; see 11.)

[63] P. I. Lukin, *Istochniki Mezhdunarodnovo Prava* [Sources of International Law] (Moscow: Publishing House of the Academy of Sciences of the U.S.S.R., 1960), p. 74.

basis for the Soviet approach to aggression and unjust wars.[64] Notwithstanding their view of the coverage of the provisions of the Charter of the United Nations, the Soviets see great utility in the conclusion of nonaggression pacts as a means of strengthening the Charter.[65] The legal rationale for this position is that ". . . an international agreement may confirm norms of existing international law and there is nothing in the Charter which forbids the repetition or reinforcement of its principles in other international acts."[66] Similarly, despite the claimed illegality of nuclear warfare under existing international law it is said that a special agreement prohibiting nuclear warfare would be useful "since the confirmation of the general principles of international law through special conventions serves to consolidate the principles of legality and law in international relations."[67] Soviet efforts to achieve such an agreement are supported by this position:

> The illegality of nuclear warfare imposes an international legal obligation upon all states to reach agreement concerning the complete and unconditional prohibition of nuclear and all other weapons of mass destruction. This also means that the refusal of any state to accept such prohibition contravenes contemporary international law. . . . The position of the U.S.S.R. and other states insisting upon the unconditional and complete prohibition of nuclear weapons is the only correct one which meets the vital interests and legal consciousness of all peoples.[68]

The legal prohibitions against aggressive, unjust, and nuclear wars are bolstered by a new, socialist-inspired concept of state responsibility under which:

> Responsibility does not result from harm to the property of foreign capitalists but rather from aggression and military crimes, the colonial enslavement of peoples, racial and national persecution—generally, from crimes against mankind in the broadest sense of the term.[69]

---

[64] V. I. Lisovskii, *Mezhdunarodnoe Pravo* [International Law] (2d ed.; Moscow: State Publishing House "Higher School," 1961), p. 409.

[65] Sharmazanashvili, *op. cit., supra* note 31, pp. 109–111.

[66] *Ibid.*, pp. 109, 110.

[67] Korovin, "The Way to Peace," *op. cit., supra* note 56, pp. 73, 74.

[68] Talalaev, *op. cit., supra* note 56, pp. 308, 309.

[69] D. B. Levin, "Ob Otvetstvennosti Gosudarstv v Sovremennom Mezhdunarodnom Prave" [The Responsibility of States Under Contemporary International Law], *SGIP*, No. 5 (1966), pp. 75–83; see 83. This development in international law is directly attributed to the epoch of socialism and the decisive role of "the countries of socialism and the developing countries" (*Ibid.*).

In addition, the new law of peaceful coexistence complements the legal prohibitions with other principles such as those requiring the resolution of international disputes by peaceful means,[70] and abstention from propaganda for war.[71]

Thus, "peaceful coexistence," despite its attractiveness as a formulation, means only that nuclear wars and unjust wars, so-called wars of aggression, or wars serving the interests of the forces of Western imperialism, are barred. The Soviets consider wars of national liberation and defensive wars to be just wars and, as such, permissible. In practice, just wars are those which are waged in the Soviet interest. To be recalled in this connection is the claim that in 1950-1953 an aggressive, unjust war was waged against the Korean people by the United States and its allies.[72] In this area as in others, the Soviets rely upon their own characterization of a situation to determine the legalities involved.

The Right of Self-Defense. The Soviet approach to the right of self-defense reflects the ambivalence of an effort to limit the use of the right by capitalist states, while expanding it to accommodate the needs of the Soviet Union. The Soviets restrict the "nonsocialist" use of self-defense by subordinating it to the law of peaceful coexistence under cover of the Charter of the United Nations. The effect of this subordination is to provide a basis for denouncing self-defense that is hostile to Soviet interests, and to license that which is deemed necessary to meet the policy requirements of coexistence.

[70] G. I. Tunkin, "Printsip Mirnovo Sosushchestvovaniia—General'naia Liniia Vneshepoliticheskoi Deiatel'nosti KPSS i Sovetskovo Gosudarstva" [The Principle of Peaceful Coexistence—The General Line of the Foreign Policy of the CPSU and the Soviet State], *SGIP*, No. 7 (1963), pp. 26–37; see 33.

[71] Ramundo, *op. cit., supra* note 1, pp. 84, 85 (note 303). The existence of domestic criminal legislation prohibiting propaganda for war in all the countries of socialism is used as documentation of the thesis that the socialist camp is the camp of peace. It is also the basis for the Soviet proposals in various disarmament forums that all states adopt criminal legislation proscribing propaganda for war.

[72] *Mezhdunarodnoe Pravo, op. cit., supra* note 2, p. 389. See also Stepan Molodtsov, "United Nations—Twenty Years," *Moscow News*, No. 43 (October 23, 1965), p. 6.

Soviet jurists use a two-pronged approach in coping with the problem of self-defense. The principal position is that this right has been limited by Article 51 of the Charter of the United Nations, so that resort to self-defense must be compatible with the requirements of that Article. The United Nations system in its entirety is the secondary bulwark. In the Soviet view, the right of self-defense has no existence apart from Article 51 of the Charter which in recognizing the right has placed extensive limitations upon its exercise.[73]

It is generally recognized that the Charter eliminated the right of states to resort to self-help in the sense of independent and uncontrolled resort to any measures for the protection of rights and interests against the acts of other states.[74]

The single most important limitation under the terms of Article 51 is the requirement that an "armed attack" must precede the resort to self-defense. Further, the employment of force in self-defense must be terminated as soon as the Security Council takes action, unless that action calls for continuance of measures of self-defense. The same rules apply to regional organizations, i.e., force may be utilized only to repel an armed attack or as a measure of compulsion sanctioned by the Security Council.[75] Emphasis upon Securit Council action, rather than the General Assembly, is to ensure th availability of the Soviet veto to exercise a measure of control upo the use of force in self-defense. Soviet jurists extol their "objective' criteria of self-defense as a welcome substitute for the subjective standard of national interest reflected in the practice of imperialist states.

[Under] the U.N. Charter. . .the right to self-defense lawfully arises "if an armed attack occurs" against a state. Acceptance of [the Western]. . .concept would furnish legal opportunities for misuse of armed force in selfish interests in cases when acts of nationalism, demands for the abrogation of

---

[73] Sobakin, Kollektivnaia Bezopasnost', op. cit., supra note 44, pp. 301 and 324. See also V. M. Chkhikvadze, "Voprosy Mezhdunarodnovo Prava na XX Sessii General'noi Assamblei OON," [Problems of International Law at the Twentieth Session of the General Assembly of the U.N.], SGIP, No. 3 (1966), pp. 67–78; see 74.
[74] Ibid., p. 300.
[75] Chkhikvadze, op. cit., supra note 73, p. 74.

fettering treaties, the social system and many other circumstances are arbitrarily fitted into the concept of "aggression" or "threat of aggression."[76]

Intervention under the Monroe, Eisenhower, and Truman Doctrines is cited as a specific type of illegality resulting from the use of a subjective standard.[77] The objectivity claimed for the "armed attack" formulation appears to be less than clear-cut if one recalls the Soviet denial of an armed attack by the North Koreans in 1950.[78] The objectivity intended is "socialist objectivity," i.e., a formulation which, like similar formulations in the Soviet lexicon, (e.g., "socialist realism," "socialist democracy," and "socialist internationalism") invites characterizations in the Soviet interest.

Apart from the specific language of Article 51, there are, in the Soviet view, general limitations upon the right of self-defense which flow from the Charter of the United Nations. Having been limited to the United Nations context, the right of self-defense is easily subordinated to peaceful coexistence, the red thread said to run through the Charter. Building on this basic premise, the Soviets argue that, given the United Nations system for the maintenance of peace and security, the resort to self-defense is an exceptional measure.

The U.N. Charter contemplates a centralized system for the application of sanctions for the purpose of protecting the security and rights of states. . . Under these conditions, resort to the right of self-defense is exceptional rather than the general rule. It is an extraordinary and auxiliary measure because the principal measures to protect peace and international security are entrusted to the Organization, which for this purpose operates through the Security Council.[79]

Other Charter principles such as self-determination, abstention from the threat or use of force, collective measures for the maintenance of peace and security, and the unanimity of the permanent

[76] S. V. Molodtsov, "Mirnoe Uregulirovanie Territorial'nykh Sporov i Voprosov o Granitsakh" [Peaceful Settlement of Territorial Disputes and Border Questions], *Sovetskii Ezhegodnik, 1963, op. cit., supra* note 13, pp. 70–84; see 82.

[77] Sobakin, Kollektivnaia Bezopasnost', *op. cit., supra* note 44, p. 302. See also Modzhorian, Amerikanskie Doktriny, *op. cit., supra* note 46.

[78] *Ibid.,* p. 71.

[79] *Ibid.,* pp. 300, 301.

members of the Security Council, are also relied upon to shape the right of self-defense:

> ... having recognized that right, the Charter of the United Nations indicated the specific limitations upon it which result from the general system of collective security established by the Charter. Directly related to the right of self-defense are the principles of self-determination of nations and peoples, abstention from the threat or use of force, collective action in the maintenance of international peace and security, unanimity amongst the permanent members of the Security Council, and abstention from assisting any states against whom the U.N. is taking preventive or enforcement action ... Article 51 cannot be interpreted or understood as superseding or weakening any of these principles or their realization in practice.[80]

This line of reasoning leads to the inevitable conclusion that the only actions permissible under Article 51 are those "which proceed from the principle of peaceful coexistence and ensure its realization."[81]

The Soviets have little difficulty in contesting the legality of any resort to the right of self-defense which is considered inimical to the interests of the Soviet Union. The existence of an armed attack may be denied; the situation may be considered one appropriate for the collective security apparatus of the United Nations, rather than the exceptional measure of self-defense; or one of the general principles of the Charter, such as the unanimity of the permanent members of the Security Council, may be invoked.[82] The Soviets also seek to insulate their seemingly unrelated policy objectives against possible interference from the very existence of a right of self-defense. For example, although it is recognized that the right of self-defense includes the right of military preparedness, the latter right cannot be invoked to obstruct the realization of general and complete disarmament.[83] Soviet international legal specialists look forward to the day when the right of self-defense and all of the related rationalizations necessary to protect Soviet interests will have

---

[80] *Ibid.*, p. 301.

[81] *Ibid.*, p. 320.

[82] "Action taken under the right of self-defense must not undermine the unity of action of the great powers and render impossible agreement amongst the permanent members of the Security Council. Otherwise it would be impossible for the Council to adopt any effective decisions or measures." (*Ibid.*, p. 315.)

[83] *Ibid.*, p. 309.

disappeared as a concomitant feature of a disarmed world.[84] As long as the right of self-defense continues as a fact of international life, however, they must attempt to gain some advantage from it for the Soviet Union.

To expand the socialist use of self-defense, the Soviets also rely upon the Charter of the United Nations, principally the Charter right of self-determination. At least one Soviet international legal specialist asserts the availability of the right of self-defense to combat any imperialist violation of the Charter. "Article 51 of the U.N. Charter recognizes peoples' inherent right of individual or collective self-defense against imperialist powers' actions forbidden by the Charter."[85] Thus the Soviets have laid the basis for expanding self-defense to include the use of force to resist or punish violations of the new law of coexistence which is said to be embodied in the Charter. This would seem to be a logical development in view of the basic Soviet technique of first seeking to neutralize a potentially hostile institution, and, after neutralization, turning it to the advantage of the Soviet Union. The current emphasis upon the general commitment not to resort to force in international relations may be the prelude to a modification of that commitment in the Soviet interest to justify the use of force as a sanction for noncompliance with the policy and law of coexistence. The plausibility of this conjecture is supported by current claims that wars of national liberation are "a sanction against the colonialist law breaker."[86]

Just as self-determination is a right enjoyed by states and nations, so too is the right of self-defense. This right is said to be involved in a struggle for national liberation under the somewhat tortured reasoning that it constitutes an "act of national self-defense against the armed attack which was perpetrated at the time of the seizure of

---

[84] *Ibid.*, pp. 324, 325.

[85] Starushenko, "Fiction and Truth," *op. cit., supra* note 53, p. 5.

[86] P. A. Tuzmukhamedov, "Ustav Organizatsii Afrikanskovo Edinstva v Svete Mezhdunarodnovo Prava" [The Charter of the Organization of African Unity in the Light of International Law], *Sovetskii Ezhegodnik, 1963, op. cit., supra* note 13, pp. 109–128; see 127.

the colonies by the imperialist powers."[87] States supporting wars of national liberation are claimed to be acting under the right of "collective self-defense. . .and assisting in restoring international law and order which has been, or is being, violated."[88] Thus, the right of self-defense can be invoked as another basis for sustaining the legality of wars of national liberation and their support by "peace-loving states."

The Soviet position on the right of self-defense reflects the need to support the duality of defense and offense in the policy objectives of the Soviet Union. By restricting self-defense to the United Nations context, the Soviets actually superimpose the policy of peaceful coexistence upon this right, thereby seeking legal support for minimum and maximum policy goals. At the minimum, it is in the Soviet interest to inhibit Western resort to force under color of the right of self-defense. The Soviet Union would derive maximum, benefit from that right if, at the same time, the socialist use of it (e.g., in support of national liberation) could remain unimpaired or be expanded. The effectiveness of the Soviet approach in this area as in others depends upon the acceptability to the West of the more basic proposition that the Charter of the United Nations embodies the principles of peaceful coexistence.

Subversion, Insurgency, and Counterinsurgency. Despite historical evidence to the contrary, the Soviets disclaim any intent to subvert governments, and frequently repeat in this connection Lenin's quotation concerning the nonexportability of revolution.[89] The ideological pronouncement is supported by the legal concept of indirect aggression, which proscribes subversive activity by one state in another (i.e., the training, financing or supplying a group for the purpose of changing the economic and social system of another

[87] Sobakin, Kollektivnaia Bezopasnost', *op. cit., supra* note 44, p. 302. See also Chkhikvadze, *op. cit., supra* note 73, p. 76.

[88] Tuzmukhamedov, Ustav Organizatsii, *op. cit., supra* note 86, p. 127.

[89] See, for example, Starushenko, Fiction and Truth, *op. cit., supra* note 53, p. 5. "Socialism is the result of the revolutionary creative activity of the broad masses and not of the efforts of the socialist states" (*Ibid.*) "All talk of exporting revolution . . . is ballyhoo. Revolution is made by the masses of people." ("Your Questions on Communism," *Soviet Life*, No. 1 [1966], pp. 20–21, answer to the question, "Why do not Communists apply the principle of peaceful coexistence to

state).[90] "Indirect aggression includes encouragement by one state of subversion against another. . .; [as well as] complicity in the fomenting of civil war, a coup, or a change in policy favorable to the intervening state."[91] In addition, reliance is placed upon the principles of nonintervention and self-determination to bolster further the case against subversion. Although the Soviets formally reject the legality of subversion, they approve of support to the forces of national liberation, and draw a self-serving distinction between the two types of intervention. When insurgency favorable to Soviet interests develops, they openly support it under the general banner of assistance to national liberation movements. The Soviets vehemently deny that support for wars of national liberation constitutes a form of aggression or unlawful intervention.[92] Their rationale for support of national liberation in the face of the general prohibition against intervention in the internal affairs of states is neither logical nor legally persuasive. Logically, the position is little more than characterization in the Soviet interest through invocation of the sanctifying grace of the designation "national liberation."[93] The legal rationale for the support for national liberation is based principally upon the outlawry of colonialism.

---

the ideological sphere?", p. 21). See also Zadorozhnyi, Mirnoe Sosushchestvo-vanie, *op. cit.*, *supra* note 54, pp. 23, 157 and 166; Sobakin, Kollektivnaia Bezopasnost', *op. cit.*, *supra* note 44, p. 41. Events in Eastern Europe after World War II and elsewhere have demonstrated that subversion of hostile governments is a covert tactic of world revolution. (See "Goldberg Blasts Soviets for Aiding Subversion," *The Washington Post* [December 11, 1965], p. A–20 and "OAS Set to Discuss Denunciation of Soviet Backing of Subversion" *Ibid.* [January 22, 1966], p. A–9.) Sobakin dismisses charges of Soviet subversion as a cover for the Western world's policy of intervention (Sobakin, Kollektivnaia Bezopasnost', *op. cit.*, *supra* note 44, pp. 59, 60).

[90] A. P. Movchan, "O Znachenii Kodifikatsii Printsipov Mezhdunarodnovo Prava" [The Importance of the Codification of the Principles of International Law], *SGIP*, No. 1 (1965), pp. 46–55; see 50, 51, 52.

[91] *Mezhdunarodnoe Pravo, op. cit., supra* note 2, p. 391.

[92] Starushenko, Fiction and Truth, *op. cit., supra* note 53, p. 5.

[93] The Soviet policy to support national liberation movements reflects the view that this tide of revolution, although not socialist in character, can be used in the struggle against capitalism and its international manifestation, imperialism, as a means of weakening it by enlisting the support of the emerging states in combating it.

"The Soviet Union advocates the use of every form of struggle for national liberation. The peoples' right to freedom and independence, whether estab-

By outlawing colonialism [by the Declaration on the Granting of Independence to the Colonial Countries and Peoples, adopted on December 14, 1960] the General Assembly legitimized every form of struggle for national liberation and every form of assistance to the national liberation movements and fighters.[94]

The Soviets also rely upon the principle of self-determination and the general obligation to assist in its realization.

As principles of equality and self-determination of nations are included in the Charter, assistance to national liberation movements is not in law an unfriendly act towards the state concerned.[95]

Utmost support by the peace-loving states to the national liberation, anti-colonial struggle of the peoples constitutes not only collective self-defense but also assistance in restoring international law and order which has been, or is being, violated.

Neither national-liberation struggle, including armed struggle, nor assistance to it run counter to the principle of peaceful coexistence. On the contrary, by reinforcing an integral element of peaceful coexistence, the right of all peoples to self-determination, these actions eliminate a threat to international peace and respect for international law.[96]

Whenever necessary, however, the illegality of colonialism and the right of self-determination are turned about to inhibit opposition to national liberation by capitalist states.[97] "Opposition of a colonial

---

lished by peaceful means or in armed struggle is sacred. The Soviet Union gives comprehensive assistance to the peoples fighting with weapons in hand against imperialism and colonialism." ("Pravda on U.S.S.R. and National Liberation Movement," trans. from *Pravda* [June 28, 1965], in *CDSP*, XVII, No. 26, pp. 3–5; see 4.)

See also "The Noble Aims of Soviet Foreign Policy," trans. from *Pravda* (August 8, 1965), in *CDSP*, XVII, No. 32, pp. 3–6; see 4, 5.

The community of interest in this struggle provides the basis for the view that the socialist and neutralist states take a common stand in their approach to the basic problems of coexistence.

"In the basic questions of the struggle for peace and security of nations, against colonialism and imperialism, the positions of these neutralist states coincide with the positions of the socialist states." (*Mezhdunarodnoe Pravo*, *op. cit.*, *supra* note 2, p. 270.)

[94] Y. Bochkaryov, "Colonial Bastions Under Attack," *New Times*, No. 50 (December 15, 1965), pp. 8, 9; see 8. See also Tuzmukhamedov, Ustav Organizatsii, *op. cit.*, *supra* note 86, p. 127.

[95] Bobrov, Mezhdunarodnoe Pravo, *op. cit.*, *supra* note 49, p. 8.

[96] Tuzmukhamedov, Ustav Organizatsii, *op. cit.*, *supra* note 86, p. 127.

[97] Bochkaryov, *op. cit.*, *supra* note 94, p. 9.

power to the realization of freedom by the people of a colonial or dependent country is the most flagrant violation of international law."[98]

Attempts to suppress Soviet-supported insurgency are denounced as unjust wars and violations of the principles of self-determination and nonintervention. Such attempts are characterized as interventionist, colonialist, and aggressive and the "imperialist export of counterrevolution" (a counter to the charge of Soviet export of revolution) forbidden by international law.[99] The double standard in invoking legal principles in support of policy objectives seriously detracts from the credibility of the Soviet position.

The propaganda line supporting the inhibiting force of the legal principles notes that Western (principally United States) counterrevolution, originally directed against the socialist states, is now directed at crushing the national liberation movement.[100] Korea, Cuba, and most recently, Vietnam provide excellent examples of the manner in which these situations are handled. For example, with respect to Vietnam, it is said that:

They [American imperialist circles] are now attempting to strangle the national-liberation movement in South Vietnam and in all of Southeast Asia. The imperialists of the U.S.A. are waging a "dirty war" against the whole South Vietnamese people, who refuse to submit to the colonialists, and are seeking to arrest the forward movement of history by force of arms.[101]

Propaganda, however strident, is not a substitute for a sound legal position.

Thus, when it is in the Soviet interest to combat subversion, the prohibitions against aggressive, unjust war and intervention are

[98] Tunkin, Voprosy Teorii, *op. cit., supra* note 7, p. 47.

[99] Sobakin, Kollektivnaia Bezopasnost', *op. cit., supra* note 44, pp. 45–50.

[100] *Ibid.*, p. 46. See also "The Noble Aims of Soviet Foreign Policy," *op. cit., supra* note 93, p. 3.

[101] Nersisyan, *op. cit., supra* note 62, p. 25. See also M. E. Volosov, "Agressiia Amerikanskovo Imperializma protiv V'etnamskovo Naroda—Prestuplenie protiv Mira i Mezhdunarodnoi Bezopasnosti" [American Imperialist Aggression Against the Vietnamese People—A Crime Against Peace and International Security], *SGIP*, No. 6 (1965), pp. 134–136; and G. A. Onitskaia, "Voina SShA v Indokitae—Gruboe Narushenie Mezhdunarodnovo Prava" [The U.S. War in Indo-China—A Flagrant Violation of International Law], *Ibid.*, No. 11 (1965), pp. 40–48.

invoked, overshadowing the principle of self-determination. When insurgency favored by the Soviet Union develops, however, priority is accorded the principle of self-determination and the cause of national liberation to support Soviet actions and inhibit counter-insurgency. In every case, the flexible legal rationale lends support to, and in turn is supported by, a propaganda tirade which condemns the reactionary imperialist policy favoring the perpetuation of colonialism and extols the enlightened, unselfish Soviet assistance to national liberation.

Apart from the principles of the law of peaceful coexistence, the Soviets also invoke their "higher law" of social development for the support of national liberation. In the *Communist Manifesto*, Karl Marx urged support for any and all revolutionary movements in the struggle against capitalism.[102] This passage from the sacred scripture of international communism is the apparent basis for the view that national liberation and the liquidation of colonialism are, like the struggle of the two systems, the ever-growing strength of the socialist system, the peaceful coexistence of states, and the impermissibility of supranational international organizations, parts of the "basic law of contemporary society" (i.e., *jus cogens*).[103] The result is a messianic strain in Soviet commentaries which speak of the international duty of the Soviet Union to assist peoples struggling for national liberation.[104]

[102] "Communists everywhere support every revolutionary movement against the existing social and political order of things." (*Manifesto of the Communist Party*, contained in the *Selected Works* of Karl Marx and Frederick Engels [Moscow: Foreign Languages Publishing House, 1950], Vol. 1, pp. 14–61; see 61.)

[103] G. I. Tunkin, "Organizatsiia Ob'edinennykh Natsii: 1945–1965 (Mezhdu-narodnopravovye Problemy)" [The United Nations Organization 1945–1965 (International Legal Problems)], *SGIP*, No. 10 (1965), pp. 58–68; see 60, 61.

[104] Bobrov, Mezhdunarodnoe Pravo, *op. cit.*, *supra* note 49, pp. 8, 9. See also "Vysshii Internatsional'nyi Dolg Strany Sotsializma" [The Supreme International Duty of a Socialist Country], *Pravda* (October 27, 1965), pp. 3, 4. At the Twenty-third Party Congress, Gromyko appeared to extend this "messianism" as follows: "The Soviet Union cannot help having an interest in the situation in every part of the world. Wherever international peace, freedom and independence are in issue, so too are the interests of the Soviet Union." (Rech' Tovarishcha A. A. Gromyko" [The Speech of Comrade Gromyko], *Pravda* [April 3, 1966], pp. 4, 5; see 5.)

The Law of War. As war is still a possibility in relations between capitalist and socialist states, the rules of war remain operative as part of the law of peaceful coexistence.[105]

Although wars are no longer fatally unavoidable, there is, so long as imperialism exists, a dangerous threat of war. Therefore, and because it is realistic, the Soviet science of international law includes coverage of the laws and rules of war.[106]

In the socialist commonwealth, the principle of everlasting, permanent peace has rendered surplusage the laws and customs of war.[107] Actually, the rules of war have become more important in the Soviet scheme of things as they are principally relied upon to support the claim that nuclear warfare is prohibited by international law.[108] In the Soviet view, the rules of war are applicable to international conflicts as well as civil wars and wars of national liberation.[109] The reason for this extended coverage is to ensure that nuclear weapons are not employed in these types of struggle and, in addition, to provide a protective cover for the forces of national liberation. For example, the Soviets are relying upon the rules of war to discredit and, as a possible consequence, to inhibit the United States military effort in Vietnam.

American armed forces have committed many military crimes, i.e., crimes against the laws and customs of war, as provided in subparagraph 6(*b*) of the Charter of the International Military Tribunal. Included among these are: the bombardment of peaceful cities and populations in South and North Vietnam, the use of such prohibited barbaric means as napalm and the use of chemical agents for the destruction of crops [defoliants].[110]

Further, it is said that ". . .the American militarists make a mockery of generally-recognized legal principles and norms of international

[105] *International Law, op. cit., supra* note 2, pp. 405, 406.

[106] *Mezhdunarodnoe Pravo* (Kozhevnikov), *op. cit., supra* note 17, p. 65.

[107] V. M. Shurshalov, "Mezhdunarodno-pravovye Printispy Sotrudnichestva Sotsialisticheskikh Gosudarstv" [International Legal Principles of the Collaboration of Socialist States], *SGIP*, No. 7 (1962), pp. 95–105.

[108] See *Mezhdunarodnoe Pravo, op. cit., supra* note 2, pp. 393 and 397. The bombing of Hiroshima and Nagasaki is treated as a lawless, senseless act. (*Ibid.*, p. 397.)

[109] *Ibid.*

[110] Volosov, *op. cit., supra* note 101, p. 135.

morality" by using napalm and chemical means of waging war.[111] The use of these means is characterized as a "crime against peace and against mankind."[112] The effectiveness of this type of propaganda can be best understood in the context of the United States' use of chemical riot-control agents in Vietnam. Concern for the U.S. image, blackened by continuing Soviet propaganda attacks, actually inhibited for a time the use of an effective and humane means of separating combatant and refugee personnel.

Even before the Vietnam tirade, the Soviets had branded the imperialist powers as habitual violators of the law of war.[113] In contrast, the Soviet Union claimed for itself the position "at the head of progressive mankind in the campaign for the further humanization of the laws and customs of war."[114] The claim is also made that the Soviet Union "unswervingly" observes the laws and customs of war.[115]

The Soviet legal positions on the vital questions of peace and war reflect a general fact of contemporary international life: the need to take account of world public opinion. As a powerful state in a world dominated numerically by legally equal, but smaller and weaker, states possessed of an effective forum in the General Assembly of the United Nations, the Soviet Union is constrained to "play to the gallery." This courtship of the gallery lies at the heart of many of the Soviet positions on international law. Soviet legal

[111] *Ibid.*, pp. 135, 136. See also N. Ushakov, "Obuzdat' Narushitelei Mezhdunarodnoi Zakonnosti!" [Restrain the Violations of International Legality!], *Pravda* (March 18, 1966), p. 4, for an attack on the legality of U.S. use of chemical agents in Vietnam.

[112] *Ibid.* As a rule, the Soviets strongly endorse individual criminal liability for persons who start or wage aggressive war or who violate the laws of war as a further means of deterring aggressive war and such violations (*Mezhdunarodnoe Pravo, op. cit., supra* note 2, pp. 412, 413, and *International Law, op. cit., supra* note 2, pp. 451, 452).

[113] *Mezhdunarodnoe Pravo, op. cit., supra* note 2, p. 394, and *International Law, op. cit., supra* note 2, pp. 415, 416. See also Bernard A. Ramundo, "Soviet Criminal Legislation in Implementation of the Hague and Geneva Conventions Relating to the Rules of Land Warfare," 57 *AJIL* 73–84 (1962), pp. 82–84.

[114] *International Law, op. cit., supra* note 2, pp. 408 and 409–415. See also Ramundo, "Soviet Criminal Legislation," *op. cit., supra* note 113, pp. 82–84.

[115] *Ibid.*, pp. 416–418.

-»»)«««-

specialists and propagandists work in tandem in this effort. The former state the standards of legality and propriety, while the latter demonstrate that these standards have been met by the Soviet Union.

CHAPTER SEVEN

COLONIALISM

THE POLICY

The Soviet Union vociferously opposes colonialism as the political, economic, and ideological enslavement of nations by imperialist powers.[1] The Soviet position is reflected in the slogans of the Central Committee of the Communist Party of the Soviet Union in commemoration of the forty-eighth anniversary of the Bolshevik Revolution:

People of the countries of socialism, people struggling for national liberation, workers of the world! Join forces in the struggle for national liberation. Workers of the world! Join forces in the struggle against imperialism and colonialism, for national liberation, for peace, democracy and socialism.

People of the world! Fight for the complete and final liquidation of the shameful system of colonial slavery, against all forms of dependence on imperialism and against racial aggression.[2]

The Twenty-third Party Congress of the Communist Party of the Soviet Union (1966) specifically "instructed" the Party "to continue supporting the peoples fighting against colonial oppression and neo-colonialism."[3] The appeal to "have not" national elements is

[1] *Mezhdunarodnoe Pravo* [International Law], ed. D. B. Levin and G. P. Kaliuzhnaia (Moscow: Publishing House "Legal Literature," 1964), pp. 115, 116.

[2] Slogans Nos. 9 and 10, *Pravda* (October 23, 1965), p. 1. See also "Prigovor Kolonializmu" [Condemnation of Colonialism], *Pravda* (December 14, 1965), p. 1.

[3] "Resolution of the Twenty-third Congress of the Communist Party of the Soviet Union on the Report of the Central Committee of the CPSU," trans. from *Pravda* (April 9, 1966), in *Moscow News*, Supplement to No. 16 (April 16, 1966), pp. 2–10; see 3.

intended to solicit general support for Soviet foreign policies. Courtship of these elements takes the form of vocal support for national and racial equality[4] and praise for the initiative of the Soviet Union in combating the reactionary forces of Western imperialism through direct assistance to national liberation and participation in such activities as the 1966 Havana Conference of Solidarity of the Peoples of Asia, Africa and Latin America.

The entire policy of our country throughout the 48 years of its existence has invariably been directed at supporting the national-liberation movements, and the expansion of friendship and cooperation with the countries of Asia, Africa and Latin America.
[There is a need for] the further consolidation of the revolutionary forces in the struggle against US [sic] aggression, against imperialism and colonialism in all its forms. . . . There can be no coexistence with the colonialists—be they old-fashioned or "modern." The support and sympathies of the Soviet people are always for the oppressed, for all who are struggling for freedom and independence.[5]

Support for the forces seeking to undermine colonialism is considered an important aspect of the struggle of the socialist countries against the forces of capitalism. In the hierarchy of historical materialism the collapse of the colonial system is ranked "second in historical importance to the formation of the world socialist system."[6]

---

[4] It is claimed that the Soviet Union was the first state to sign the convention (adopted at the Twentieth Session of the General Assembly) prohibiting all forms of racial discrimination. "It [the convention] can and should be used for intensifying the struggle for the complete liquidation of the shameful system of colonialism and racism." (V. Chkhikvadze, "Likvidirovat' Rasovuiu Diskriminatsiiu vo Vsekh ee Proiavleniiakh" [Eliminate All Forms of Discrimination], *Pravda* [March 14, 1966], p. 3). Racism is characterized as "a more brutal form of colonialism." ("Panorama of World Events," trans. from *Izvestiia* [December 30, 1965], in *CDSP*, XVII, No. 52, pp. 17, 18.)

[5] Nikolai Pastukhov, "Slogans of the Soviet People," *Moscow News*, No. 44 (October 30, 1965), p. 3. See also *Mezhdunarodnoe Pravo, op. cit., supra* note 1, pp. 116–118.

[6] *OON i Aktual'nye Mezhdunarodyne Problemy* [The U.N. and Contemporary International Problems], ed. V. A. Zorin and G. I. Morozov (Moscow: Publishing House "International Relations," 1965), p. 4. See also O. E. Tuganova, "OON i Likvidatsiia Kolonial'noi Sistemy" [The U.N. and the Liquidation of the Colonial System], Review of S. A. Krasil'shchikova, *Organizatsiia Ob'edinennykh Natsiı i Natsional'no-osvoboditel'noe Dvizhenie* [The United Nations and the National Liberation Movement] (Moscow: Publishing House "International Relations," 1964), *SGIP*, No. 3 (1966), pp. 147, 148; see 148.

Soviet policy condemns direct as well as indirect forms of colonialism. The Soviets include under the former capitulations, vassal state, protectorate, mandate, and trustee relationships.[7] The indirect forms of colonialism, characterized as neocolonial because of the departure from more traditional, direct forms, include unequal economic and political arrangements, aggressive military alliances, and the establishment of military bases in the territory of developing countries.[8] Just as the Soviet Union is portrayed as the champion of the weak in the struggle against colonialism, the United States is cast in the role of the prime mover of the world forces of imperialism in their efforts at "economic penetration of underdeveloped countries and military suppression of national liberation movements."[9] The Soviets claim that as a result of the initiatives of the Soviet Union and "all the progressive forces of the world which support freedom and independence. . .contemporary international law condemns colonialism in all its forms and manifestations."[10]

THE LEGAL POSITION

In the Soviet view, contemporary international law (the law of coexistence) is anticolonial in orientation because of its bias in favor of the principle of self-determination.

The old international law contained norms and institutions constituting tools for the colonial enslavement of peoples and giving sanctification and legality to the system of colonialism. International law of today is anticolonial in its direction.[11]
With the acknowledgement of the general acceptance of the principle of self-determination of nations, international law was turned against the colonial system. From a means of enslaving people, it has become a weapon of struggle for the freedom of the people of colonies and dependent countries.

---

[7] *Mezhdunarodnoe Pravo, op. cit., supra* note 1, pp. 120–124.

[8] *Ibid.*, pp. 118–127. It is said that the "open door" and "equal opportunity" policies are devices for economic penetration. (*Ibid.*, p. 127.)

[9] *Ibid.*, p. 118.

[10] *Ibid.*

[11] G. I. Tunkin, "The Twenty-second Congress of the CPSU and the Tasks of the Soviet Science of International Law," *Soviet Law and Government* (New York: International Arts and Sciences Press, Winter 1962/63), Vol. 1, No. 2, pp. 18–27; see 24.

Colonialism contradicts the very basis of contemporary international law.[12]

Since the Charter of the United Nations is allegedly based upon the principles of peaceful coexistence, the Soviets claim a similar anti-colonial orientation for the United Nations.[13]

Basically, the right of a nation or people to throw off "the colonial yoke" is related to realization of self-determination, "an anti-imperialist, and anticolonial principle."[14]

Since the principle of self-determination became through the efforts of the Soviet Union. . .an effective principle of international law, the forcible retention of an alien people within a state is illegal.[15]

One commentary derives a right-duty national liberation relationship from the principle of self-determination.

An unconditional right of colonies is the right to create independent nation-states. Colonial powers are obliged to grant independence to all countries and nations under their sovereign jurisdiction.[16]

Another notes that "world public opinion condemns colonialism in all its manifestations as a crime against mankind [and that] the illegality of colonialism has become a generally recognized norm of

[12] G. I. Tunkin, *Voprosy Teorii Mezhdunarodnovo Prava* [Problems of the Theory of International Law] (Moscow: State Publishing House of Legal Literature, 1962), p. 209.

[13] V. M. Chkhikvadze, "Voprosy Mezhdunarodnovo Prava na XX Sessii General'noi Assamblei OON" [Problems of International Law at the Twentieth Session of the General Assembly of the U.N.], *SGIP*, No. 2 (1966), pp. 67–78; see 68.

[14] *Mezhdunarodnoe Pravo, op. cit., supra* note 1, p. 128.

[15] R. L. Bobrov, "Mezhdunarodnoe Pravo i Istoricheskii Progress" [International Law and Historical Progress], *SGIP*, No. 12 (1963), pp. 3–11; see 8. The Soviets claim that it was the initiative of the Soviet Union at the San Francisco Conference which resulted in the inclusion of the principle of self-determination in the Charter of the United Nations as a fundamental principle. (Tuganova, *op. cit., supra* note 6, p. 147.)

[16] N. A. Ushakov, "Poslanie N. S. Khrushcheva i Mirnoe Uregulirovanie Territorial'nykh Sporov mezhdu Gosudarstvami" [N. S. Khrushchev's Message and the Peaceful Settlement of Territorial Disputes between States], *SGIP*, No. 5 (1964), pp. 3–10; see 8.

international law."[17] The element of *jus cogens* is injected by the assertion that the "illegality of colonialism" is a new fundamental principle of the law of peaceful coexistence.[18]

> The preservation of the colonial system based on the oppression of peoples runs counter to the basic principles of international law.[19]
> The illegality of colonialism flows from the principles of the United Nations and, above all, from the provisions of the Charter concerning the equality of large and small nations (Preamble), equality and self-determination of peoples (Article 1, para. 2), and respect for the basic rights of the individual "without distinction based upon race, sex, language, and religion" (Article 1, para. 3; Article 31, para. "B"; Article 76, para. "C").[20]

Whether colonialism is directly proscribed by international law or only derivatively proscribed (i.e., on the basis of the principle of self-determination) matters little, because self-determination has been expanded to provide adequate legal basis for attacks upon traditional as well as new relationships which the Soviet Union chooses to treat as colonial.

In championing the cause of national liberation, the Soviets have greatly expanded the principle of self-determination. The principle is said to include the right of peoples and nations to independent statehood, territorial integrity, utilization of natural resources, choice of social and economic systems, and resolution of internal problems without outside interference and without regard for race or the degree of economic, political, and cultural development.[21]

[17] B. I. Melekhin, "Vozdeistvie Mirovovo Obshchestvennovo Mneniia na Sovremennoe Mezhdunarodnoe Pravo" [The Impact of World Public Opinion on International Law], *SGIP*, No. 2 (1964), pp. 75–83; see 83.

[18] L. A. Modzhoryan, "Raspad Kolonial'noi Sistemy Imperializma i Nekotorye Voprosy Mezhdunarodnovo Prava" [The Break-up of the Colonial System of Imperialism and Some Problems of International Law], *Sovetskii Ezhegodnik, 1961* (Moscow: Publishing House of the Academy of Sciences of the U.S.S.R., 1962), pp. 36–49. See also G. I. Tunkin, "Printsip Mirnovo Sosushchestvovaniia —General'naia Liniia Vneshnepoliticheskoi Deiatel'nosti KPSS i Sovetskovo Gosudarstva" [The Principle of Peaceful Coexistence—The General Line of the Foreign Policy of the C.P.S.U. and the Soviet State], *SGIP*, No. 7 (1963), pp. 26–37; see 33.

[19] G. Osnitskaya, "The Downfall of Colonialism and International Law," *International Affairs*, No. 1 (1961), pp. 38–43; see 39.

[20] *Mezhdunarodnoe Pravo, op. cit., supra* note 1, p. 118.

[21] *Ibid.,* p. 128.

Self-determination is said to be closely related to the concept of sovereignty as national sovereignty (i.e., the sovereignty possessed prior to statehood) and state sovereignty include the rights associated with self-determination.[22]

The possession of sovereignty gives the nations struggling [for national liberation] the right to be free from interference in their internal affairs by other states, to have states maintain neutrality towards them, to defend themselves from attack, etc.[23]

The right of self-determination is also related to the international legal personality of nations and peoples struggling for national liberation, since possession of this right provides the rationale for such personality.[24] As subjects of international law, they "have the right to have their sovereignty and [national and racial] equality respected,[25] and specifically, to denounce the oppressive obligations imposed upon them when they were in a colonial status. Additional support for this "clean-slate" approach is provided by the agreement theory of norm formulation under which a former colony, being the object of, rather than a participant in, the agreements concluded during the colonial period, has the sovereign right to accept or renounce them.[26]

Soviet legal specialists hold that the right of self-determination can be realized through peaceful as well as nonpeaceful means:

...contemporary international law recognizes the legality of the armed struggle of oppressed people to realize their right of self-determination.[27]

In support of this position, they have expanded the concept of self-defense under Article 51 of the United Nations Charter to include "the use of armed force to defend [as well as support] the

[22] *Ibid.*, p. 129. See also *Mezhdunarodnoe Pravo* [International Law], ed. F. I. Kozhevnikov (Moscow: Publishing House "International Relations," 1964), pp. 125–130; see 132.

[23] *Ibid.*, p. 135.

[24] *Ibid.*

[25] *Ibid.* See also G. P. Zadorozhnyi, *Mirnoe Sosushchestvovanie i Mezhdunarodnoe Pravo* [Peaceful Coexistence and International Law] (Moscow: Publishing House "International Relations," 1964), pp. 144 and 400.

[26] *Ibid.*, p. 136.

[27] *Ibid.*, p. 133.

right of self-determination."[28] The Soviets also say that wars of liberation are just wars which should be supported by all progressive, peace-loving states as part of their commitment to the principles of peaceful coexistence. The basis for these positions is the view that the forcible retention of colonies and neocolonialism are illegal as forms of aggression. Although Western states contest the Soviet approach to wars of national liberation, the Soviets claim that the absolute majority of the states of the world and world public opinion unconditionally recognize the legality and just, progressive character of wars of liberation.[29] If pressed on this claim, they can mitigate the effect of Western-state dissent by characterizing self-determination or the illegality of colonialism *jus cogens*, thereby providing a legal basis, independent of the agreement theory of norm formulation, for the anticolonial policy of militant support for national liberation. The inconsistency of avoiding the agreement theory in the case of Western state dissent, and invoking it on behalf of a former colony to permit it to select the obligations binding upon it, is one of logic rather than purpose.

Soviet expansion of the right of self-determination has resulted in a broader concept of that which is considered to be illegal as a form of colonialism. "Neocolonialism," principally in the form of Western economic, cultural, and military ties, shares the same illegality as the older, more traditional forms of colonialism. Both are treated as Western institutions, since similar ties with the Soviet Union or socialist countries are characterized as unselfish, fraternal assistance. In the context of continuing socialist support for the anti-colonialist forces, this assistance cannot be, by definition, colonial or neocolonial. In attacking Western direct and indirect aggression against the national liberation movements in Asia and Africa, a Soviet commentary describes the "new look" of neocolonialism as follows:

[28] *Ibid.* See also P. A. Tuzmukhamedov, "Ustav Organizatsii Afrikanskovo Edinstva v Svete Mezhdunarodnovo Prava" [The Charter of the Organization of African Unity in the Light of International Law], *Sovetskii Ezhegodnik, 1963* (Moscow: Publishing House "Science," 1965), pp. 109–128; see 127.

[29] G. Starushenko, "Fiction and Truth About Wars of Liberation," translated from *Kommunist* (August 1965), in *CDSP*, XVII, No. 34, pp. 5, 6; see 5.

->>)(<<-

Imperialist aggression not only changes its location, but takes on many different forms—from the crude methods of armed intervention in the 19th century colonial style to the sophisticated paraphernalia of neo-colonialist aggression. All available methods—both economic and ideological—are being used, sometimes so skillfully disguised that people frequently confuse it with goodwill. Take for example, the economic and cultural "aid programmes," the Peace Corps, and so on, which look quite respectable on the surface but which are in reality mere tools of the imperialist powers for achieving a single goal: to enmesh one or other independent Asian or African country and to keep it under imperialist domination.[30]

Similarly, it is said that if the capital investments of a colonial power remain in a former colony, independence is a sham as the new state has merely traded a traditional colonial status for a form of neo-colonialism.[31] The same is said of military base arrangements:

Bilateral agreements for the preservation or creation of new military bases, which frequently are conditions of the grant of independence, are a form of neo-colonialism.[32]

The Soviet position is intended to discredit and undermine Western influence among emerging nations and states.

The Soviets also appear to be expanding the principle of self-determination and national liberation to include all forms of revolutionary struggle. A 1964 Soviet commentary derives from the principle of self-determination the additional, specific principle that every nation or people has the right to choose its social and economic systems, as well as the form of its government and state organization, and to have its choices respected by other states.[33] A later commentary draws upon this principle in stating that "the usual method whereby new sovereign entities and governments rise at the present time is socialist and national liberation revolutionary

[30] Vladimir Kudryavtsev, "Asia and Africa: Solidarity v. Aggression," *Moscow News*, No. 40 (October 2, 1965), p. 7.

[31] *Mezhdunarodnoe Pravo* (Kozhevnikov), *op. cit., supra* note 22, p. 165.

[32] Ushakov, "Poslanie N. S. Khrushcheva," *op. cit., supra* note 16, p. 9. "See also Viktor Maevskii, "Bazy i Nezavisimost" [Bases and Independence], *Pravda* (October 24, 1966), p. 5.

[33] Zadorozhnyi, Mirnoe Sosushchestvovanie, *op. cit., supra* note 25, p. 399.

action."[34] The basic principle is said to include a corresponding obligation on the part of other states to abstain from any action interfering with the right of choice, including "hostile propaganda which foments hatred between peoples."[35] Thus, the legal rationale is being broadened to encompass all revolutionary activity, whether it is directed against a colonial power or domestic exploitation by a ruling group. This rationale has the flexibility to support policies contemplating complete independence and statehood, union with an existing state, or the establishment of a state smaller than the nation.[36] It also provides the legal basis for socialist revolutions, the break up of colonial empires, formation of a world-socialist state, and the statehood of split nations, such as Germany, Korea, and Vietnam. At the same time, the legal position can be invoked to inhibit all action directed against revolutionary activity, and to attack the legality of any such action. In effect, the Soviet approach to self-determination and the illegality of colonialism provides a legal basis for all revolutionary struggle, its support by friendly elements, and its protection from hostile elements, all in the interest of the Soviet Union. Under this comprehensive, "scatter gun" approach, all that is necessary in a given situation is an appropriate characterization to provide legal support for a Soviet policy position.

By attacking the legality of "neo-colonialistic," Western policies such as economic and military assistance to developing countries, collective security and mutual defense arrangements, and the maintenance of foreign military bases, the Soviets mass and reinforce their legal armament. For example, they say that economic and

[34] D. I. Fel'dman, *Priznanie Gosudarstv v Sovremennom Mezhdunarodnom Prave* [The Recognition of States in Contemporary International Law] (Kazan': Publishing House Kazan' University, 1965), p. 90. A recent commentary speaks of the struggle against imperialism in terms of "peoples battling for national and social liberation." (Yuri Bochkaryov, "Washington's New Tactics," *New Times*, No. 27 [July 6, 1966], pp. 4–6; see 6.)

[35] Zadorozhnyi, Mirnoe Sosushchestvovanie, *op. cit., supra* note 25, p. 399.

[36] See Tunkin, Voprosy Teorii, *op. cit., supra* note 12, p. 47, and S. V. Chernichenko, "Pravo Natsii na Samoopredelenie i Voprosy Grazhdanstva" [The Right of Nations to Self-determination and Problems of Citizenship], *SGIP*, No. 1 (1964), pp. 110–114; see 110. See also L. A. Modzhorian, *Osnovnye Prava i Obiazannosti Gosudarstv* [The Fundamental Rights and Duties of States] (Moscow: Publishing House "Legal Literature," 1965), p. 18.

military assistance arrangements are unequal treaties which are therefore illegal. These arrangements violate at least two other basic proscriptions of the law of peaceful coexistence, because they constitute interference in the internal affairs of states and are forms of economic and military (indirect) aggression. The same reasoning is applied to attack the legality of foreign military bases and collective security arrangements. The use of mutually reinforcing principles, an identifiable characteristic of Soviet legal positions, is of interest because this evidence of the preoccupation and concentrated effort of Soviet international legal specialists indicates the areas of principal concern to the policy-makers they serve.

CHAPTER EIGHT

COLLECTIVE SECURITY

THE POLICY

In its original form, the concept of collective security stands for "the proposition that aggressive and unlawful use of force by any nation against any other nation will be met by the combined force of all other nations."[1] In the West, the term has become corrupted through usage and is applied loosely to any arrangement providing for concerted action in a crisis by two or more states.[2] The Soviet approach to collective security also varies from the original concept. It is not, however, a similar case of misnomer. The concept of collective security has been carefully tailored to support the foreign policy of peaceful coexistence.

In the Soviet view, collective security includes any arrangement which ensures the peaceful coexistence of states. It is conceived of "as the guarantee of the peaceful coexistence of states with different social economic systems."[3] As a consequence, "the international legal principles and organizational forms of collective security must be defined and structured in complete agreement with the principles of peaceful coexistence."[4] The Soviets distinguish between collective security systems on the basis of their compatibility with the require-

[1] Inis L. Claude, Jr., *Swords Into Plowshares: The Problems and Progress of International Organization* (New York; Random House, 1956), p. 251.

[2] *Ibid.*, p. 252.

[3] V. K. Sobakin, *Kollektivnaia Bezopasnost'—Garantiia Mirnovo Sosushchestvovaniia* [Collective Security—Guarantee of Peaceful Coexistence] (Moscow: Publishing House of the Institute of International Relations, 1962), pp. 22, 23.

[4] *Ibid.*

151

ments of peaceful coexistence, rather than their organizational forms as international, regional, or bilateral systems.[5]

Any state acts which, although taking the technical legal forms of collective security, conflict with the principles of peaceful coexistence are in fact a negation of collective security. This consideration governs the content of the international legal principles of collective security and its legal forms.[6]

Applying this criterion, organizations such as The North Atlantic Treaty Organization (NATO), Southeast Asia Treaty Organization (SEATO) and Central Treaty Organization (CENTO) are denounced as military blocs incompatible with the concept of collective security.[7] On the other hand, the United Nations and Warsaw Treaty Organizations are considered fully compatible; with the former, because of its embodiment of peaceful coexistence, said to be the principal contemporary system of collective security.

. . . the practice of the creation of blocs of imperialist states which divide the world into hostile groupings and seek to undermine the United Nations Organization [e.g., NATO, SEATO and CENTO] contradicts both peaceful coexistence and the Charter of the United Nations.[8]

The Soviets denounce the United States as the principal user of aggressive blocs to undermine the system of collective security established by the Charter of the United Nations.[9]

In essence, the Soviet approach to collective security envisions arrangements compatible with the foreign policy objectives of the Soviet Union. As a consequence, collective security arrangements must contribute to, or at the very least be compatible with, the attainment of such objectives as general and complete disarmament, peaceful settlement of disputes, withdrawal of foreign military forces, liquidation of foreign bases, creation of nuclear-free zones, further growth of the national liberation movement and the forces of revolution, and the dissolution of aggressive military blocs.

[5] *Ibid.*, p. 101.
[6] *Ibid.*, p. 23.
[7] *Ibid.*, p. 462.
[8] G. P. Zadorozhnyi, *Mirnoe Sosushchestvovanie i Mezhdunarodnoe Pravo* [Peaceful Coexistence and International Law] (Moscow: Publishing House "International Relations," 1964), pp. 236, 237.
[9] *Ibid.*, p. 237.

Collective security can be recognized as the guarantee of peaceful coexistence only if it contributes to the realization of stronger, material guarantees of peaceful coexistence. . .[e.g., the realization of the program of general and complete disarmament].[10]

Arrangements which are not compatible are denounced as hostile groupings which, directed against the socialist commonwealth and the national liberation movement, seek the perpetuation of the use of force in international relations.[11]

THE LEGAL POSITION

In the Soviet view, collective security is a fundamental principle of international law.[12] To ensure that collective security arrangements serve as "the guarantee of peaceful coexistence," the Soviets have formulated six "international legal principles of collective security" which purport to set forth the conditions of the "legality" of such arrangements.[13] Three of these principles (sovereign equality of states and peoples, protection of sovereignty and territorial integrity, and noninterference in internal affairs) are included in the fundamental principles of peaceful coexistence. The remaining principles (unity of action of the great powers; maintenance of international peace and security; and struggle against the threat to peace, violations of peace and acts of aggression) are encompassed by the principle of collective security, another of the principles of peaceful coexistence. All of these principles are said to be included in the framework of collective security established by the Charter of the United Nations.[14]

The principle of unity of action of the great powers prohibits the establishment of any arrangement which is directed against any of the great powers by other great powers. On this basis, the Soviets attack the legality of Western collective security organizations which

[10] Sobakin, Kollektivnaia Bezopasnost', *op. cit., supra* note 3, p. 23. See also *Ibid.*, p. 203.

[11] *Ibid.*, p. 97.

[12] Zadorozhnyi, Mirnoe Sosushchestvovanie, *op. cit., supra* note 8, p. 234.

[13] Sobakin, Kollektivnaia Bezopasnost', *op. cit., supra* note 3, pp. 24–72.

[14] *Ibid.*, pp. 24, 25. See also, Zadorozhnyi, Mirnoe Sosushchestvovanie, *op. cit., supra* note 8, p. 400.

were formed in response to the Soviet challenge in the "cold war."[15] Specifically, they claim that such organizations are not collective security arrangements because they are "a weapon in the hands of a group of states of one system for the compulsion of countries belonging to the opposing system."[16] Under this approach, the Western powers legally cannot enter into alliances or other arrangements designed to counter foreign policy moves of the Soviet Union because of the legal requirement for unity of action of the great powers in maintaining general peace and resolving important international problems.[17] The propaganda support for this position discounts the existence of a Soviet threat by pointing to the frequently stated desire of the Soviet Union for peaceful competition and coexistence, describes Western apprehension as anti-communist hysteria, and stresses the many positive achievements that would be possible if the United States and the Soviet Union were to work together for peace and friendly relations among all nations.[18]

The principle of the sovereign equality of states and peoples includes the right of all states and peoples to participate in collective security arrangements and to shape their development. In international organizations this is a bid for universality; in regional organizations, for participation by all states and peoples in the area. In the United Nations context, this principle can be relied upon to support the seating of the Peoples Republic of China and the German Democratic Republic.[19] It can be used also to insist upon

[15] *Ibid.*, pp. 27–32. In Soviet political terminology, the "cold war" is described as a policy "diametrically opposite to the policy of peaceful coexistence," with the following its principal elements: "creation and maintenance of international tension, rejection of international cooperation on an equal footing, coercion, blackmail and pressure." ("What It Means. . .A Brief Guide to Political Terminology." *New Times*, No. 36 [September 7, 1966], p. 13.)

[16] *Ibid.*

[17] Zadorozhnyi, Mirnoe Sosushchestvovanie, *op. cit., supra* note 8, pp. 239–245.

[18] *Ibid.*

[19] The universality argument was invoked on behalf of the application for membership of the German Democratic Republic by the Soviet delegate to the United Nations on April 20, 1966. "Zaiavlenie Sovetskovo Pravitel'stva po Voprosu o Prieme GDR v OON" [The Statement of the Soviet Government Concerning Admission to the U.N. of the G.D.R.,] *Pravda* (22 April 1966), p. 4. See also G. Tunkin, "Zakonnoe Pravo, Germanskaia Demokraticheskaia Respublika Dolzhna Byt' Priniata v OON" [A Legal Right, The German Democratic Republic Should Be Admitted to the U.N.], *Pravda* (September 15, 1966), p. 3.

factual equality in the sense that no state should have military advantage over any other, thereby providing legal support for many specific policy objectives of the Soviet Union; such as the withdrawal of military forces, liquidation of foreign bases, creation of nuclear-free zones, nuclear disarmament, and general and complete disarmament.[20] Regionally, the principle can be used to attack the legality of the North Atlantic Treaty Organization and similar organizations because they do not provide for participation by all states in the region. Moreover, to the extent that regional participation is permitted in these organizations, it is said to be unequal and result in the unlawful exploitation of weaker members. In contrast, the Soviets claim that the Warsaw Treaty Organization is a true collective security arrangement because the Treaty of Friendship, Cooperation and Mutual Assistance of May 14, 1955 provides for (1) accession by other states regardless of their social and state orders (Article 9), and (2) state participation on the basis of sovereign equality (Article 8).[21] The inclusion of Article 9 in the so-called "Warsaw Pact" reflects the care of Soviet international legal specialists in formulating and maintaining legal positions.

The principle of maintenance of international peace and security is intended to limit collective security to international security, "that is, protection of political independence from infringements by other states."[22] Thus, the Soviets carefully avoid a legal basis for maintenance of the status quo or interference with national liberation or domestic revolutionary forces.

Collective security provides only for international security, not assurances that an internal social order will be preserved.[23]

Peaceful coexistence does not mean guarantees against the further growth of the national liberation movement of colonial and dependent nations and the growth of the influence of communist ideas in the world. Consequently collective security cannot serve these objectives.[24]

State actions interfering with the forces of revolution under the color of collective security are characterized as a distortion of the concept,

[20] Sobakin, Kollektivnaia Bezopasnost', *op. cit.*, *supra* note 3, p. 37.
[21] *Ibid.*, pp. 33, 34.
[22] *Ibid.*, p. 50.
[23] *Ibid.*, p. 41.
[24] *Ibid.*, p. 20.

155

->>><<<-

resulting from a subjective approach (i.e., other than "peaceful coexistence") to the values or interests protected under collective security.[25] Soviet writers claim that capitalist states reject objective standards and other legal controls on regional and collective security organizations in order to preserve military blocs directed against the socialist world and their fellow sufferers, and hoped-for travellers, the peoples struggling for national liberation.[26]

Related to the principle of the maintenance of international security is the principle of protection of sovereignty and territorial integrity. The point of relation is protection of revolutionary movements and new states from imperialist interference.

> In the framework of such a system of collective security [i.e., one based upon the principle of peaceful coexistence], the change in the social order of a state will depend on the struggle of internal social forces within the country without any external interference.[27]

> The object of collective security should be protection of states not only from war but also from all possible "peaceful" attempts at limiting their sovereignty.[28]

The Soviets specifically allow for national liberation and other revolutionary movements by holding that this principle of protection of sovereignty and territorial integrity cannot "conflict with the right of nations to self-determination."[29]

> ...collective security cannot mean collective protection of a certain regime against the actions of internal forces within the state or protection of a colonial empire or colonial privileges.[30]

The complementary operation of these principles is further reinforced by the principle of noninterference in the internal affairs of states and nations.

As may be expected the principle of noninterference is selectively applied in the Soviet interest. Its principal area of operation is to

---

[25] *Ibid.*, pp. 25, 26.
[26] *Ibid.*, p. 320.
[27] *Ibid.*, p. 53.
[28] *Ibid.*, p. 51.
[29] *Ibid.*, p. 56.
[30] *Ibid.*, p. 308.

prevent "the interference of imperialist states in the internal affairs of other states" as a means of forestalling "the export of counterrevolution."[31]

The system of collective security must prevent the export of counterrevolution. It must be structured so that the peoples of all countries can mobilize all their forces. . .and, relying upon the strength of the world socialist system, prevent or defeat the intervention of imperialists in the affairs of the people of a country who are in revolt and thereby prevent imperialist export of counterrevolution. The prevention of the export of counterrevolution will be easier if the masses, insisting upon national sovereignty, effect the elimination of foreign military bases and withdrawal from aggressive military blocs.[32]

The principle of nonintervention and the related principles of maintenance of international peace and security and protection of sovereignty and territorial integrity, individually and collectively, provide the legal basis for the revolutionary process which is an integral part of the policy of peaceful coexistence. They effectively convert collective security into a principle of socialist revolutionary change.

The remaining principle of collective security, "struggle against the threat to peace, violation of peace and acts of aggression" is directed against nuclear wars, unjust wars, and wars of aggression. A corollary of this principle is the indivisibility of peace (i.e., a violation of peace in one place is a violation of the general peace) and the concept that an act of aggression against one state is aggression against all other states.[33] This borrowing from the original concept of collective security is said to be even more compelling in the age of missiles and nuclear weapons. Its use, however, is not, as in the basic concept, to provide for collective action against any unlawful resort to force; rather, in effect, it is invoked to establish a legal requirement for the peaceful coexistence of states.

In its previous formulation, the principle of the indivisibility of peace was limited by the concept of the priority and necessity for collective action *at the time of the commission of aggression.*

---

[31] *Ibid.*, pp. 58 and 60.
[32] *Ibid.*, p. 60.
[33] *Ibid.*, p. 62 and 65, 66.

At the present time, the principle of the indivisibility of peace must be understood not only as a requirement for collective opposition to aggression, but also for collective collaboration by states and peoples to avert the very *possibility* of aggression.[34]

In connection with this principle, the Soviets cite the need for an agreed definition of aggression in order to ensure the effectiveness of collective security. The stated reason for this need is that the absence of such a definition makes unity of action in a crisis impossible.[35] Actually, the call for definition is a ploy in the continuing Soviet effort to codify the principles of peaceful coexistence; in this case, the definition of aggression, and with it, the concept of just war.

The Soviet legal position on collective security is a thinly-veiled effort to provide a legal basis for the unfettered pursuit of the objectives of the Soviet Union under the policy of peaceful coexistence. The principal technique is to limit the possibility of subjective approaches to collective security, and with it a corresponding flexibility in foreign policy formulation, by the West, while reserving to the Soviet Union the inherent subjectivism of the peaceful coexistence formulation. The Soviet approach to collective security is an excellent example of law in the service of policy as peaceful coexistence, the guarantee of which is the function of collective security, is, in fact, the present strategy of the Soviet Union.

[34] *Ibid.*, pp. 62, 63. See also G. I. Tunkin, *Voprosy Teorii Mezhdunarodnovo Prava* [Problems of the Theory of International Law] (Moscow: State Publishing House of Legal Literature, 1962), p. 53.

[35] *Ibid.*, p. 68.

CHAPTER NINE

﹣⟫⟩⟨⟨﹣

INTERNATIONAL ORGANIZATION

The Soviet approach to international organization reflects the same selectivity in support of peaceful coexistence encountered in the concept of collective security:

...the vitality of any such organization [international], even though created by states, is determined in the first instance by the extent to which its character, its fundamental principles correspond to the laws of social development.[1]

Although there is recognition of the increased interdependence of states and the consequent general need for greater international organization, the Soviet Union and the socialist countries are said to

...react positively to those international organs and organizations which serve the cause of strengthening peace and security and the development of international collaboration . . . [but] tirelessly unmask the imperialist character of various organizations created by capitalist states for purposes hostile to the interests of peace and international collaboration.[2]

The thrust of the Soviet position is that acceptable international organizations are those which operate on the basis of the principles of peaceful coexistence and the sovereign equality of states.[3] In

[1] G. I. Tunkin, "Organizatsiia Ob'edinennykh Natsii: 1945–1965 (Mezhdunarodnopravovye Problemy)" [The United Nations: 1945–1965 (International Legal Problems)], *SGIP*, No. 10 (1965), pp. 58–68; see 60.

[2] *Mezhdunarodnoe Pravo* [International Law], ed. D. B. Levin and G. P. Kaliuzhnaia (Moscow: Publishing House "Legal Literature," 1964), pp. 269, 270; see 270. See also M. V. Ianovskii, "Iuridicheskaia Sila Rezoliutsii General'noi Assamblei i Ustav OON" [The Juridical Force of Resolutions of the General Assembly and the Charter of the U.N.], *SGIP*, No. 9 (1965), pp. 120–124.

[3] *Ibid.*, p. 270. See G. I. Morozov, "Poniatie i Klassifikatsiia Mezhdunarodnykh Organizatsii" [The Concept and Classification of International Organizations], *SGIP*, No. 6 (1966), pp. 67–76.

159

effect, international organization is supported only if socialist in character (e.g., Warsaw Treaty Organization and Council for Mutual Economic Assistance), possible of manipulation in the socialist interest (e.g., the Organization of African Unity and the League of Arab States), or, as in the case of the United Nations and the administrative international organizations, participation is essential as a fact of international life and socialist interests can be served by it. In Soviet jargon, the position is that "the Soviet Union. . .participates in those [organizations] which in the slightest degree serve the cause of strengthening peace and security."[4] Organizations which are hostile to the socialist countries or which purport to be supranational in character are viewed as contradictions of the principles of peaceful coexistence.

GLOBALISM

Soviet insistence upon respect for the sovereign prerogatives of the nation-state as an essential element of peaceful coexistence is incompatible with global approaches to international organization. Efforts to create supranational bodies or other institutional forms approaching world government are rejected: legally, as an infringement upon state sovereignty; and ideologically, as incompatible with "the basic law of contemporary society" which prescribes the coexistence of two opposed world social systems.[5] The legal objection is stated as follows:

As the participants in international organizations are states, the legal character of these organizations is international and not supranational. These organizations are the institutional instruments for the international collaboration of sovereign states. They do not, nor can they, act as an "international administration" standing above the states.[6]

---

[4] V. I. Lisovskii, *Mezhdunarodnoe Pravo* [International Law] (2d ed.; Moscow: State Publishing House "Higher School," 1961), p. 312.

[5] Tunkin, "Organizatsiia Ob'edinennykh Natsii," *op. cit., supra* note 1, pp. 60, 61.

[6] *Mezhdunarodnoe Pravo, op. cit., supra* note 2, p. 269. See also Edward McWhinney, *Peaceful Coexistence and Soviet-Western International Law* (Leyden: A. W. Sythoff, 1964), p. 53.

On the ideological side, the Soviets say that "more effective" international organization is the answer to the increased interdependence of states resulting from technological advances. World government cannot be realized at this time because of the existence of the two opposed social systems, and the contradictions inherent in the capitalist system.[7]

...in the conditions of the existence of states of two systems, international organizations with broad supranational powers are not possible, and the creation of such organizations in the framework of the capitalist world leads to the policy of diktat and interference in the internal affairs of states.[8]

In addition to raising the spectre of interference in internal affairs as an inescapable consequence of supranational organization, the Soviets claim that world government would invariably have a status quo orientation which would stifle the movement for national liberation.[9]

In opposing globalism, criticism is heaped upon those Western jurists who view the present stage of international law as primitive and hold that, as in the case of domestic law, international law will become true law only with the development of centralized authority approaching world government.[10] Tunkin notes in this regard that as eminent a Western international legal authority as Anzilotti shares the view that if a world state is achieved, international law would cease to exist because it would be replaced by the domestic law of the world state.[11] Tunkin, therefore, rejects the "mechanical"

[7] G. I. Tunkin, *Voprosy Teorii Mezhdunarodnovo Prava* [Problems of the Theory of International Law] (Moscow: State Publishing House of Legal Literature, 1962), pp. 191, 192.

[8] B. Mikhailov, "Konferentsiia Iuristov-Mezhdunarodnikov" [Conference of International Jurists], *SGIP*, No. 10 (1963), pp. 147–149; see 149.

[9] V. K. Sobakin, *Kollektivnaia Bezopasnost'—Garantiia Mirnovo Sosushchestvovaniia* [Collective Security—Guarantee of Peaceful Coexistence] (Moscow: Publishing House of the Institute of International Relations, 1962), pp. 44, 45.

[10] Tunkin, Voprosy Teorii, *op. cit.*, *supra* note 7, pp. 186 and 190, citing D. Anzilotti, *Corso di Diritto Internazionale* [Course in International Law] (Rome [sic] [should be Padova]: Cedam, 1955), I, 47, as an example of the Western view of the primitive state of international law and the need for its further development.

[11] *Ibid.*

-»»«««-

application of domestic legal developmental concepts to international law in Western commentaries. He suggests, instead, an approach which takes account of the present need for cooperation of the great powers in ensuring the peaceful coexistence of the states of the two systems (i.e., the Soviet view of the United Nations system).[12]

> Increasing the role of international law in international relations is being accomplished not through a movement towards a world state and the liquidation of state sovereignty, but as a result of the development and strengthening of the basic principles and norms of present international law and instilling in it new principles and norms directed towards the development of international collaboration and ensuring the peaceful coexistence of states on the basis of equality, respect for sovereignty and non-interference in internal affairs.[13]

In an effort to bolster their position, the Soviets predict (and in effect threaten) that linking the effectiveness of international law to world government will result in reduced reliance upon law to maintain international peace and security.[14]

Soviet rejection of world government, however, does not extend to socialist groupings which contribute to the building of communism (i.e., the emergence of a Soviet-oriented "world communist society where there will be no states, national or world.").[15]

> On the way to the classless, stateless communist society many forms of state groupings of socialist states are possible. The creation of a world federation or another form of combination of free states and nations is thinkable only as a means of eliminating exploitation, class and national contradictions and the creation of socialism and communism.[16]

The level of political, economic and military collaboration within the socialist commonwealth of nations, heralded by the Soviets as international relations of a new, higher type, is directed toward the eventual integration of all socialist states into a single state and society. The socialist commonwealth, said to be a natural grouping

---

[12] *Ibid.*, pp. 194, 195.
[13] *Ibid.*, p. 197.
[14] *Ibid.*, pp. 193 and 196, 197.
[15] *Ibid.*, p. 192.
[16] *Ibid.*, pp. 192, 193.

rather than an alliance or other creature of agreement, actually achieves political and military collaboration within the institutional framework of the Warsaw Treaty Organization, and economic collaboration through the Council for Mutual Economic Assistance. Of course, the level of collaboration possible in the commonwealth cannot be realized in relations with capitalist states because of the class barrier. Therefore, in the Soviet view, "the concept of [nonsocialist] world government under present conditions is utopian and reactionary."[17] The only feasible basis for nonsocialist international cooperation is international organization structured along the lines of the United Nations[18] because "the Charter ideals of broad and all-around collaboration between states is nothing more than the ideas of peaceful coexistence."[19]

UNIVERSALISM

Confronted with the complexities of contemporary international relations, the Soviet Union is torn between the fear of limitations upon freedom of action stemming from membership in a nonsocialist universal òrganization, and the need for such membership as a fact of international life and a means of enhancing the effectiveness of its foreign policies and molding world opinion. The competing considerations are political restriction versus political isolation. In opting for membership to avoid the latter, the Soviets have attempted to minimize the former by harnessing international organization to the building of communism.

Soviet jurists endorse the United Nations as a universal, world organization which provides an effective basis for international peace and collaboration because it embodies the principles of peaceful coexistence in its Charter.

[17] *Ibid.*, p. 193.
[18] *Ibid.*, p. 196.
[19] O. V. Bogdanov, *Vseobshchee i Polnoe Razoruzhenie* (*Mezhdunarodnopravovye Voprosy*) [General and Complete Disarmament (International Legal Problems)] (Moscow: Publishing House "International Relations," 1964), p. 114.

The principal instrument for the maintenance of peace and the settling of international disputes by peaceful means should be the U.N. which makes it possible to reconcile the actions of all sovereign state-members in the interests of the peaceful coexistence of states and the settlement of international disputes by peaceful means.[20]

In view of the element of change implicit in peaceful coexistence (i.e., in the direction of a socialist world), the United Nations is said to be a distinct departure from the status quo orientation of its predecessor, the League of Nations, which was doomed to failure because of commitment to that orientation.[21] The United Nations is looked upon as a dynamic organization with every opportunity of becoming "an effective instrument for the maintenance of international peace and the development of. . .peaceful coexistence."[22] Great care is taken to emphasize that "the organization is not a State and still less . . . a super-State" as "it is based upon the . . . sovereign equality of all its members."[23] Emphasis upon sovereign equality sits well with the emerging states as does lip service to their important role in the ability of the United Nations to "handle the new task facing it":[24] "Now, not a single important decision can be made without taking into account the views of the Afro-Asian countries."[25] Western jurists are critized for holding "that the main principle of the United Nations Charter is not the peaceful coexistence of states with different economic and social systems but the

[20] Mikhailov, op. cit., supra note 8, p. 149.

[21] E. S. Pchelintsev, "Mezhdunarodnopravovye Voprosy Ekonomicheskovo i Sotsial'novo Sotrudnichestva Gosudarstv" [International Legal Problems Concerning Economic and Social Collaboration of States], Voprosy Mezhdunarodnovo Prava [Problems of International Law], ed. V. I. Menzhinskii (Moscow: Publishing House of the Institute of International Relations, 1963), pp. 177–217; see 177.

[22] OON i Aktual'nye Mezhdunarodnye Problemy [The U.N. and Contemporary International Problems], ed. V. A. Zorin and G. I. Morozov (Moscow: Publishing House "International Relations," 1965), p. 18.

[23] International Law (Moscow: Foreign Languages Publishing House, n.d.), p. 347.

[24] OON i Aktual'nye Mezhdunarodnye Problemy, op. cit., supra note 22, p. 198.

[25] O. E. Tuganova, "OON i Likvidatsiia Kolonial'noi Sistemy" [The U.N. and the Liquidation of the Colonial System], Review of S. A. Krasil'shchikova, Organizatsiia Ob'edinennykh Natsii i Natsional'no-osvoboditel'noe Dvizhenie [The United Nations Organization and the National Liberation Movement] (Moscow: Publishing House "International Relations," 1964), SGIP, No. 3 (1966), pp. 147, 148; see 148.

'primacy' of international law."[26] This position is attacked on the general basis that it negates "national sovereignty which is of primary importance for the peaceful coexistence of states."[27] Actually, the issue here is one of deciding whose law is to have primacy. The Soviet objection is to the rejection of peaceful co-existence as the main Charter principle rather than the concept of the primacy of law as peaceful coexistence is said to be "unthinkable without international legality," "possible only if the generally recognized norms of international law are observed," and, finally, "generally recognized international law in action."[28]

As in the case of collective security, the criterion of acceptability of the United Nations Organization is its relationship to peaceful coexistence.

The United Nations' contribution to history will depend upon the degree to which it promotes the development of international cooperation and safeguards peaceful coexistence.[29]

Although the term "peaceful coexistence" is not encountered in the Charter of the United Nations, the principle of peaceful coexistence is the basis of the organization.[30]

Linking the United Nations and peaceful coexistence serves the Soviet Union well. It provides a means of alleviating the basic "predicament. . .of a state with a 'two camp' world view trying to operate in a 'one world' organization."[31] It does this by postulating a basis for judging in the Soviet interest the legality of activities of the organization and its members, for shaping its further development, and for claiming that "peaceful coexistence" has become the fundamental principle of international law, a claim which is not unmindful of the precedence accorded Charter obligations over inconsistent provisions of other agreements (Article 103).

[26] Y. Korovin, "Peace Through Law: Two Views," *International Affairs*, No. 7 (1963), pp. 100–102; see 101.

[27] *Ibid.*

[28] G. P. Zadorozhnyi, *Mirnoe Sosushchestvovanie i Mezhdunarodnoe Pravo* [Peaceful Coexistence and International Law] (Moscow: Publishing House "International Relations," 1964), pp. 7, 69 and 293.

[29] *International Law, op. cit., supra* note 23, p. 334.

[30] Tunkin, Organizatsiia Ob'edinennykh Natsii, *op. cit., supra* note 1, p. 61.

[31] Alexander Dallin, *The Soviet Union at the United Nations* [An Inquiry into Soviet Motives and Objectives] (New York: Praeger, 1962), p. 6.

→»)«←

The Charter of the United Nations is a treaty of a special type. . .states have given it a place above all their other agreements.[32]

For example, the failure to seat the People's Republic of China in the Security Council is said to violate the Charter principle of the unanimity of the great powers.[33] The same principle is relied upon to attack the legality of Western "collective security" arrangements such as NATO, SEATO and CENTO. The Soviets claim that the "cold war" and Western policies based upon a "position of strength" are illegal because they do not contribute to the collaboration between states of the two systems and the great powers envisioned by the Charter of the United Nations.[34] Although the Soviets recognize that changes in the world since the signing of the Charter call for changes in the United Nations Organization, they resist any changes which are not considered compatible with the principles of peaceful coexistence. A distinction is made between basic or fundamental provisions (i.e., those which embody the principles of coexistence and therefore *jus cogens*) and other principles with the former only subject to strengthening in the interest of more effective collaboration.[35] For example, attempts to reduce the authority of the Security Council or the use of the veto therein are attacked as violations of fundamental Charter principles (i.e., the principle of the unity of the great powers and their principal responsibility for the maintenance

[32] Tunkin, Organizatsiia Ob'edinennykh Natsii, *op. cit.*, *supra* note 1, p. 64. See also *OON i Aktual'nye Mezhdunarodnye Problemy*, *op. cit.*, *supra* note 22, p. 15.

[33] *Mezhdunarodnoe Pravo*, *op. cit.*, *supra* note 2, pp. 284, 285. See also *International Law*, *op. cit.*, *supra* note 23, p. 339, where it is said: "it is necessary to underline the absolute illegality of the decisions adopted by the Security Council on the Korean question in 1950 in the absence of the permanent representatives of the U.S.S.R. and the Chinese People's Republic."

[34] Tunkin, Voprosy Teorii, *op. cit.*, *supra* note 7, p. 195. See also Zadorozhnyi, Mirnoe Sosushchestvovanie, *op. cit.*, *supra* note 26, pp. 103–121, where the "cold war" and the policy of "position of strength" are rejected as negations of peaceful coexistence; and *OON i Aktual'nye Mezhdunarodnye Problemy*, *op. cit.*, *supra* note 22, p. 3. In their codification efforts the Soviets seek express confirmation of the "obligation of states to collaborate with one another in accordance with the Charter [of the United Nations]" (V. M. Chkhikvadze, "Voprosy Mezhdunarodnovo Prava na XX Sessii General'noi Assamblei OON" [Problems of International Law at the Twentieth Session of the General Assembly of the U.N.], *SGIP*, No. 3 [1966], pp. 67–78; see 70.)

[35] Tunkin, Organizatsiia Ob'edinennykh Natsii, *op. cit.*, *supra* note 1, p. 63.

of peace and security).[36] Similarly, they view any change in the relationship between the General Assembly and the Security Council or expansion of the role of the Secretary General as an abuse of the Charter, aimed at transforming the organization of peaceful coexistence into a supranational body directed against the countries of socialism and the national liberation movement.[37] On the other hand, support for Soviet proposals, (e.g., the troika concept for the office of the Secretary General, or increased representation for neutralist states in the Security Council) is solicited on the basis of their strengthening fundamental principles. The heart of the Soviet position is the larger claim that the Charter of the United Nations embodies the fundamental principles of peaceful coexistence. The Charter, as a fundamental source of international law, is the standard against which other norms are to be measured and judged.[38]

A review of the principles of the United Nations Charter indicates that all the basic and most important aspects of peaceful coexistence are incorporated in that most important code of contemporary international law.[39]

The United Nations Charter has become the basic code of postwar international law and no government should violate it.[40]

The Charter of the United Nations being the juridical basis of the peaceful coexistence of states. . .is one of the most important sources of contemporary international law.[41]

---

[36] Tunkin, Voprosy Teorii, op. cit., supra note 7, p. 195. See also, International Law, op. cit., supra note 23, p. 337, where it is said: "Organs set up contrary to the Charter, in particular with the aim of weakening and undermining the authority of the Security Council, can not be considered as subsidiary organizations."

[37] Sobakin, Kollektivnaia Bezopasnost', op. cit., supra note 9, pp. 293–294. See also L. A. Modzhorian, Osnovnye Prava i Obiazannosti Gosudarstv [The Fundamental Rights and Duties of States] (Moscow: Publishing House "Legal Literature," 1965), pp. 19, 20.

[38] Zadorozhnyi, Mirnoe Sosushchestvovanie, op. cit., supra note 26, pp. 372–381.

[39] Mezhdunarodnoe Pravo [International Law], ed. F. I. Kozhevnikov (Moscow: Publishing House "International Relations," 1964), p. 88.

[40] Observer, "We the Peoples of the United Nations," New Times, No. 43 (October 27, 1965), pp. 1–3; see 3.

[41] Mezhdunarodnoe Pravo, op. cit., supra note 2, p. 282.

For example, the Charter is used as the basis for judging the legality of opinions of the International Court of Justice.[42] Similarly, the legality of international agreements is judged on the basis of Article 103 of the Charter. An example of the latter use is the Soviet treatment of the "colonial treaty of 1903" between the United States and Panama.

Article 103 of the Charter explicitly states that if any international agreement runs counter to this Charter, obligations under the Charter shall prevail. The 1903 Treaty undoubtedly runs counter to the United Nations Charter.[43]

In the Soviet view, however, not all provisions of the United Nations Charter have this fundamental validity (i.e., are part of the *jus cogens*).[44] Therefore, the Soviets can selectively invoke the proposition that the Charter is "a major code of international law" which should be strictly adhered to.[45]

In insisting upon strict compliance with the Charter of the United Nations the Soviets are not unmindful that the concept and functioning of the United Nations as an instrument of, or weapon against, peaceful coexistence depends upon the manner in which the Charter is interpreted. Specifically, they resist the "inherent and implied competence" and "organization practice" bases suggested by Western jurists for expanding the powers of the United Nations at the expense of the sovereign prerogatives of its members.[46] When in the Soviet interest, however, Soviet jurists have no difficulty in urging a broad construction. Apart from their ambivalent, self-serving positions on specific questions (e.g., self-determination, aggression and self-defense), a bid is made to apply the Charter concept of breach of the peace broadly to any state action deemed incompatible with peaceful coexistence.

[42] See G. Morozov and Y. Pchelintsev, "Behind the U.N. Financial Crisis," *International Affairs*, No. 6 (1964), pp. 23–29; see 28.

[43] O. Khlestov, "International Law Is on the Side of Panama," *International Affairs*, No. 4 (1964), pp. 92, 93; see 92.

[44] Ianovskii, *op. cit., supra* note 2, p. 124.

[45] Georgi Zadorozhny, "Strict Adherence to UN Charter—Basis of International Relations," *Moscow News*, No. 26 (June 26, 1965), p. 5. See also V. Nekrasov, "Vysokaia Otvetstvennost' OON" [The Great Responsibility of the U.N.], *Pravda* (September 25, 1965), p. 5.

[46] Tunkin, Organizatsiia Ob'edinennykh Natsii, *op. cit., supra* note 1, pp. 61–68.

The concept of peace in the Charter of the U.N. is the equivalent of the concept of peaceful coexistence which is something more than the absence of war between states. It follows therefore that the concept of breach of the peace is considerably broader than the concept of armed aggression.

In the sense of the Charter of the U.N. breach of the peace must be understood in the broad sense of any violation of friendly relations between peoples. A breach of the peace is not only a threat to the peace; it may also take the form of a breach of friendly relations between states. [For example], any violation of the principle of self-determination of peoples is a breach of the peace.[47]

Having provided themselves with sufficient flexibility under the Charter, the Soviets reject the Western view that "U.N. Law" has a limited range of operation.[48] As in the case of their basic approach to international law, the Soviets are vigorous proponents of universality once the interests of the Soviet Union have been adequately provided for (i.e., a basis has been established for inhibiting Western foreign policies and unfettering those of the Soviet Union on the same issues).

The Soviet Union covers its own position of convenience towards the United Nations by paying vigorous lip service to the universality of the United Nations in the sense of its need to serve the interests of the entire international community:

...the United Nations bears no resemblance to its predecessor. For one thing, the international situation today differs fundamentally from that of the League of Nations years. The League was representative chiefly of the imperialist powers, their weapon for maintaining the unjust system of Versailles, a centre of anti-Soviet intrigue. The United Nations, in contrast, represents the overwhelming majority of the world's nations, and its purpose is to maintain peace and promote co-operation.[49]
The United Nations organization must become a genuinely universal international organization and serve the interests of the world in general, and not the interests of a group of states.[50]

---

[47] Sobakin, Kollektivnaia Bezopasnost', *op. cit., supra* note 9, p. 67.

[48] Professor S. Molodtsov, "Frontiers and International Law," *International Affairs*, No. 4 (1964), pp. 9–14; see 10.

[49] "We the Peoples of the United Nations," *op. cit., supra* note 40, p. 2.

[50] *Mezhdunarodnoe Pravo, op. cit., supra* note 2, p. 288.

It is quick to point out and resist the attempts of "imperialist states who have sought to use the United Nations as an instrument of their policy which is incompatible with the interests of peace and international security."[51]

The United Nations Organization is of key importance in the Soviet campaign on behalf of the policy and law of peaceful coexistence. The Soviet attempt to superimpose peaceful coexistence upon the Charter of the United Nations is intended to provide a basis for "capture" of the Organization in its present form, shaping its future development, and manipulating the international legal order. The importance of the Organization is twofold: (1) the Charter is invoked as the "legislative" basis for the principles of peaceful coexistence which are universally binding and changeable, expressly or by interpretation, only with the consent of the socialist world; and (2) the Organization serves as the principal forum and instrument for achieving specific policies of coexistence.

> Discussion in the Sixth Committee [of the General Assembly] gave the Soviet delegation the opportunity of using the tribune of the U.N. for explanation and propaganda of the peace-loving foreign policy of the Soviet Union, and also to demonstrate the attitude of Soviet diplomacy and juridical science to questions of international law which is an important instrument for preserving and strengthening peace.
>
> It assisted in making clear the essence of the different international legal systems of the world and the basic differences which exist in the approach of socialist states and Western countries to the unavoidable problems of war and peace.[52]

The Soviet effort is concentrated on the United Nations because of its near-universal membership, and the realization that utilization of it in the terms above stated will in large measure achieve Soviet objectives vis-à-vis the international political and legal order.

REGIONALISM

The Soviet position on regionalism is closely related to the approach to collective security. As under collective security, the

[51] *Ibid.*, p. 285. It is said that the United States is attempting to "capture" the United Nations (*Mezhdunarodnoe Pravo* [Kozhevnikov]), *op. cit., supra* note 39, p. 54.

[52] Chkhikvadze, *op. cit., supra* note 34, p. 78.

170

needs of peaceful coexistence, under cover of the Charter of the United Nations, govern the acceptability, and therefore legality, of regional arrangements.

> The Charter of the U.N. . . . .permits the existence of regional international organizations provided these organizations and their activity are compatible with the goals and principles of the U.N.[53]

In the Soviet view, regional organizations satisfy the Charter requirements if membership is regional in character, there is no discrimination against membership based upon the type of social order in a given state, and the cause of peaceful coexistence is served.[54] Regional arrangements which the Soviets choose to characterize as "aggressive military blocs or groupings" are said to violate the basic aims of the United Nations and, therefore, to be illegal. They claim that these groupings are a means of undermining the United Nations, interventionist and aggressive by nature, and unequal because they are subject to manipulation by the big power members.[55] For example, the North Atlantic Treaty and Southeast Asia Treaty and Central Treaty Organizations are characterized as "pseudo-regional organizations of the capitalist states."[56] NATO is said to violate the Charter of the United Nations because it is not regional in its membership and is directed against the socialist countries; SEATO, because it is not regional in membership and its basic purpose is the struggle against socialist states and the national liberation movement in Southeast Asia;[57] and CENTO, because "the military and political obligations assumed by the member states . . . contradict the interests of peace and security and the Charter of the United Nations."[58] The Soviets say that the Organization of American States, despite formal provisions in its charter concerning peace, security, peaceful settlement, and economic, social and cultural cooperation, is a tool of United States imperialism

---

[53] *Mezhdunarodnoe Pravo, op. cit., supra* note 2, p. 292.

[54] Sobakin, Kollektivnaia Bezopasnost', *op. cit., supra* note 9, pp. 334 and 339.

[55] *Ibid.*, pp. 462–492.

[56] *Mezhdunarodnoe Pravo, op. cit., supra* note 2, pp. 299–302.

[57] *Ibid.*, p. 301.

[58] *International Law, op. cit., supra* note 23, p. 370.

which has been "converted into a closed military political group-ing. . .as an instrument for suppressing the growing national libera-tion movement in Latin America."[59] These organizations share the common fault of interfering with the realization of Soviet foreign policy objectives.

The rationale of the Soviet position is that regional groupings must qualify either as regional organizations or collective security arrangements under the United Nations system. A basic require-ment of a regional organization is that the membership be from a definite geographic area. A requirement of both regional and collec-tive security arrangements is that the organizations not contravene the principles of peaceful coexistence, including the prohibition against restrictive membership which is the antithesis of international collaboration and an indication of a grouping against nonmember states:

. . .these blocs . . . are not regional organizations in the sense of the Charter of the U.N. nor agreements for general collective security. The Charter of the U.N. contemplates under regional agreements the joining of states of a definite geographic area without regard to their social and state orders.
. . . .
By their very spirit, aggressive blocs contradict the concept of international security as they are structured on the negation of the principle of the peace-ful coexistence of states. They are illegal agreements directed at the prepa-ration of aggressive wars and the suppression of the national liberation movement.[60]

Of course, Western regional defense organizations do not qualify under the Soviet criteria. Nonmilitary organizations, such as the Council of Europe and the European Economic Community, are denounced on the principal basis that the exclusion of membership of socialist states is tantamount to an effort directed at those states in contravention of the United Nations Charter concept of a regional organization.[61] The whole effort at European unification, and, in particular, the European Economic Community is attacked on the

[59] *Mezhdunarodnoe Pravo, op. cit., supra* note 2, p. 298. Also, *International Law, op. cit., supra* note 23; see 359.

[60] *Ibid.,* p. 302.

[61] *International Law, op. cit., supra* note 23, p. 366.

additional ground that the supranational aspects of these organizations derogate from respect for sovereignty, a basic principle of the Charter of the United Nations (i.e., the law of peaceful coexistence.) [62]

On the other hand, Soviet-favored organizations, such as the League of Arab States and the Organization of African Unity, are said to be regional organizations within the purview of the Charter of the United Nations. [63] The shining examples of regional organizations are the Warsaw Treaty Organization and the Council for Mutual Economic Assistance (COMECON), the principal organizations of the socialist commonwealth of nations. [64] Both the Warsaw Treaty Organization and the Council for Mutual Economic Assistance were established under multilateral arrangements which stress the possibility of full regional participation and the sovereignty and independence of action of the participating states.

[62] See V. Morozov, "Equality: Cornerstone of the Socialist Countries' Economic Cooperation," *International Affairs*, No. 12 (1963), pp. 4–8; see 7. See also I. Pomelov, "30th Anniversary of the Seventh Comintern Congress," trans. from *Pravda* (August 20, 1965), in *CDSP*, XVII, No. 33, pp. 5, 6 and 36; see 6, and I. Usov, "Obshchii Rynok Protivorechit Progressivnym Tendentsiiam Mezhdunarodnykh Otnoshenii i Mezhdunarodnovo Prava" [The Common Market Contradicts the Progressive Tendencies of International Relations and International Law], *SGIP*, No. 7 (1966), pp. 137–141.

[63] *Mezhdunardnoe Pravo*, *op. cit.*, *supra* note 2, pp. 295 and 297.

[64] Morozov, Equality: Cornerstone of Cooperation, *op. cit.*, *supra* note 62, p. 4. There are other socialist organizations of lesser competence and importance, e.g., the Railway Cooperation Organization, the Joint Institute for Nuclear Research, and the Communications Cooperation Organization, designated as "the specialized agencies of the socialist countries" P. A. Tokareva, "Mezhdunarodnye Economicheskie Organizatsii Sotsialisticheskikh Stran" [The International Economic Organizations of the Socialist Countries], *Sovetskii Ezhegodnik, 1959* (Moscow: Publishing House of the Academy of Sciences of the U.S.S.R., 1960), pp. 169–180; see 179. See also *Mezhdunarodnopravovye Formy Sotrudnichestva Sotsialisticheskikh Gosudarstv* [Forms of International Legal Collaboration of Socialist States], ed. V. M. Shurshalov (Moscow: Publishing House of the Academy of Sciences of the U.S.S.R., 1962), pp. 306–316; and Kazimierz Grzybowski, *The Socialist Commonwealth of Nations, Organizations and Institutions*, (New Haven and London: Yale University Press, 1964), Chap. 4, pp. 111–171. In January 1964, the International Bank of Economic Collaboration was established as a financial organization independent of COMECON. (A. B. Al'tshuler, "Novaia Mezhdunarodnopravovaia Forma Ekonomicheskovo Sotrudnichestva (k Sozdaniiu Mezhdunarodnovo Banka Ekonomicheskovo Sotrudnichestva)" [A New International Legal Form of Economic Collaboration (Re The Creation

-≫≫)≪≪-

The Warsaw Treaty Organization was established pursuant to the Treaty of Friendship, Cooperation and Mutual Assistance which was signed at Warsaw, Poland, on May 14, 1955.[65] Reciting concern over the entry of West Germany into the North Atlantic Treaty Organization, the contracting parties (Albania, Bulgaria, Czechoslovakia, the German Democratic Republic, Hungary, Poland, Rumania and the Soviet Union) agreed, for a period of twenty years or until the conclusion of a general European treaty establishing a system of collective security for Europe; (1) to settle their disputes by peaceful means (Art. 1); (2) to consult on all important international questions involving their common interests, including collective measures of defense (Art. 3); (3) to render immediate assistance in the event of an attack upon any participating state (Art 4); (4) to establish a Unified Command (Art. 5); (5) to establish a Political Consultative Committee on which "each State Party to the Treaty shall be represented by a member of the Government or some other specially appointed representative"; (6) not to participate in any coalitions or alliances or enter into agreements not compatible with the treaty (Art. 7); and (7) to promote economic and cultural ties "in accordance with the principles of respect for each other's independence and sovereignty and of nonintervention in each other's domestic affairs" (Art. 8). The Warsaw Treaty Organization, although purporting to be a universal organization open to accession by other states without regard to their social and political systems (Art. 9), serves at the present time as a counter to the North Atlantic Treaty Organization.[66] A Soviet commentary describes the Warsaw Pact as follows:

---

of the International Bank of Economic Collaboration)], *SGIP*, No. 10 (1964), pp. 54–65.) The formation of a bilateral Soviet-Rumanian Intergovernmental Commission for Economic Collaboration was announced in a Joint Communique published in *Pravda* (September 12, 1965), pp. 1, 2; see 1. (See also "Bucharest, Moscow Sign Special Pact," *The Washington Post* [September 12, 1965], p. A-10.)

[65] Amos J. Peaslee, *International Governmental Organizations, Constitutional Documents* (2d ed. rev.; The Hague: Martinus Nijhoff, 1961), II, pp. 1860–1862. See also generally Grzybowski, "Socialist Commonwealth," *op. cit., supra* note 64, Chap. 5, pp. 172–213.

[66] Zbigniew K. Brzezinski, "The Organization of the Communist Camp," *World Politics*, XIII (1960–1961), 175–209; see 176–178 and 193, 194.

...the Warsaw Pact has become an important instrument in preserving peace in Europe and all over the world. Unlike the aggressive military blocs that the imperialist powers are slapping together, the Warsaw Pact is filled from first to last with a love of peace. Along with mutual defense, it aims at further strengthening economic and cultural relations among the countries of socialism. The Warsaw Pact is not a closed pact, it is open to other states, regardless of their political systems.[67]

Further, in contradistinction to the aggressive blocs of the West, it is said that the Warsaw Treaty Organization has not weakened the role of the United Nations or attempted to replace it by acting as a police force to suppress national liberation in Asia, Africa and Latin America.[68] In September, 1965, it was announced that the Warsaw Treaty Organization was to be reorganized, presumably to reduce the obvious primacy of the Soviet Union in directing its affairs.[69]

The Council for Mutual Economic Assistance was established in January, 1949, primarily as a device to keep the members of the socialist camp from participating in the Marshall Plan.[70] The Council remained relatively inactive until after the death of Stalin. At that time, economic cooperation was recognized to be an important unifying force in camp relationships, especially in the face

[67] A. Lukovets, "On Guard over Peace and Progress," trans. from *Pravda* (May 14, 1961), in *CDSP*, XIII, No. 19, p. 19.

[68] M. E. Volosov, "Desiatiletie Varshavskovo Dogovora" [Tenth Anniversary of the Warsaw Pact], *SGIP*, No. 8 (1965), pp. 123, 124; see 124.

[69] Victor Zorza, "Warsaw Pact Improvement Is Red Aim," *The Washington Post* (September 15, 1965), p. A-12. The Resolution adopted at the Twenty-third Party Congress of the C.P.S.U. noted that "the mechanism of the Warsaw Pact is being strengthened and improved" ("Resolution of the Twenty-third Congress of the Communist Party of the Soviet Union on the Report of the Central Committee of the CPSU", trans. from *Pravda* [April 6, 1966], in *Moscow News*, Supplement to No. 16 [April 16, 1966], pp. 2–10; see 3.) The Political Consultative Committee of the Warsaw Treaty Organization met at Bucharest during the period July 4–6, 1966, ostensibly to strengthen and improve the Organization. (See "Warsaw Treaty—Reliable Peace Shield," *Moscow News*, No. 28 [July 9, 1966], p. 3.) No significant changes in the Warsaw Treaty Organization resulted from this conference. "Communique on the Meeting of the Political Consultative Committee of the Warsaw Treaty Member-states," *Moscow News*, Supplement to No. 29 (July 16, 1966), pp. 23–26. See also, Mikhail Kapista, "Realistic Peace Program," *Moscow News*, No. 29 (July 16, 1966), p. 3.

[70] Brzezinski, "Organization of the Communist Camp," *op. cit.*, *supra* note 66, p. 179.

of the growing strength of West European political and economic unity.[71] The current Statute of the Council was adopted at Sofia, Bulgaria, on December 14, 1959.[72] The contracting states[73] established the Council for Mutual Economic Assistance for the purpose of "economic cooperation. . .for the successful development of their economies and, based on that development, raising the standards of living of their peoples."[74] Membership is open to any European state (Art. 2). The members pledge economic, scientific and technical cooperation "in accordance with the principle of full equality of rights, respect for sovereignty and national interests, mutual benefit and comradely reciprocity" (Art. 1). The Council makes recomendations for economic and technical cooperation which must be accepted by members before becoming effective (Art. 4).

The Council is described as a new type of organization for international collaboration which involves the coordination of economic planning as a means of realizing economic integration within the socialist commonwealth, i.e., the "international socialist division of labor."[75] The basic principles of socialist internationalism are said

[71] *Ibid.*, pp. 180, 181 and Otakar Shimunek, "Mezhdunarodnye Ekonomicheskie Otnosheniia i Sorevnovanie Dvukh Sistem" [International Economic Relations and Competition of the Two Systems], *Mezhdunarodnaia Zhizn'* [International Affairs], No. 12 (1962), pp. 23–31; see 28–30. See also Nikita S. Khrushchev, "The Socialist Camp and EEC," reprinted from *Kommunist*, No. 12 (1962) in *Survival*, Vol. 4, No. 6 (1962), pp. 282–285; see 283–285.

[72] Peaslee, *op. cit.*, *supra* note 65, I, 330. The text of the statute is translated on pp. 332–338. See generally, Grzybowski, *op. cit.*, *supra* note 64, pp. 64–110.

[73] The same states participating in the Warsaw Treaty Organization are also members of COMECON with the exception of Outer Mongolia which became a formal member of the latter organization in June, 1962. ("Kommiunike o Soveshchanii Predstavitelei Kommunisticheskikh i Rabochikh Partii Stran-Uchastnits Soveta Ekonomicheskoi Vzaimopomoshchi" [Communique Concerning the Meeting of Representatives of Communist and Workers' Parties of the Countries Participating in the Council for Mutual Economic Assistance], *Pravda* [June 9, 1962], p. 3. See also "International Organizations: Summary of Activities, Council for Mutual Economic Assistance," *Internationl Organization*, XVI, No. 3 [Summer, 1962], 638). Yugoslavia concluded an arrangement with COMECON for affiliate membership status in September, 1964. (*Pravda* [September 18, 1964], p. 3.)

[74] Shimunek, *op. cit.*, *supra* note 71, p. 25.

[75] See International Law, *op. cit.*, *supra* note 23, p. 375; V. I. Morozov "Mnorostoronnie Soglasheniia—Deistvennaia Forma Ekonomicheskovo Sotrudnichestva Sotsialisticheskh Stran" [Multilateral Agreements—An Effec-

to govern the operation of the organization with all of the obligations to the "world socialist economic system" that is implicit therein left unstated.[76] The goal is the realization of the Leninist ideal of "a single economy regulated by the proletariat of all nations according to a general plan. . . ."[77] The formulation "proletarian control" is actually a euphemism for party control, and especially the party of the largest member, the Soviet Union. Notwithstanding these realities, Soviet commentaries stress that:

> The relations between members of COMECON are based upon the principles of sovereignty and nonintervention. Fraternal mutual assistance, formulated as the principle of socialist internationalism in November of 1957 by the Declaration of the representatives of communist and workers' parties of the Socialist countries, is the basic element in these relations.[78]

Furthermore:

> COMECON should not be looked upon as some sort of supranational organization where the majority imposes its will upon the minority.[79]

> The Council for Mutual Economic Assistance organizes and directs the mutual economic collaboration of the European socialist countries, improves its forms and methods on the basis of genuine equality, mutual advantage and respect for the sovereignty of all the participating states. The activity of the Council—an example of the new type of international relations among the countries of socialism—is permeated by the principle of proletarian [socialist] internationalism, mutual trust and comradely mutual assistance.[80]

---

tive Form of Economic Collaboration of Socialist Countries], *SGIP*, No. 12 (1963), pp. 75–85; see 79. Also, V. A. Kikot', "Pravovye Voprosy Sotrudnichestva Sotsialisticheskikh Stran v Oblasti Sel'skovo Khoziaistva" [Legal Problems of the Collaboration of the Socialist Countries in the Field of Agriculture], *SGIP*, No. 1 (1964), pp. 64–72; see 65, 66.

[76] E. T. Usenko, "O Iuridicheskoi Prirode Rekomendatsii Soveta Ekonomicheskoi Vzaimopomoshchi" [The Juridical Nature of Recommendations of the Council of Mutual Economic Assistance], *SGIP*, No. 12 (1963), pp. 86–94; see 86. "The world socialist system is a world economic system as well as a social-political union of nations." (*Mezhdunarodnoe Pravo*, *op. cit.*, *supra* note 2, p. 97.)

[77] Kikot', *op. cit.*, *supra* note 75, p. 71.

[78] Shimunek, *op. cit.*, *supra* note 71, p. 27.

[79] *Ibid.* See also Y. Belayev and V. Tandit, "CMEA and the Six," *International Affairs*, No. 2 (1963), pp. 15–20; see 15, 16.

[80] *Mezhdunarodnoe Pravo*, *op. cit.*, *supra* note 2, p. 295.

The Warsaw Treaty Organization and the Council for Mutual Economic Assistance emerge as the ideals of regional organization.

Despite claims to the contrary, the Warsaw Treaty Organization and the Council for Mutual Economic Assistance do not fully meet the Soviet-sponsored regional and open membership requirements of regional organizations under the Charter of the United Nations. Both organizations are considered institutional forms of class struggle and, therefore, constitute groupings of states against other states. Moreover, although Article 9 of the Warsaw Pact permits the accession of "other states, without regard to their social and state order, which indicate a readiness for participation in this agreement to further the unification of the forces of peace-loving states in the interest of ensuring the peace and security of nations,"[81] it can be restrictively interpreted to bar capitalist states, given the Soviet penchant for darkly characterizing the motives of such states.[82] Further, the accession of Mongolia to the Council for Mutual Economic Assistance in June, 1962 destroyed the regional purity of the membership of that organization. Thus, it appears that political exigencies in regional groupings have, for the moment, at least, outstripped the rationale creativity of Soviet international legal specialists and that the only consistency extant is political rather than legal or logical.

FUNCTIONALISM

The Soviets recognize the conventional distinction between political and administrative international organizations and the growth in importance of the latter with the increased interdependence of states resulting from advances in technology.[83] Although these administrative organizations are said to be functional rather than political, the Soviet Union is selective in its participation.

---

[81] *Ibid.*, p. 294.

[82] Sobakin notes that the geographic exclusivity of the Warsaw Pact is attributable to the refusal of Western states to create a general European system of collective security rather than the desire of socialist states to exclude capitalist states. (Sobakin, Kollektivnaia Bezopasnost', *op. cit., supra* note 9, p. 389.)

[83] *Mezhdunarodnoe Pravo, op. cit., supra*, note 2, pp. 306, 307.

Where there is no choice, as is the case in the majority of these organizations (e.g., International Telegraphic Union and Universal Postal Union), political preferences give way to practical need. In the case of those organizations where participation is not a necessary condition of international life, the consequent luxury of choice permits selectivity and the Soviet Union refrains from participating in organizations "in which the influence of imperialist agencies is particularly pronounced" (e.g., The International Monetary Fund and the International Bank for Reconstruction and Development).[84] Lack of Soviet participation in these organizations is political rather than ideological, reflecting the pressure of a practical foreign policy objective and not a basic aversion to participation in joint endeavors with capitalist states. The realities of interdependence negate the feasibility of nonparticipation in such endeavors as a matter of principle.

The Soviet approach to international organization, like the approach to other questions of international law (e.g., sovereignty), reflects the complexity of the foreign policy needs of the Soviet Union. The opposition to nonsocialist globalism and hostile universal or regional organization clearly reflects Soviet defensism. On the other hand, the efforts to capture the United Nations (i.e., convert it into an instrument of peaceful coexistence) and to create a form of socialist globalism under the cover of socialist regionalism are related to policy offensives. Given the ambivalence of defense and offense in the policies of the Soviet Union, Soviet international legal specialists are constrained to formulate minimum and maximum legal positions in order to provide suitable support for them.

[84] *International Law, op. cit., supra* note 23, pp. 348, 349. See also, Lisovskii, *op. cit., supra* note 4, pp. 353, 354.

CHAPTER TEN

PEACEFUL SETTLEMENT OF INTERNATIONAL DISPUTES

THE POLICY

One of the basic features of the policy of peaceful coexistence is the negotiated, peaceful settlement of international disputes. Communists are said to "propose that both systems agree not to resort to arms in settlement of international disputes. . . ."[1] The policy of peaceful settlement is said to be possible only under the conditions and within the framework of coexistence.

The possibility of peaceful settlement of disputes between the countries of the camp of peace and democracy and the countries of the imperialist, anti-democratic camp arises from the possibility of the peaceful coexistence of the socialist and capitalist systems.[2]

The commitment to peaceful settlement, as formulated by the Soviets, stresses agreement of the parties as the principal method for reaching settlement.

The Government of the U.S.S.R. has frequently declared that there is no outstanding international issue that cannot be settled by peaceful means on the basis of mutual agreement between the parties concerned.[3]

---

[1] "Your Questions on Communism," *Soviet Life*, No. 1 (1966), pp. 20, 21, answer to the question, "Why do not Communists apply the principle of peaceful coexistence to the ideological sphere?" (pp. 20, 21; see 20.)

[2] V. I. Lisovskii, *Mezhdunarodnoe Pravo* [International Law] (2d ed.; Moscow: State Publishing House "Higher School," 1961), p. 380.

[3] *International Law* (Moscow: Foreign Languages Publishing House, n.d.), p. 377.

꒦꒷꒦

This policy, intended to complement the prohibition of nuclear, aggressive and unjust wars, reflects Soviet preference for political (rather than judicial) settlement because of the control it provides in a dispute situation by reserving the element of consent as an essential condition of settlement. Soviet lip service to peaceful settlement is part of the portrayal of the Soviet Union as the champion of peace.

> Soviet diplomacy uses all peaceful means if they can contribute to peace in the particular case. Soviet International Law acknowledges that the peaceful settlement of differences between the U.S.S.R. and other States is both necessary and possible in the interests of universal peace.[4]

The propaganda exploitation of this position is supported by diplomatic initiatives, such as Khrushchev's New Year's Eve (1963) proposal to all heads of state that border disputes be settled by peaceful means, and the Soviet Union's role in sponsoring the Tashkent summit conference (1966) between the heads-of-state of India and Pakistan.[5]

The Soviet desire to preserve the element of consent in effecting the settlement of international disputes is part of the basic positivist orientation of the Soviet Union which has been carried forward as part of the law of peaceful coexistence. The extreme positivism of earlier positions (i.e., settlement of an international dispute is the sole concern of the parties to it) has been relaxed, principally in recognition of the increased need for, and dependence upon, international organization to maintain international peace and security. The basic positivism of the Soviet position on peaceful settlement was affected little by the formation of the United Nations. As originally conceived, the Charter of the United Nations left intact the traditional means of peaceful settlement and, by giving the Security Council primacy in the maintenance of peace and security, allowed for the protection of Soviet interests in the form of the permanent member's "veto" under the voting rules for nonprocedural matters. At that point, Soviet concern was to insist only upon a strict construction of "procedural matters" (i.e.,

---

[4] *Ibid.*, p. 378.

[5] As to the Tashkent conference, see "Tashkent," *New Times*, No. 3 (January 19, 1966), pp. 1, 2 and Lev Stepanov, "After Tashkent," *New Times*, No. 4 (January 26, 1966), p. 6, 7.

matters not subject to the veto) and that the abstention, or absence, of a permanent member barred Security Council action on non-procedural matters.[6] The difficulties resulting from limited success in achieving these positions were far overshadowed by those inherent in the shift of influence to the General Assembly, stemming from the Uniting for Peace Resolution of 1950. This shift, in large part a reaction to the Soviet Union's use of the veto to block Security Council action of which it did not approve, required an adjustment in the Soviet position on peaceful settlement, the principal thrust of which is to insist that the Security Council be the sole international body empowered to effect the political settlement of disputes.

In effect, the Soviet effort is to revitalize the peace-keeping role of the Security Council and, thereby, the effectiveness of the Soviet veto, as the alternative to settlement by an organ over which it has no control.

In contemporary international relations the United Nations and its principal organ, the Security Council, should serve as an important means of maintaining peace and security of nations, an international forum from which it is very easy to wage the struggle for realization of the principle of the peaceful coexistence of states with different social-economic regimes.[7]

The recent refusal of the Soviet Union to pay its share of the costs of General Assembly-sponsored United Nations peace-keeping efforts is an aspect of the Soviet campaign to re-emphasize the importance of the principle of great power unity incorporated in the organization of the Security Council. In support of this campaign, Soviet propagandists took the line that the effort of the United States to collect peace-keeping costs was another of its attacks on the integrity of the United Nations Organization.

[6] *International Law, op. cit., supra* note 3, p. 339.

[7] V. N. Fedorov, "Istoriia Sozdaniia Soveta Bezopasnosti OON" (The History of the Creation of the Security Council of the U.N.), *Voprosy Mezhdunarodnovo Prava*, [Problems of International Law], ed. V. I. Menzhinskii (Moscow: Publishing House of the Institute of International Relations, 1963), pp. 147–176; see 147.

183

This attack was beaten off by the resolute opposition of the states whose concern is that the U.N. be a genuine instrument of peace and the security of peoples.[8]

Soviet support for the Security Council as the principal organ for the maintenance of peace and security is, in part, a recognition of the need for an international body for this purpose; but principally, the counter to Western proposals for increased authority for the General Assembly and greater use of judicial settlement in international disputes. It does not change the basic position that viable solutions of international disputes require settlement on the basis of equality of, and mutual acceptability of the settlement, to the disputing parties.

THE LEGAL POSITION

In the Soviet view, international law requires the use of peaceful means to settle international disputes. Although they recognize that peaceful settlement is not new, the Soviets claim that the law of peaceful coexistence has made a significant contribution. In earlier times, both war and peaceful settlement were available to resolve international disputes, but now only the latter is permitted. In effect, the law of peaceful coexistence has converted peaceful settlement from a secondary means of resolving international disputes to the only permissible one.[9]

The principle of peaceful settlement of disputes, in accordance with which all states are required to settle their differences only by peaceful means, is closely related to the principle of nonaggression. . . .If states are forbidden to resort to force in their relations with other states, it follows that only peaceful means of settlement are available.[10]

---

[8] Viktor Mayevsky, "Life Has Its Way," trans. from *Pravda* (August 27, 1965), in *CDSP*, XVII, No. 34, p. 14. See also, Nikolai Pastukhov, "International Commentary" ["In the Interests of All People"], *Moscow News*, No. 41 (October 9, 1965), p. 7.

[9] A. M. Ladyzhenskii and I. P. Blishchenko, *Mirnye Sredstva Razresheniia Sporov mezhdu Gosudarstvami* [Peaceful Settlement of Disputes Between States] (Moscow: State Publishing House of Legal Literature, 1962), p. 173.

[10] G. I. Tunkin, *Voprosy Teorii Mezhdunarodnovo Prava* [Problems of the Theory of International Law] (Moscow: State Publishing House of Legal Literature 1962), p. 32.

The preemptive role of peaceful settlement (as a necessary complement to the prohibition of war under the law of peaceful coexistence)
is confirmed by the Charter of the United Nations: "The United
Nations Charter prohibits resort to war and demands the settlement
of differences by peaceful means."[11] As part of the law of peaceful
coexistence, the principle of peaceful settlement reflects the bias of
that law toward sovereignty by preferring political to judicial
settlement.

The Soviets generally endorse the traditional means of peaceful
settlement: negotiation, inquiry, mediation, good offices, conciliation, arbitration and judicial settlement by the International Court
of Justice.[12] Typically, the Soviet endorsement reflects the desire to
ensure freedom of action for the Soviet Union and a readiness to
condemn the practice of Western states. As to negotiation, it is
said that there must be no "prior condition, . . *diktat or* coercion"
and "there have been cases when the imperialist States, pursuing
their own aggressive ends, have proposed negotiations in order
to lull the vigilance of their future victims."[13] Further, "mediation
must not give rise to interference in negotiations—something which
is frequently encountered in imperialist practice and which is prohibited by international law."[14] In practice, the Soviet Union
has demonstrated, as many other nations have, a preference for
political rather than judicial settlement. At least one Soviet commentary includes political settlement as one of the basic principles of
the law of peaceful coexistence.[15] The preference for political settlement is perfectly consistent with the basic Soviet approach of reduc-
ing the fetters of international law. Political settlement, rather than
the third-party judgment of arbitration and judicial settlement,
maximizes the freedom of action of the parties to a dispute.

Soviet jurists recognize the binding nature of an arbitration
award or a judgment of the International Court of Justice, once the

---

[11] *International Law, op. cit., supra* note 3, p. 377.
[12] *Ibid.*, pp. 378–396.
[13] *Ibid.*, pp. 378, 379.
[14] *Ibid.*, p. 381.
[15] G. P. Zadorozhnyi, *Mirnoe Sosushchestvovanie i Mezhdunarodnoe Pravo* [Peaceful
Coexistence and International Law] (Moscow: Publishing House "International
Relations," 1964), p. 401.

parties to a dispute consent to these forms of peaceful settlement. The Soviet Union withholds its consent by avoiding, wherever possible, undertakings to submit to judicial settlement. It has not accepted the compulsory jurisdication of the International Court of Justice,[16] and it has made appropriate reservations in adhering to multilateral arrangements which provide for judicial settlement of disputes under them.[17] The Soviets pay lip service to the increased importance of judicial settlement under present conditions and in a disarmed world, although they resist all attempts to change the consent basis of the jurisdiction of arbitral tribunals or to place them under the general competence of the International Court of Justice.[18] It is said that the Soviet Union will continue "to react positively" to international arbitration so long as it remains voluntary. Any attempt to make arbitration compulsory would be considered a violation of state sovereignty, a fundamental principle of contemporary international law.[19]

The Soviet Union opposes all proposals to create a comprehensive system of international courts and to expand the compulsory jurisdiction of the International Court of Justice. These proposals are attacked as the attempts of capitalist states to compensate for their loss of control in the General Assembly by increasing the power, competence and authority of international tribunals which they control.[20] On their part, the Soviets have proposed changes in

[16] *International Law, op. cit., supra* note 3, p. 393.

[17] For example, "the Declaration regarding the Soviet Union's adherence to the Convention on the privileges and immunities of the United Nations approved on February 13, 1946, was accompanied by the reservation that the Soviet Union does not consider itself bound by the clause in Section 30 of the Convention regarding the compulsory jurisdiction of the International Court of Justice and that the Soviet Union will adhere to its former position regarding the need for the submission of a dispute to the International Court of Justice with the agreement of all parties to the dispute in each individual case." (*Ibid.*, pp. 270, 271.)

[18] Ladyzhenskii and Blishchenko, *op. cit., supra* note 9, pp. 130–132.

[19] *Mezhdunarodnoe Pravo* [International Law], ed. D. B. Levin and G. P. Kaliuzhnaia (Moscow: Publishing House "Legal Literature," 1964), p. 376.

[20] V. A. Kartashkin, "Rol' Mezhdunarodnovo Suda OON v Mirnom Razreshenii Territorial'nykh Sporov" [The Role of the International Court of the U.N. in the Peaceful Settlement of Territorial Disputes], *Sovetskii Ezhegodnik, 1963* (Moscow: Publishing House "Science," 1965), pp. 501–503; see 502.

the organization of the International Court of Justice which would increase socialist and neutralist representation. Soviet jurists invoke the United Nations Charter principle of geographic representation in support of their proposals, and claim that the authority of the Court would be enhanced by their adoption and international disputes would be decided more justly "in the interest of. . .universal peace and the peaceful coexistence of states."[21]

The Soviet approach to the International Court of Justice has been one of suspicion and reluctance to submit to its nonsocialist, third-party judgment. The Soviets suspect that greater competence for the Court would reduce the settlement of disputes by the United Nations, with a consequent lessening of deference to the sovereign prerogatives of the nation-state and the special role of the Security Council in the maintenance of peace and security.

The majority in the United Nations have tried to use the International Court of Justice to infringe [sic] the United Nations Charter and to replace the Security Council.[22]

The reluctance stems from a fear that a greater role for the Court would be a step in the direction of world government.[23]

In the West major attention is devoted to further expanding and increasing the competence of the International Court, to giving it automatic, compulsory jurisdiction which would convert the Court into a world universal court—a basic departure from the basic principles of contemporary international law. Western plans for the reorganization of international tribunals is directed at the creation of a whole system of such international judicial organs as an international court of justice, with compulsory jurisdiction over all dangerous international disputes not of a legal nature; and a universal conciliation chamber for the settlement of any international dispute in which diplomatic efforts have failed but which are possible of

---

[21] *Ibid.*, p. 503. See also Professor F. Kozhevnikov, "International Court at the Crossroads," *New Times*, No. 36 (September 7, 1966), pp. 3, 4; see 4.

[22] *International Law, op. cit., supra* note 3, p. 396.

[23] B. Mikhailov, "Konferentsiia Iuristov-Mezhdunarodnikov" [Conference of International Legal Specialists], *SGIP*, No. 10 (1963), pp. 147–149; see 148, 149. See also N. M. Minasian, Review of A. M. Ladyzhenskii and I. P. Blishchenko, *Mirnye Sredstva Razresheniia Sporov mezhdu Gosudarstvami* [Peaceful Settlement of International Disputes] (Moscow: State Publishing House of Legal Literature, 1962), *SGIP*, No. 2 (1964), pp. 160, 161.

settlement. They also contemplate a whole system of regional courts of the U.N., subordinated to the International Court and whose decisions are subject to its review. Such plans proceed from the reactionary idea of world government.[24]

The Soviets also feel that there is little possibility of obtaining a "correct" decision in a given case "because the Court is not one which can be counted upon to be sympathetic to socialism."[25]

There are only two judges from the Socialist world on the present [1963] panel of the Court, and it is hard to expect it to be fair in deciding cases which reflect the social and political conceptions existing in the world.[26]

The Soviet predilection to view the world as split along class lines into capitalist and socialist camps and the pragmatic rather than ethical approach to law (i.e., to support foreign policy objectives) confirm the belief that nonsocialist third-party judgment would, of necessity, be hostile to Soviet interests.[27] In the Soviet view, the practice of the International Court of Justice reflects many decisions which depart from contemporary international law (i.e., the law of peaceful coexistence) and "decisions which express a one-sided interpretation thereof."[28] . . ."As a whole, the practice of the International Court attests to the fact that the majority of judges more frequently adopt reactionary positions."[29] Where the Court has rendered decisions acceptable to the Soviet Union, it is said to "have served the cause of international legality and peaceful coexistence."[30]

[24] *Ibid.*, p. 148. See also *Mezhdunarodnoe Pravo, op. cit., supra* note 19, pp. 383, 384.

[25] Bernard A. Ramundo, Review of Kazimierz Grzybowski, *The Socialist Commonwealth of Nations* (New Haven and London: Yale University Press, 1964), in 17 *Journal of Legal Education* 476–479 (1965), p. 478.

[26] Y. Korovin, "Peace Through Law: Two Views," *International Affairs*, No. 7 (1963), pp. 100–102; see 101. The July 18, 1966 decision of the International Court of Justice concerning the status of Southwest Africa has been roundly condemned as reactionary approval of the racist and criminal policy of South Africa toward its mandate. (Kozhevnikov, *op. cit., supra* note 21; p. 4.)

[27] George Schwarzenberger, *The Frontiers of International Law* (London: Stevens & Sons, Ltd., 1962), pp. 150–154. See also *International Law, op. cit., supra* note 3, p. 396.

[28] Tunkin, Voprosy Teorii, *op. cit., supra* note 10, p. 140. See also Kozhevnikov, *op. cit., supra* note 21; p. 3.

[29] Kartashkin, *op. cit., supra* note 20, p. 502.

[30] Ladyzhenskii and Blishchenko, *op. cit., supra* note 9, p. 155.

Moreover, as general proponent of a socialist world order, the Soviet state from its earliest days has not accepted international law *in toto*. It has always reserved to itself the right to select those "democratic" and "progressive" principles to which it would submit. The general absence of Western acquiescence in this selective submission has made the Soviet Union wary of what it considers to be capitalist state-controlled judicial institutions. The Soviets are even more wary of nonsocialist judicial institutions in view of their campaign to gain acceptance of the new law of peaceful coexistence. They do not wish to risk the disruptive effect of a decision of an international tribunal—the persuasiveness which they concede—which either rejects or otherwise undermines the existence of the new law.

In addition to avoiding subordination to nonsocialist third-party judgment, the Soviet Union attempts to limit the legal consequences of judicial settlement. Decisions of courts of arbitration and the International Court of Justice are not considered to be a part of the international norm formulation process. These decisions, representing the views of tribunal members (who are not considered representatives of states for this purpose), are regarded as a form of international practice relating to the existence and interpretation of international law which gains normative force only upon acceptance by the states of both systems. In effect, the Soviets reject any attempt to give international tribunals the "law-making" power wielded by courts under the common law system.[31] If forced to accept judicial settlement, the Soviet Union prefers arbitration to the International Court of Justice for the stated reason that the decisions under the former are closer to international law[32] and the unstated reason that the parties to an arbitration have greater control over procedure and substance. Whenever possible, however, the Soviet Union opts for political settlement because it is considered "the most effective means of resolving international differences."[33]

If resort to an institutional mechanism is necessary to effect political settlement, the Soviet Union considers the Security Council

---

[31] Tunkin, Voprosy Teorii, *op. cit.*, *supra* note 10, pp. 139 and 146.
[32] *Ibid.*, p. 141.
[33] Ladyzhenskii and Blishchenko, *op. cit.*, *supra* note 9, p. 2.

of the United Nations the ideal forum for the obvious reason that effective use of the veto can be made to protect Soviet interests. In support of this position, Soviet jurists claim that "as contemplated by the Charter, the Security Council. . .is . . .the main agency for the settlement of international disputes."[34]

The principal instrument for the maintenance of peace and the peaceful settlement of international disputes should be the U.N. which is not a world government. It is the U.N. which makes possible reconciling the acts of all sovereign state-members in the interests of the peaceful coexistence of states and the peaceful settlement of disputes. Fulfillment of the principal task—maintenance of international peace and security—is accomplished by one of the principal organs of the U.N., the Security Council.[35]

The Soviets recognize that world developments since the establishment of the United Nations have made improvement in the mechanism of the organization necessary;[36] however, they resist any attempt to change the Charter provisions concerning the authority of the Security Council or the use of the veto as violations of the principle of the unity of the great powers and their primary responsibility for the maintenance of the peace. These provisions, said to be basic to the law of peaceful coexistence, are given a special sanctity because of Soviet political needs.

Attempts to explain the lack of effectiveness of the U.N. on the basis of the principle of the unanimity of the great powers in the Security Council and proposals for the liquidation of the "right of veto" clearly reflect the desire of the imperialist powers to subordinate completely the U.N. to their aggressive purposes. The principle of the unanimity of the great powers in the Security Council is dictated by life and is under contemporary conditions a keystone of the United Nations Organization.

The Soviet government has repeatedly stated its position on this question, underscoring the importance of the principle of the unity of the great powers.[37]

---

[34] International Law, *op. cit., supra* note 3, pp. 398, 399.

[35] Mikhailov, *op. cit., supra* note 23, p. 149.

[36] V. K. Sobakin, *Kollektivnaia Bezopasnost'—Garantiia Mirnovo Sosushchestvovaniia* [Collective Security—Guarantee of Peaceful Coexistence] (Moscow: Publishing House of the Institute of International Relations, 1962), p. 101.

[37] Tunkin, Voprosy Teorii, *op. cit., supra* note 10, pp. 195, 196.

Recently, in connection with the twentieth anniversary of the United Nations Charter, it was said that:

The U.N. Charter. . .is a great charter for peace and a major code of international law.
. . .the noble principles enshrined in the U.N. Charter have weathered all storms. Strict adherence to them is even more important today, because the aggressive imperialist powers are seriously endangering world peace.
All that [Soviet diplomatic initiatives] is evidence of the steadfast desire of the Soviet Union to strengthen world peace and security, to strictly adhere to the principles of the U.N. Charter, and to strengthen that Organization.[38]

This Soviet position again reflects the importance attached to consent—in this case, retention of the primacy of the Security Council and the great power veto therein—as a means of lightening the burden of compliance with the international legal order upon policy formulation.

Within the socialist commonwealth of nations there is no formal agency for the settlement of political disputes. In theory, all differences between member states are settled on the basis of the spirit of fraternal cooperation and collaboration which permeates socialist relationships under the principle of socialist internationalism.[39] Extant dispute-settling agencies operate in the technical areas of commercial arbitration, frontier problems, and status-of-forces arrangements.[40]

The narrow scope given to the arbitral function within the socialist commonwealth of nations is a natural result of the attitude that considered pacific settlement of international disputes not vital for promoting peace and cooperation among socialist countries. Permanent peace among them was supposed to rest upon their identical social and economic structures.[41]

When political differences arise—and past events have demonstrated that, at least in the cases of Yugoslavia, Albania, China, and now, Rumania, socialist internationalsim, is not a panacea for the ills of international differences—attempts are made to resolve them at

[38] George Zadorozhny, "Strict Adherence to UN Charter—Basis of International Relations," *Moscow News*, No. 26 (June 26, 1965), p. 5.
[39] *International Law, op. cit., supra* note 3, pp. 197, 198.
[40] Grzybowski, "The Socialist Commonwealth," *op. cit., supra* note 25, pp. 214–245.
[41] *Ibid.*, p. 214.

꘏꘏꘏

multilateral meetings of party leaders where commonwealth foreign policy objectives and goals are formulated.[42] In practical effect, "the multilateral meetings of national party leaders. . .[are] the principal element in the ordering of camp relationships."[43] Although national sovereignty is characterized as "an important integral part of socialist internationalsim," the requirement for unity and solidarity in the commonwealth is said to be paramount. National sovereignty must be socialist in content: "the Marxist-Leninist party of each socialist country needs to be able to solve these problems [of mutual relations] in such a way as to combine national interests with the general interests of the socialist camp."[44] The invocation of socialist internationalism by the Soviet Union, the principal member of the commonwealth, has, at the very least, great persuasive force in the ordering of socialist relationships. The attempt to instill a measure of discipline in dispute-settling within the commonwealth, which is implicit in the concepts of socialist internationalism, fraternity and solidarity, sharply contrasts with the bid for freedom-of-action in the settlement of disputes with capitalist states.

[42] Zbigniew K. Brzezinski, "The Organization of the Communist Camp," *World Politics*, XIII (1960–1961), pp. 175–209; see 190, 191. It is said that bilateral meetings of party leaders are also utilized in the policy formulation process (*Ibid.*).

[43] Ramundo, Review of Grzybowski's Socialist Commonweatlh, *op. cit.*, *supra* note 25, p. 477.

[44] O. W. Kuusinen, *Fundamentals of Marxism-Leninism* (2d ed.; Moscow: Foreign Languages Publishing House, 1961), p. 773; and the Declaration of Representatives of the Eighty-one Communist Parties (November–December 1961) in *The New Communist Manifesto*, ed. Dan N. Jacobs (2d ed.; Evanston, Illinois and Elmsford, New York: Low, Peterson and Co., 1962), p. 21. See also, V. M. Shurshalov, "Mezhdunarodno-pravovye Printsipy Sotrudnichestva Sotsialisticheskikh Gosudarstv" [International Legal Principles of the Collaboration of Socialist States], *SGIP*, No. 7 (1962), pp. 95–105; see 103.

CHAPTER ELEVEN

ARMS CONTROL

Historically, whenever the Soviet Union has been beset with internal difficulties or concentrating on internal development, it has been a vociferous proponent of arms control. This was true of the young Soviet state in the twenties, the maturing state in the thirties, and still applies to the more mature, but still developing, Soviet Union of today. This tradition dictated by necessity is used as a basis of convenience for the claim that the Soviet Union has always been the principal proponent of arms control measures in its continuing struggle for peace. At the present time, the Soviets go beyond merely seeking acceptance of the desirability of a policy of arms control (i.e., as a means of eliminating the "material-technical bases of wars" of aggression).[1] Their current claim is that disarmament and other arms control measures embodied in their policy of peaceful coexistence have become principles of the new international law of peaceful coexistence.[2] This claim has a threefold purpose. It seeks to gain (1) acceptance of Soviet proposals on arms control, an aspect of the international *detente* deemed necessary for the building of communism; (2) support for peaceful coexistence as the basic principle of contemporary international law, using the appeal of arms control as a bootstrap; and (3) an additional basis for the claim of primacy in the struggle for peace and international law and order. Again international law is tailored to provide a supporting rationale for basic policy objectives.

[1] R. L. Bobrov, "Mezhdunarodnoe Pravo i Istoricheskii Progress" [International Law and Historical Progress], *SGIP*, No. 12 (1963), pp. 3–11; see 9.

[2] See e.g., Y. Korovin, "The Way to Peace" (Review of O. V. Bogdanov, *General and Complete Disarmament* (Moscow: Publishing House "International Relations," 1964), *International Affairs*, No. 11 (1964), pp. 73–75; see 73.

->>)((<-

THE POLICY

Peaceful coexistence is, in effect, an arms control policy that basically seeks to reduce the risk of nuclear and general warfare in the interest of furthering the values of the Soviet system. The policy reflects a realistic awareness of the destructiveness of nuclear conflict and the realization that the building of communism requires a period of general international peace. Peaceful coexistence, however, is less than a complete arms control policy in that it envisages and supports nonnuclear conflicts of national liberation and wars characterized as "just" in the Soviet lexicon. This incompleteness is ignored in the propaganda effort which supports Soviet arms control measures. The technique is to finesse the gaps in Soviet arms control policy by emphasizing that (1) the Soviet Union has consistently been in the forefront of the struggle for peace, general and complete disarmament, national liberation and the relaxation of international tensions, and (2) the socialist camp, led by the Soviet Union, is pitted against the forces of capitalism which are fostering the arms race, planning aggressive war and seeking to restore colonialism.[3]

The Communist Party of the Soviet Union and the Soviet government are waging a consistent and persistent struggle for the strengthening of universal peace, for the halting of the arms race and for general disarmament.

. . . .

The whole history of the Soviet Union's stand in favor of disarmament, from the first proposals on general disarmament submitted on V. I. Lenin's instructions at the 1922 Genoa Conference on down to the U.S.S.R.'s latest steps in this field—the Moscow treaty banning nuclear tests in three environments, the agreement not to place vehicles bearing nuclear weapons

---

[3] *Mezhdunarodnoe Pravo* [International Law] ed. D. B. Levin and G. P. Kaliuzhnaia (Moscow: Publishing House "Legal Literature," 1964), pp. 416, 417. See S. Viskov, *Za Mir bez Oruzhiia, za Mir bez Voin* [For a World Without Arms and War] (Moscow: Publishing House of Social Economic Literature "Thought," 1964), pp. 40–105, and 123–175, describing Soviet efforts to relax international tensions, resolve the unfinished business of World War II, halt the arms race and achieve general and complete disarmament, promote international collaboration, support national liberation and defend neutralist states (in fact it is claimed that the support of the Soviet Union has made neutralism possible [p. 126]), substitute peaceful competition for hostilities in relations with capitalist states, and prevent a thermonuclear war.

-»»)«(-

in orbit around the earth, the Soviet government's readiness to reduce the production of fissionable materials for military purposes—bears testimony to its tireless and consistent struggle for the strengthening of universal peace and for the delivering of mankind from the horrors of war.... [the Soviet Union has] taken important foreign policy steps to unmask the aggressive imperialist forces that threaten the people with nuclear weapons and to counterpose to these forces' program of war [its]...own peace-loving program corresponding to the aspirations of the peoples of all countries. [4]

The emphasis upon struggle and goals generally desired by all is intended to serve as a lightning rod to draw attention away from the failure of Soviet policy to contain an unambiguous commitment to peace.

Specifically, Soviet propaganda and diplomatic initiatives are intended to demonstrate the peaceful intentions of the Soviet Union and its support for effective arms control. While it would prefer the big leap to "general and complete disarmament," the Soviet Union endorses the functional approach to arms control.

In the struggle to extricate mankind from wars, success in specific aspects of disarmament have great significance. Each new success in this cause clears the way for further progress, bringing mankind closer to the final goal—complete elimination of the means of waging war. [5]

Soviet initiatives in the United Nations, in the Eighteen Nation Disarmament Committee, and elsewhere include plans for general and complete disarmament; proposals for limiting the utilization of outer space to peaceful purposes, nuclear-free zones, and complete cessation of nuclear testing; readiness to reduce the production of fissionable materials for military purposes; and the December 1964 proposal for a summit conference on arms control. [6] On December 7, 1964, the Soviet Government circulated a memorandum at the

[4] V. A. Zorin, "Disarmament Problems and Peking's Maneuvers," trans. from *Izvestiia* (June 30, 1964), in *CDSP*, XVI, No. 26, p. 11.

[5] *OON i Aktual'nye Mezhdunarodnye Problemy* [The U.N. and Contemporary International Problems], ed. V. A. Zorin and G. I. Morozov (Moscow: Publishing House "International Relations," 1965), pp. 128, 129. See also, Vasily Emelyanov, "Needed: The Next Step," *New Times*, No. 33 (August 17, 1966), pp. 5, 6.

[6] See Zorin, *op. cit., supra* note 4, p. 11; Viskov, *op. cit., supra* note 3, pp. 40–105; and "Gromyko Proposes World Arms Summit," *The Evening Star* (December 7, 1964), p. A-1.

United Nations which enumerated the standard Soviet measures "for the further relaxation of international tensions and limiting the arms race": (*1*) reduction of military budgets, (*2*) recall or reduction of foreign based troops, (*3*) liquidation of foreign bases, (*4*) prevention of further proliferation of nuclear weapons (and, of course, the NATO multilateral force), (*5*) prohibition against the use of nuclear weapons, (*6*) creation of nuclear-free zones, (*7*) destruction of bombers, (*8*) prohibition against underground nuclear testing, (*9*) conclusion of a nonaggression pact between the North Atlantic Treaty Organization and Warsaw Pact countries, (*10*) prevention of surprise attack, and (*11*) reduction of the over-all strength of the armed forces.[7] A "new Soviet initiative" in the United Nations Disarmament Commission on June 1, 1965, took the form of two draft resolutions calling for (*1*) the immediate liquidation of foreign bases and the withdrawal of forces stationed abroad and (*2*) a prohibition against the use of nuclear and thermonuclear weaponry.[8] At the Twentieth Session of the General Assembly in the fall of 1965, the Soviet delegation tabled a Draft Treaty on the Non-Dissemination of Nuclear Weapons as "a watertight agreement" against proliferation of nuclear weapons.[9] On February 1, 1966, Kosygin, the Chairman of the Council of Ministers of the Soviet Union, solicited the support of the Eighteen-Nation Disarmament Committee for the Soviet draft nonproliferation treaty, and announced Soviet readiness to (*1*) agree to a prohibition against the use of

[7] "Memorandum Sovetskovo Pravitel'stva o Merakh po Dal'neishemu Smiagcheniiu Mezhdunarodnoi Napriazhennosti i Ogranicheniiu Gonki Vooruzhenii" [Memorandum of the Soviet Government Concerning Measures for the Further Relaxation of International Tensions and Limiting the Arms Race], *Pravda* (December 8, 1964), pp. 1 and 4.

[8] "Novaia Sovetskaia Initsiativa" [A New Soviet Initiative], *Pravda* (June 2, 1965), p. 1.

[9] "The General Assembly," *New Times*, No. 40 (October 6, 1965), pp. 1, 2; see 2. The text of the Soviet nonproliferation treaty is in the Documents section of the cited issue at pp. 31, 32. An interesting provision of this treaty which substantially detracts from its watertightness is Article VI which provides pertinently:

"Every party shall be entitled, in the exercise of its state sovereignty, to withdraw from the treaty if it finds that exceptional circumstances involving the Treaty provisions imperil the supreme interests of its country." (*Ibid.*, p. 32.)

nuclear weapons against nonnuclear powers (i.e., states not having nuclear weapons in their territory), (2) support and respect for nuclear-free zones, if other nuclear powers do likewise, (3) agree to prohibit underground nuclear testing with national rather than international inspection controls, and (4) undertake not to be the first to use nuclear weapons, if the other nuclear powers give a similar undertaking. He reiterated the need for the recall of foreign-based troops and the elimination of foreign bases, and also called for the destruction of nuclear stockpiles, a ban on the production of nuclear weapons, and the destruction of weapon delivery vehicles.[10] Unilateral measures such as reduction in the strength of the armed services in the late fifties[11] and the decision in December 1964 to reduce defense expenditures (the so-called "peace budget"),[12] are also parts of the portrayal of Soviet commitment to arms control in pursuit of the policy of peaceful coexistence. Similarly, the 5 per cent increase in the Soviet military budget for 1966 was said to be dictated by the "growing activity of the aggressive forces of the imperialist states."[13] Many of these generally appealing propaganda-diplomatic initiatives of the Soviet Union have not been acceptable to, or given credibility in, the West. Reviewed against the backdrop of the fundamental militancy of the policy of peaceful coexistence, they are not regarded as meaningful negotiating commitments or actions. Soviet writers describe the failure of the West to welcome these initiatives as part of a continuing effort to block progress on arms control.

[10] "Poslanie Predsedatelia Soveta Ministrov S.S.S.R.Uchastnikam Komiteta 18 Gosudarstv po Razoruzheniiu v Zheneve" [Message of the Chairman of the Council of Ministers of the U.S.S.R. to the Participants in the Eighteen Nation Disarmament Committee], *Pravda* (February 3, 1966), pp. 1, 2.

[11] V. A. Romanov "Vseobshchee i Polnoe Razoruzhenie i Mezhdunarodnoe Pravo" [Universal and Complete Disarmament and International Law], *Sovetskii Ezhegodnik, 1960,* (Moscow: Publishing House of the Academy of Sciences of the U.S.S.R., 1961), pp. 80–91; see 90.

[12] "Reds Cut '65 Budget for Arms," *The Washington Post* (December 10, 1964), p. A-1. See also Kosygin's Speech to the Supreme Soviet (December 9, 1964) on the State Economic Plan for 1965 in *Pravda* (December 10, 1964), pp. 3, 4.

[13] "Kosygin Says U.S. Policy Foments War and Forces Soviet Arms Budget Rise," *The New York Times* (December 8, 1965), pp. 1 and 20; see 1.

—»»)«(«—

There is such strong support all over the world for the Soviet Union's consistent and firm demand for some earnest measures in nuclear disarmament that the Western Powers could not afford to retain their openly negative stand on this issue. . . .The Soviet Government has proposed agreement on the following concrete issues: withdrawal of foreign troops from the territory of other countries; reduction in the total numerical strength of the armed forces of states; reduction of military budgets; conclusion of a nonaggression pact between the NATO and Warsaw Treaty countries; the setting up of atom-free zones; prevention of the further spread of nuclear weapons; measures to prevent surprise attack; destruction of the bomber air force; and prohibition of underground nuclear tests.

It is clear, therefore, that the Western Powers in the Eighteen-Nation Committee took a negative stand on all concrete proposals aimed at mitigating the threat of war, and this is what has brought about the impasse and prevented any progress in its deliberations over the period.[14]

...the Soviet Union needs not war but the peaceful coexistence of states with different social systems, not an arms race but general and complete disarmament. But, as is known, the reactionary imperialist forces have not abandoned their schemes for wiping out the U.S.S.R. and other socialist countries by military means. The military preparations of the imperialist powers are aimed against the U.S.S.R. and the entire socialist camp. It is this that compels the Soviet Union to prepare plans for the repulse of imperialist aggression.[15]

The Soviet Union emerges from the propaganda smoke screen as the patient proponent of peace and arms control; the capitalist states as an aggressive, obstructionist force.

The propaganda exploitation of Soviet diplomatic initiatives is enhanced by the specific claim that arms control provides the material guarantee for the realization of peaceful coexistence, collective security, and an effective international legal order.[16] They claim

---

[14] K. Semyonov, "Geneva: Another Impasse," *International Affairs*, No. 11 (1964), pp. 10–16; see 10–15. See also "Pochemu Oni Blokiruiut Razoruzhenie?" [Why Do They Block Disarmament?], *Pravda* (October 10, 1964), p. 3; and Y. Mikhailov, "Fifth Year at Geneva" (Eighteen-Nation Disarmament Committee Resumes Work), *International Affairs*, No. 3 (1966), pp. 43–45.

[15] "Marshall Sokolovsky on Art of War in Nuclear Age," trans. from *Krasnaia Zvezda* [Red Star], in *CDSP*, XVI, No. 38, pp. 14–18; see 14.

[16] G. P. Zadorozhnyi, *Mirnoe Sosushchestvovanie i Mezhdunarodnoe Pravo* [Peaceful Coexistence and International Law] (Moscow: Publishing House "International Relations," 1964), p. 219; V. K. Sobakin, *Kollektivnaia Bezopasnost'— Garantiia Mirnovo Sosushchestvovaniia* [Collective Security—Guarantee of Peaceful Coexistence] (Moscow: Publishing House of the Institute of International Relations, 1962), pp. 203, 204.

that arms control will ensure peace, respect for state sovereignty, and elimination of all forms of colonialism, imperialism, and military intervention in the internal affairs of any state.[17] Only Soviet-supported arms control measures can have this beneficial effect, since indiscriminate arms control can lead to the undermining of the security of states and new opportunities for Western imperialism.[18] To avoid this possibility, arms control must be an integral part of the policy and law of peaceful coexistence.

The Soviets are not unmindful of the economic advantages of arms control:

> The arms race implies, on the one hand, the accumulation of means of warfare, which enhances the danger of an outbreak of war, and, on the other, the diversion of huge forces and resources needed for satisfying the peaceful requirements of society.[19]

Intent upon further rapid industrialization ("the development of the material and technical bases of communism") and utilizing a resource pie that can be cut only so many ways, the Soviet leadership has long been confronted with the need to juggle the competing demands of various sectors of the economy (e.g., housing, agriculture, and consumer-oriented production versus armaments and heavy industry). Resource expenditure for armaments above minimal security requirements is wasteful in terms of the industrialization effort.

> The. . .nature of the U.S.S.R. as a socialist country objectively calls for only the planning of the development of the national economy in the interests of the victory of communism and the creation of an abundance of material and spiritual benefits for the people. For this the Soviet Union

---

[17] B. Mikhailov, "Konferentsiia Iuristov-Mezhdunarodnikov" [Conference of International Jurists], *SGIP*, No. 10 (1963), pp. 147, 148; see 148. See V. K. Sobakin, Review of N. A. Ushakov, *Suvernitet v Sovremennom Mezhdunarodnom Prave* [Sovereignty in Contemporary International Law] (Moscow: Publishing House of the Institute of International Relations, 1963), *SGIP*, No. 3 (1964), pp. 153, 154; see 154; and Bobrov, *Mezhdunarodnoe Pravo, op. cit., supra* note 1, p. 9.

[18] *Ibid.*, p. 147.

[19] Konstantin Ivanov and Boris Batsanov, *What Disarmament Will Give to Developing Countries* (n. p.: Novosti Press Agency Publishing House, n.d.), p. 24.

needs not war but the peaceful coexistence of states with different social systems, not an arms race but general and complete disarmament.[20]

Support for national liberation movements, an integral part of the struggle for communism, and the Soviet Union's self-assumed role of defender of peoples seeking national independence and of the socialist camp broaden the concept of minimal security requirements. Nevertheless, Soviet military expenditures could be reduced if the proper international environment (i.e., peaceful coexistence and, specifically, general and complete disarmament, Soviet-style) were created. Economic considerations are even more compelling in the present era of "goulash communism" and the new leadership's attempts to improve the performance of a faltering economy.[21] Thus, Soviet arms control policy is principally motivated by foreign and domestic needs in the building of communism.

THE LEGAL POSITION

To reinforce its propaganda and diplomatic initiatives, the Soviet Union has embarked upon a legal offensive in support of its arms control policies. The arms race is denounced as illegal. As a consequence, it is claimed that states are obligated to disarm.[22] Moreover, the rejection of aggressive war has converted the political need for disarmament into a legal norm.[23]

---

[20] Sokolovsky, *op. cit., supra* note 14, p. 14. See also *U.S.S.R., Soviet Life Today*, No. 12 (1964), pp. 7, 8, the answer to the question "What Part Will Science Play as a Direct Productive Force?" and p. 37, the answer to the question, "What are Communists Really Interested In—International Tension and Wars, Or a Stable International Situation and Peace?"

[21] It has been suggested that the 1964 cuts in the Soviet military budget were dictated by pressing internal developmental needs. (Charles Bartlett, "Reds Turn Their Attention to Internal Needs," *The Sunday Star* [December 13, 1964], p. A-20. See also Richard Fryklund, "U.S. and Soviet Union Slow Up Arms Race," *Ibid.*, pp. A-1 and A-22. See also Kosygin's Speech to the Supreme Soviet, *op. cit., supra* note 12, pp. 3, 4.)

[22] Zadorozhnyi, Mirnoe Sosushchestvovanie, *op. cit., supra* note 16, p. 400.

[23] R. L. Bobrov and S. A. Malinin, Review of O. V. Bogdanov, *Vseobschee i Polnoe Razoruzhenie* (*Mezhdunarodnopravovye Voprosy* [General and Complete Disarmament (International Legal Problems)], (Moscow: Publishing House "International Relations," 1964), *SGIP*, No. 8 (1964), pp. 152–154; see 152.

->>)<<-

Disarmament is today not only a political problem, but also a problem of international law. Operative international law contains a number of principles designed to determine the approach of states to disarmament as a whole and to its individual aspects. The struggle for disarmament is now to a certain extent the struggle for the implementation of international law.[24]

Further, disarmament is described as an indispensable principle of the law of peaceful coexistence as that law "demands the striving of states towards the strengthening of peace and not preparation for a new war."[25]

The necessity of disarmament . . . follows from the generally recognized principles and norms of contemporary international law which prohibit war as a means of resolving international disputes.[26]

Based upon the foregoing and the fact that disarmament is mentioned as an organizational objective in the Charter of the United Nations and in unanimously adopted resolutions of the General Assembly, it is said that disarmament is recognized as a principle of international law.[27] The Soviet-sponsored principle of general and complete disarmament, on the other hand, is considered a new

[24] O. V. Bogdanov, "O Znachenii i Soderzhanii Printsipa Razoruzheniia v Sovremennom Mezhdunarodnom Prave" [The Significance and Essence of the Principle of Disarmament in Contemporary International Law], *Sovetskii Ezhegodnik, 1961* (Moscow: Publishing House of the Academy of Sciences of the U.S.S.R., 1962), pp. 94–117; see 116.

[25] G. I. Tunkin, "Printsip Mirnovo Sosushchestvovaniia—General'naia Liniia Vneshnepoliticheskoi Deiatel'nosti KPSS i Sovetskovo Gosudarstva" [The Principle of Peaceful Coexistence—The General Line of the Foreign Policy of the *CPSU* and the Soviet State], *SGIP*, No. 7 (1963), pp. 26–37; see 33.

[26] Mikhailov, *op. cit., supra* note 17, p. 147.

[27] O. V. Bogdanov, *Vseobshchee i Polnoe Razoruzhenie (Mezhdunarodno-pravovye Voprosy)* [General and Complete Disarmament (International Legal Problems)] (Moscow: Publishing House "International Relations," 1964), pp. 101–125. In an earlier commentary, Bogdanov (most active in the legal obligation approach to disarmament) had referred to disarmament "as one of the principles advanced by socialism which had received in recent years wide international acceptance" (O. V. Bogdanov, "Mezhdunarodnopravovye Aspekty Osushchestvleniia Vseobshchevo i Polnovo Razoruzheniia" [International Legal Aspects of the Realization of General and Complete Disarmament], *SGIP*, No. 6 (1962), pp. 87–99; see 99). See also G. I. Tunkin, *Voprosy Teorii Mezhdunarodnovo Prava* [Problems of the Theory of International Law] (Moscow: State Publishing House of Legal Literature, 1962), pp. 56, 57; and Zadorozhnyi, Mirnoe Sosushchestvovania, *op. cit., supra* note 16, pp. 226–233.

principle of great importance which is in the process of being established in modern international law;[28] although it is claimed that "One can already say that agreement has been reached on the goal of general and complete disarmament."[29] As the principle has not been established as yet, "states still enjoy the right to maintain armies and arms";[30] however, the principle does operate to the extent that "it imposes an obligation on states to work out in the shortest possible time a document which would clearly and un-equivocally establish the manner and times for the elimination of the armed forces and arms of all countries."[31] The preamble to the Limited Test Ban Treaty (1963) with its reference to the major goal of an agreement for general and complete disarmament under strict international control, is characterized "as an obligation which broadens the scope of the treaty and constitutes a step in the strengthening of the principle of general and complete disarma-ment."[32] The Soviet Union claims the principal role in the con-firmation of disarmament as a general principle of international law and in seeking similar confirmation for general and complete disarmament.[33]

The Soviets claim that "the conclusion of an agreement . . . for general and complete disarmament would create effective juridical and material guarantees of the principle of nonaggression, and, as a consequence, the principle of peaceful coexistence."[34] To be effec-tive, however, such agreement must be complemented by other arms control measures strengthening peaceful coexistence.

[28] Bogdanov, *Vseobshchee i Polnoe Razoruzhenie, op. cit., supra* note 27, pp. 128, 129.

[29] *OON i Aktual'nye Mezhdunarodnye Problemy, op. cit., supra* note 5, p. 340.

[30] Bogdanov, *Vseobshchee i Polnoe Razoruzhenie, op. cit., supra* note 27, p. 130.

[31] *Ibid.*

[32] I. G. Usachev, "Moskovskii Dogovor o Chastichnom Zapreshchenii Ispytanii Iadernovo Oruzhiia i Mezhdunarodnoe Pravo" [The Moscow Treaty Concerning the Partial Prohibition of the Testing of Nuclear Weapons and International Law], *SGIP*, No. 3 (1964), pp. 72–78; see 77. The preamble of the Draft Treaty on the Non-Dissemination of Nuclear Weapons also contains a reference to the goal of "general and complete disarmament under strict inter-national control" ("Documents", *New Times, op. cit., supra* note 9, p. 31).

[33] Bobrov and Malinin, *op. cit., supra* note 23, p. 152.

[34] Tunkin, Voprosy Teorii, *op. cit., supra* note 27, p. 59.

➤➤)《《◄

Before general and complete disarmament can be accomplished other measures strengthening peaceful coexistence are needed such as the creation of nuclear-free zones, withdrawal of troops stationed abroad, liquidation of foreign bases, prohibition of nuclear testing, dissolution of military blocs, etc.[35]

To add appeal to their proposal for general and complete disarmament, the Soviets include the requirement that the disarmament be effected under "strict international control."

The Soviet concept of "strict international control" contains a special, positivist wrinkle which affects its salability to the West. Under the Soviet view, international control must be based upon the sovereign equality of states, and must not infringe upon the basic rights of sovereign states.[36] This dilution of control by the primacy accorded sovereign prerogatives lies at the heart of the inability to conclude a general arms control agreement. Western demands for "inspection" and "control" are characterized as "excessive" and dismissed as ruses to "torpedo" constructive Soviet proposals.[37]

In support of their policies against proliferation and nuclear-testing by the West, the Soviets claim that even in the absence of treaty, such testing would violate international law when conducted outside of a state's own territory (e.g., United States testing in trust territories), or in areas of the high seas.[38] Utilizing the double standard, Soviet jurists hold that past Soviet testing, done only in response to testing by the West and conducted within the territory

[35] Zadorozhnyi, Mirnoe Sosushchestvovanie, *op. cit.*, *supra* note 16, p. 233.

[36] Mikhailov, *op. cit.*, *supra* note 17, p. 148. See also Ivanov and Batsanov, *op. cit.*, *supra* note 19, pp. 9–23, for a discussion of the Soviet proposal for general and complete disarmament.

[37] G. Deinichenke, "Geneva Disarmament Talks," *New Times*, No. 38 (September 22, 1965), pp. 4–6; see 5.

[38] Usachev, *op. cit.*, *supra* note 32, pp. 74, 75. See also A. N. Talalaev, Review of O. V. Bogdanov, *Iadernoe Razoruzhenie* [Nuclear Disarmament] (Moscow: Publishing House of the Institute of International Relations, 1961), *Sovetskii Ezhegodnik, 1962* (Moscow: Publishing House of the Academy of Sciences of the U.S.S.R., 1963), pp. 308–310; see 309. See Nikolai Fedorenko, "The U.N. and Nuclear Weapons," *New Times*, No. 44 (November 2, 1965), pp. 3–5, for a statement of the Soviet policy against proliferation.

of the Soviet Union, was not illegal.[39] The claim of illegality based upon infringement of the territorial sovereignty of another state or the high seas is bolstered by the socialist content attributed to international medical law. (These three arguments formed the basis of the Soviet protest following the Palomares incident [1966] involving the temporary "loss" of a United States nuclear device as a result of an air accident.)[40] The Western approach to this law as a part of the law of war (e.g., related to the Geneva and other conventions dealing with the law of war) is said to be outdated in light of the law of peaceful coexistence. The socialist content of international medical law requires protection of the health of mankind in time of peace and war, with special emphasis upon the former because of the reduced importance of the latter under the law of coexistence. Drawing upon this new appealing content, the Soviets claim that international medical law should govern the resolution of the problems of nuclear disarmament, nuclear testing and the peaceful use of nuclear-energy, and call for its codification to that end.[41] The Soviet approach here demonstrates the art of the international legal

---

[39] *Ibid.* The claim is, of course, that Soviet tests do not violate the territory of another state or the freedom of the high seas. Insofar as air pollution is relied upon as another legal objection to nuclear testing. See *Soviet Impact on International Law* [External Research Paper 156] (Washington, D.C.: U.S. Department of State, Bureau of Intelligence and Research, May 1964), p. 4; and Talalaev, *op. cit., supra* note 38, p. 310, the Soviets note that when they test, all necessary measures are taken to minimize the adverse effects. (Usachev, *op. cit., supra* note 23, pp. 75 and 76.)

[40] Soviet Government Memorandum to the United States Government, dated February 16, 1966, trans. from *Pravda* and *Izvestiia* (February 18, 1966), in *CDSP*, XVIII, No. 7, p. 19.

[41] O. S. Padbil', "Nekotorye Problemy Mezhdunarodnovo Meditsinskovo Prava" [Some Problems of International Medical Law], *Sovetskii Ezhegodnik, 1963* (Moscow: Publishing House "Science," 1965), pp. 303–307; and V. S. Mikhailov, "K Voprosu o Mezhdunarodnom Meditsinskom Prave" [Concerning International Medical Law], *Ibid.*, pp. 308–322. It is said that although Soviet jurists agree with Western commentators that international medical law is already an independent branch of international law, the former broaden the concept to protection of the health of mankind in peace as well as war, with particular emphasis upon peacetime because of the need for greater protection as a result of advances in nuclear weaponry and technology (Mikhailov, *op. cit., supra*, pp. 310–321). In calling for codification, it is said that the most important problem area to be covered by the new law is nuclear disarmament and the use of nuclear energy for peaceful means (Padbil', *op. cit., supra*, pp. 304–306).

specialist. Building upon Western acceptance of the existence of a separate body of international medical law, Soviet scholars expand it to serve a policy need of the Soviet Union under the cover of a new progressive, socialist content, and then call for codification to express this new content. This masterful use of the bootstrap is intended to supplement the Limited Test Ban Treaty which has made express the prohibition on nuclear-testing (with the exception of those tests conducted underground).

The Moscow Treaty has completely clarified and confirmed the conclusion of international legal specialists who support progressive norms of international law. Nuclear-weapon testing resulting in radioactive pollution of man's environment is prohibited by an international document supported by more than 100 states.[42]

The Soviets can be expected to continue their efforts, through creative interpretation of extant international legal principles and campaigns for codification, to achieve the nuclear disarmament objectives of the Soviet Union. In all probability, Western resistance to Soviet creativity or codification proposals will continue to be subjected to virulent propaganda attacks which attribute sinister motives to Western caution in reaching agreements with the Soviet Union on nuclear disarmament.[43]

The Soviet Union has frequently proposed the creation of nuclear-free or demilitarized zones for strategic areas, including the atmosphere. Although they continually cite the 1959 Agreement concerning the Antarctic as a persuasive legal precedent for a formal arrangement,[44] the Soviets say that such zones can also result from

[42] Usachev, *op. cit., supra* note 32, pp. 75, 76. "The Moscow partial test ban treaty is of great importance and it is a basic source of international medical law." (Mikhailov, *op. cit., supra* note 41, p. 322.)

[43] The failure of the West in 1965 to accept a Soviet proposed convention forbidding the use of nuclear and thermonuclear weapons is laid to the "strategy of 'atomic intimidation' of the peoples of Asia, Africa and Latin America. . .to impede the. . .national liberation struggle and the strengthening of young independent states." (Victor Mayevsky, "Before the Return to Geneva," trans. from *Pravda* [July 25, 1965], in *CDSP*, XVII, No. 30, pp. 23, 24; see 23.)

[44] B. M. Klimenko, "Demilitarizatsiia Territorii v Svete Problemy Razoruzheniia" [The Demilitarization of Territory and the Problem of Disarmament], *SGIP*, No. 4 (1962), pp. 98–108; see 107. See also B. M. Klimenko, "K Voprosu o Neitralizatsii Territorii v Sovremennom Mezhdunarodnom Prave" [The Problem of the Neutralization of Territories in Contemporary International Law], *Sovetskii Ezhegodnik, 1961, op. cit., supra* note 24, pp. 208–219.

unilateral or joint declarations.[45] They claim that demilitarization and neutralization of outer space have already become a part of international law, by virtue of the unanimous approval of the December 20, 1961 Resolution of the General Assembly on the peaceful use of outer space.[46]

The question of neutrality is related to demilitarization and neutralization. The Soviet approach to neutrality and neutralism has varied to meet the needs of the Soviet Union. From absolute rejection during World War II as a form of connivance and the handmaiden of aggression, it is now considered a positive aid in realizing peaceful coexistence.[47] The rationale for this variation is stated as follows:

> The status and rules of neutrality change in each historical epoch to suit specific economic, social and political conditions and, particularly, the nature of each war . . . . There can be no absolute criteria in an evaluation of the varieties and instances of neutrality in different historical epochs. . . . Specific analysis of a specific situation is the decisive factor in defining the significance of neutrality in various periods of history.[48]

At the present time, Soviet commentators wholeheartedly endorse neutrality and neutralism (in the sense of nonalignment with military blocs) as institutions promoting world peace and peaceful coexistence.[49]

---

[45] B. M. Klimenko, "Osnovnye Printsipy Sozdaniia Bez'iardernykh Zon" [The Basic Principles for the Creation of Nuclear-free Zones], *SGIP*, No. 12 (1964), pp. 110–115; see 112.

[46] G. P. Zhukov, "Demilitarizatsiia i Neitralizatsiia Kosmicheskovo Prostranstva" [Demilitarization and Neutralization of Outer Space], *SGIP*, No. 3 (1964), pp. 79–89, for a discussion of subsequent actions in the United Nations and elsewhere confirming the author's conclusion.

[47] E. Korovin, "Likvidirovat' Posledstviia Kul'ta Lichnosti v Nauke Mezhdunarodnovo Prava [Eliminate the Consequences of the Cult of the Individual in the Science of International Law], *Sotsialisticheskaia Zakonnost'* [Socialist Legality], No. 8 (1962), pp. 46–49; see 48.

[48] D. Melnikov, "Neutrality and the Current Situation," *International Affairs*, No. 2 (1965), pp. 74, 75.

[49] A. Galina, "Problema Neitraliteta v Sovremennom Mezhdunarodnom Prave" [The Problem of Neutrality in Contemporary International Law], *Sovetskii Ezhegodnik, 1958* (Moscow: Publishing House of the Academy of Sciences of the U.S.S.R., 1959), pp. 200–229. See also, S. Beglov, "Neitralitet v Sevodniashnem Mire" [Neutrality in Today's World], *Pravda* (April 19, 1965), p. 3.

Under contemporary conditions neutrality is understood in international law as a legal status of a state in time of peace as well as war. This is related to the general change in the content of international law which now is directed not only against aggression which has been committed but also and, above all, its prevention.[50]

Neutrality and the policy of neutrality are of great importance in present day international law and practice as a means of promoting peaceful coexistence and of demonstrating devotion to peace.

The policy of neutrality is that consistently pursued by a peace-loving state in remaining outside military blocs and wars.[51]

...the status of neutrality not only does not exclude, but actually contemplates membership and active participation in international organizations which contribute to the strengthening of general peace, and also active participation in the struggle against the unleashing of wars of aggression and for the creation of an effective system of collective security.[52]

In addition to transforming neutrality from a wartime to a peaceful status, the Soviets have created new forms of neutrality to further Soviet objectives. The new formulations include "active, positive neutrality" (the policy of nonalignment with support of Soviet positions)[53] and "nuclear neutrality."

"Active, positive neutrality,"..."a form of peaceful coexistence of states with different systems,"[54] is actually the policy of nonalignment with a Soviet label to indicate support for the progressive principles of the socialist camp not otherwise inferable from the blander nonalignment formulation. To some extent "neutrality" is a misnomer, since active and positive support for, rather than neutrality towards, "preventing a world military holocaust and abolishing colonialism" is claimed. The Soviets look upon the

---

[50] *Mezhdunarodnoe Pravo* [International Law], ed. V. I. Kozhevnikov (Moscow: Publishing House "International Relations," 1964), p. 630.

[51] V. N. Durdenevsky, "Neitralitet i Atomnoe Oruzhie (v Svete Printsipa Mirnovo Sosushchestvovaniia)" [Neutrality and Atomic Weapons (In the Light of the Principle of Peaceful Co-existence)], *Sovetskii Ezhegodnik, 1960, op. cit.,* *supra* note 11, pp. 104–108; see 108.

[52] L. A. Modzhorian, *Osnovnye Prava i Obiazannosti Gosudarstv* [The Fundamental Rights and Duties of States] (Moscow: Publishing House "Legal Literature," 1965), p. 53.

[53] *The Evening Star* (June 18, 1965), p. A-2, quoting Kosygin.

[54] M. I. Lazarev, "Mezhdunarodnopravovye Voprosy Dvizheniia Narodov za Mir" [International Legal Aspects of the Peoples' Movement for Peace], *Sovetskii Ezhegodnik, 1963, op. cit., supra* note 41, pp. 45–69; see 61.

specific basis of active, positive neutrality (i.e., support for the Soviet-sponsored legal bans on colonialism and aggression) as the foundation for wider nonalignment in the sense of accepting all of the principles of coexistence. Pursuit by many states of the policy of active, positive neutrality or nonalignment confirms the Soviet belief that the principles of peaceful coexistence can unite all peace-loving states, irrespective of continent or race, in the struggle against imperialism and colonialism.[55]

Nuclear neutrality, on the other hand, more closely resembles neutrality in that it involves, on the part of the state concerned, an obligation

. . . to refrain from the production, acquisition or possession of such weapons, and also not to permit the stationing of nuclear weapons of any kind on its territory, and also not to permit the establishment on its territory of installations and equipment servicing nuclear weapons, including rocket-launching installations.[56]

Nuclear neutrality is said to be similar to permanent neutrality, except that under the latter, the maintenance of weapons is permitted for defensive purposes. The former contemplates the complete absence of nuclear weapons, thereby providing the legal basis for national nuclear-free zones.[57] As in the case of nuclear-free and demilitarized zones, a unilateral declaration of nuclear or permanent neutrality "can have international legal significance if. . .recognized by other states or confirmed in international agreements.[58] To assist in the normative process, the Soviets say that the recognition of neutrality can be express or tacit. The positivist strain of Soviet positions reflected in the importance generally accorded the consent of states is relaxed in the Soviet interest, and they hold that (1) "the absence of protest signifies that neutrality has been tacitly recognized," and (2) states are obliged to

[55] P. A. Tuzmukhamedov, "Ustav Organizatsii Afrikanskovo Edinstva v Svete Mezhdunarodnovo Prava," [The Charter of the Organization of African Unity in the Light of International Law], *Sovetskii Ezhegodnik, 1963, op. cit., supra* note 41, pp. 109–128; see 127.

[56] Durdenevsky, *op. cit., supra* note 51, p. 108.

[57] Klimenko, "Osnovnye Printsipy Sozdaniia Bez'iardernykh Zon," *op. cit., supra* note 45, p. 113.

[58] *Ibid.*, p. 114.

⇉⦉⦉

recognize neutrality because war is no longer legal.[59] As a compensating, protective device, however, it is specified that only those declarations of neutrality which are consistent with peaceful coexistence should be respected:

...to the extent that [nuclear neutrality] does not infringe upon the sovereign rights of third states and is directed, in accordance with the provisions of the Charter of the United Nations, at the maintenance and strengthening of international peace and security, it should be respected by all states.[60]

The reference to the provisions of the Charter is a euphemism for consistency with the requirements of peaceful coexistence.

The collateral attack on Western bases implicit in the concept of nuclear-free and demilitarized zones is reinforced by the more direct claim of growing support for a universal rule prohibiting military bases on foreign territory as the logical outgrowth of the principles of peaceful coexistence and general and complete disarmament.[61] The Soviets hold that such a prohibition can also be implied from a nonaggression treaty which "presupposes the prohibition on the territory of both contracting parties of foreign military bases spearheaded against the other party."[62] (This approach would indicate hidden pitfalls in the conclusion of the oft-Soviet proposed nonagression pact between the North Atlantic Treaty Organization and Warsaw Pact countries.) A more extensive attack on Western

[59] *Ibid.*

[60] *Ibid.*

[61] M. I. Lazarev, "Zapreshchenie Inostrannykh Voennykh Baz na Chuzhikh Territoriiakh Normami Mezhdunarodnovo Prava" [Prohibition of Foreign Military Bases by Norms of International Law], *Sovetskii Ezhegodnik, 1962* (Moscow: Publishing House of Academy of Sciences of U.S.S.R., 1963), pp. 64–77; see 76. In an earlier commentary (M. I. Lararev, "Vopros ob Inostrahnykh Voennykh Bazakh i Vooruzhennykh Silakh na Chuzhikh Territoriiakh v Mezhdunarodno-pravovoi Literature" [The Problem of Foreign Military Bases and Armed Forces Abroad in Writings on International Law], *Sovetskii Ezhegodnik, 1960, op. cit., supra* note 11, pp. 371–380; see 380), Lazarev notes that present day international law makes no provision for military bases or the stationing of forces abroad and criticizes Western writers for accepting them as institutions of international law and ignoring the need to prohibit such bases and stationing "in the present epoch of peaceful coexistence and the struggle for disarmament."

[62] *Ibid.*

military bases in a 1964 Soviet commentary notes their incompatibility with peaceful coexistence because: they (*1*) violate the principles of respect for territorial integrity and sovereignty, nonaggression, noninterference, and equality and mutual benefit, and (*2*) "abuse the UN Charter."[63] Further, the Soviets say that "the establishment of military bases in the territory of other countries today is an. . .international crime" and that violations of base agreements by the host state do not entail any legal responsibility for that state, presumably because the agreements are unenforceable because illegal.[64] The cited commentary suggests that the express banning of foreign bases by international agreement should be couched in terms of "strong points" rather than military bases, since the latter formulation is not broad enough to cover Western devices to camouflage them (e.g., civil airfields, concessions, ship anchorages, and supply depots). To further ensure its effectiveness, the agreement should contain a universal prohibition on the deployment of armed forces abroad.[65] Another commentary suggests widespread support for such an agreement:

> In the changed international conditions, sovereign states struggling to strengthen their political independence. . .demand the dissolution of unjust and illegal, from the point of view of contemporary international law, agreements for territorial concessions and the liquidation of foreign military bases and the withdrawal of foreign forces.[66]

The Soviet position here reinforces the other legal bases for attacks on Western military bases considered previously (i.e., that the agreements providing for such bases are invalid as "unequal" treaties and that foreign bases are a form of neo-colonialism).

[63] A. Pirodov, "Bases and International Law," *International Affairs*, No. 5 (1964), pp. 98, 99; see 99. Piradov essentially repeats the thesis of M. I. Lazarev, *Imperialisticheskie Voennye Bazy na Chuzhikh Territoriakh i Mezhdunarodnoe Pravo* [Foreign Military Bases of Imperialist Countries and International Law] (Moscow: Publishing House of the Institute of International Relations, 1963), pp. 74–208.

[64] *Ibid.*

[65] *Ibid.*

[66] N. A. Ushakov, "Poslanie N. S. Khrushcheva i Mirnoe Uregulirovanie Territorial'nykh Sporov mezhdu Gosudarstvami" [N. S. Khrushchev's Message and the Peaceful Settlement of Territorial Disputes Between States], *SGIP*, No.5 (1964), pp. 3–10; see 9.

-》》《《-

Although Polaris submarines are not barred by the principle against territorial bases they are said to be illegal "as mobile missile bases. . . designed to conceal preparations for striking a surprise nuclear blow. Such actions are a conspiracy against the peace and are condemned by the Statute of the International Military Tribunal [Charter of the International Military Tribunal, October 6, 1945] as preparations for aggression, as an international crime."[67] The rationale of the illegality of the Polaris submarine (i.e., its offensive nuclear character) has recently been extended to military bases by Kosygin. In his February 1, 1966, message to the Eighteen-Nation Disarmament Committee, he calls for their liquidation because they are used to store nuclear weapons, and increase the threat of a nuclear war.[68]

Soviet bases, on the other hand, are not illegal because they are dictated by the struggle against imperialism and colonialism and are provided for by special agreements the most important characteristics of which are "strict observance of the sovereignty of the country where stationed, noninterference in its internal affairs, absolute observance of national legislation and subordination to its jurisdiction, and respect for the rights and interest of the peaceful population."[69] The equality and fairness of these agreements result in the Soviet soldier abroad being "considered a guardian of peace, friend and ally of our brothers in the common struggle for socialism and communism."[70] It is apparent that the Soviets rely upon a double standard of characterization to resolve the dilemma of a state which seeks to maintain its own base arrangements and, at the same time, to eliminate those of states potentially hostile to it.

In pursuing their arms control policy, the Soviets have not neglected the "legal basis in [sic] relationships between disarmed states."[71] To minimize restrictions upon the freedom of action of the

[67] Lazarev, *op. cit., supra* note 61, p. 77.
[68] Poslanie, *op. cit., supra* note 10, p. 1.
[69] M. E. Volosov, "Desiatiletie Varshavskovo Dogovora" [Tenth Anniversary of the Warsaw Pact], *SGIP*, No. 8 (1965), pp. 123, 124; see 124.
[70] *Ibid.*
[71] O. V. Bogdanov, "Security of States in a Disarmed World and International Law," trans. from *SGIP*, No. 9 (1963), in *The Daily Review* (Moscow), IX, No. 87 (November 12, 1963), pp. 1, 12.

Soviet Union in a disarmed world, they have reiterated their traditional aversion to world government, "world law," and non-socialist judicial settlement by insisting upon an expanded concept of respect for state sovereignty and noninterference in domestic affairs.[72]

There is no reason to assume that the liquidation of the instruments of war will create favorable conditions for the institution of "world" government bodies or a system of "world" law. Disarmament does not abolish the social distinctions between states. Hence every state will, as before, possess the sovereign right to resolve its domestic problems as it thinks fit. To ensure the inviolability of this right it will be necessary to fortify the principle of sovereignty and all the principles stemming therefrom.
The objective laws of social development in our time . . . exclude in very principle the possibility of applying for this purpose conceptions of "supranational authority" and a system of "world" law based on a negation of the sovereignty of states. That is why the imperialist international and legal doctrines and practices which propagate a "supranational" approach to regulating relations between disarmed states is totally unacceptable.[73]

The rationale for the Soviet position is that social and political contradictions and conflicts will remain in a disarmed world and require a greater role for international law (i.e., the law of peaceful coexistence).[74] The increased role of law will be to accord greater protection to state sovereignty in the interest of coexistence, rather than to strengthen the international legal order.

In the Soviet view, world disarmament will not change the nature of international relations, so long as the two systems exist except that "armed force as an instrument of foreign policy will be not only illegal as it now is, but actually beyond the capability of states."[75] Therefore, the principles of the United Nations—"nothing other than the principles of peaceful coexistence"—will continue to be applicable until the world victory of socialism:[76]

---

[72] *Ibid.*, pp. 11, 12.

[73] *Ibid.*

[74] Mikhailov, *op. cit.*, *supra* note 17, p. 148.

[75] *OON i Aktual'nye Mezhdunarodnye Problemy*, *op. cit.*, *supra* note 5, p. 341. It is said, however, that there will be a greater tendency towards justice rather than might in the settling of international disputes (*Ibid.*, p. 342).

[76] *Ibid.*, p. 342.

...the means of ensuring international security under complete disarmament . . . [will be] the general principles of international law and the machinery for cutting short breaches of the peace as provided by the U.N.
Charter (U.N. sanctions).[77]

The Soviets recognize, however, that the United Nations system will
have to be strengthened, along with the procedures for the peaceful
settlement of disputes, including the International Court of Justice.
The Soviet concept of strengthening the United Nations system
involves a greater role for the Security Council and a reorganization
of the Secretariat and the Security Council to reflect existence of the
three groups of states: socialist, capitalist, and neutralist. The
International Court of Justice would be "strengthened," not through
expanded competence or jurisdiction, but by a similar reorganization of Court membership to ensure adequate representation of the
three groups of states.[78]

The legal positions in support of Soviet arms control policies
provide an excellent example of the use of law in a policy offensive.
They highlight the general Soviet view that extra mileage can be
obtained from the persuasive force of law in pursuing foreign policy
objectives.

The Socialist states call for strict observance of the principles and rules of
international law. At the same time they fight unswervingly for the incorporation into international law of new progressive principles and rules
furthering peaceful coexistence.[79]

As is apparent, law must be given a socialist content to have the
desired persuasive effect.

[77] Korovin, "The Way to Peace," *op. cit., supra* note 2, p. 74.
[78] Mikhailov, *op. cit., supra* note 17, p. 148.
[79] G. I. Tunkin, "Vstupitel'naia Stat'ia" [Introduction], *Sovetskii Ezhegodnik,
1960, op. cit., supra* note 11, pp. 15–27; see 22, 23.

CHAPTER TWELVE

INTERNATIONAL RELATIONS

Peaceful coexistence is the Soviet political and legal formula for international relations during the present epoch. The requirement that the capitalist and socialist systems coexist, stemming from the need to compete "peacefully" because of the impermissibility and unacceptability of a thermonuclear war, is the stated foundation for the policy and law of peaceful coexistence. The policy and the law are said to require "the normalization of relations between states without regard to their social orders," "broad, mutually profitable collaboration on all questions, joint solutions to problems and. . .friendly, good neighborly relations."[1] These formulations tend to conceal the revolutionary character of peaceful coexistence as the best method in the Soviet view—but the bone of contention with the Chinese—of overcoming, peacefully and in the interest of world socialism, "the main contradiction" of contemporary international relations, i.e., the existence of the two contending social economic systems. Under this view, the victory of socialism is assured by the objective laws of social development, with peaceful coexistence providing the political and legal environment for the operation of these laws.[2]

The principle of peaceful coexistence is directed at the maintenance and strengthening of peaceful relations between states while the two systems

---

[1] G. P. Zadorozhnyi, *Mirnoe Sosushchestvovanie i Mezhdunarodnoe Pravo* [Peaceful Coexistence and International Law] (Moscow: Publishing House "International Relations," 1964), pp. 19 and 248.

[2] Mark Rosenthal, *Contradictions and Motive Forces of Present Epoch* (Pamphlet) (n.p.: Novosti Press Agency Publishing House, n.d.), pp. 13–15.

compete peacefully in economic, scientific, technical, cultural and other fields of peaceful construction.[3]

International law ensures the peaceful condition for competition between the two systems in the course of which the superiority of a system is established not by weapons but by the level of satisfaction of the national and cultural needs of mankind.[4]

In effect, peaceful coexistence is the formula and strategy for the peaceful victory of socialism over capitalism.[5]

INTERNATIONAL COLLABORATION

Contemporary international law, in the Soviet view, includes the obligation to develop political, economic and cultural collaboration on the basis of complete equality and mutual advantage without regard to the nature of the social systems of the states concerned.[6] As contemporary international law is the law of peaceful coexistence, the collaboration called for is that which contributes to coexistence:

... the principal idea of international collaboration is the necessity of mutual agreement in deciding international problems in a manner which takes account of the interests of the states of the different social systems in the interest of securing peace and peaceful coexistence.[7]

Thus, the Soviets claim, all states are obligated to collaborate actively "to eliminate all that interferes with peaceful coexistence." Specifically, it is said that respect for sovereignty, the equality of states and systems, noninterference in internal affairs, the impermissibility of aggression, and all the other principles of peaceful coexistence provide the legal basis for, and therefore require, "broad, fruitful and mutually advantageous international collaboration on all matters under conditions of peace."[8] The Charter of the

[3] G. I. Tunkin, *Voprosy Teorii Mezhdunarodnovo Prava* [Problems of the Theory of International Law] (Moscow: State Publishing House of Legal Literature, 1962), pp. 53, 54.

[4] Zadorozhnyi, Mirnoe Sosushchestvovanie, *op. cit., supra* note 1, p. 314.

[5] Rosenthal, *op. cit., supra* note 2, p. 15.

[6] Tunkin, Voprosy Teorii, *op. cit., supra* note 3, p. 53.

[7] *OON i Aktual'nye Mezhdunarodnye Problemy* [The U.N. and Contemporary International Problems] ed. V. A. Zorin and G. I. Morozov (Moscow: Publishing House "International Relations," 1965), p. 3.

[8] Zadorozhnyi, Mirnoe Sosushchestvovanie, *op. cit., supra* note 5, p. 401.

United Nations, said to impose the legal obligation to conclude arrangements for international collaboration and for developing and strengthening friendly relations between states, is used to confirm the Soviet position.[9] The principal arrangement contemplated is codification of the "obligation of states to collaborate with one another in accordance with the Charter [of the United Nations]," the cover for peaceful coexistence.[10]

The legal rationale is intended to provide a persuasive basis for attacking policies which "obstruct" peaceful coexistence and the realization of the particular type of collaboration required under it (i.e., collaboration, which will demonstrate the superiority of socialism). The desired result is freedom of action for the Soviet Union with all other states, capitalist, neutralist, and socialist, "legally" bound to cooperate in collaboration favorable to the "cause of socialism." To appreciate the possibilities of this aspect of the law of coexistence, one need only to consider that the process of creating norms of international law is said to involve the struggle and cooperation of states.[11] The failure to agree, and thereby give effect, to progressive principles of international law can be attacked as a violation of the obligation to collaborate in the interest of eliminating obstacles—in this case, a political obstacle—to peaceful coexistence. This legal bootstrap in support of the transformation of international law along progressive lines provides a basis for limiting, in the Soviet interest, the freedom of choice said to be essential in the creation of international legal norms.[12] In effect, the requirement that states collaborate in the interest of peaceful coexistence can be invoked to harness positivism to the foreign policy needs of the Soviet Union.

The general obligation to collaborate in the realization of coexistence includes economic and cultural collaboration. Soviet commitment to this all-around collaboration is stated in the broadest of terms.

[9] *Ibid.*, p. 273.

[10] V. M. Chkhikvadze, "Voprosy Mezhdunarodnovo Prava na XX Sessii General'noi Assamblei OON" [Problems of International Law at the Twentieth Session of the General Assembly of the U.N.], *SGIP*, No. 3 (1966), pp. 67–78; see 70.

[11] Tunkin, Voprosy Teorii, *op. cit.*, *supra* note 3, p. 86.

[12] See *Ibid.*, p. 211.

->>><<<-

The Soviet Union, like the other countries of socialism, is ready to proceed to all-around peaceful cooperation and normal relations with all capitalist countries. It favors the broad development of mutually advantageous trade, economic, scientific, technical and cultural ties between them, [and] cooperation in behalf of peace and the security of peoples.[13]

The economic and cultural collaboration contemplated, however, is that which serves the cause of peaceful coexistence and all that is subsumed under it.

The principle of peaceful coexistence includes the obligation to develop friendly relations and economic and cultural collaboration between states on the basis of equality and mutual advantage without regard to social systems, and consequently, includes rejection of political boycott of individual countries because of dislike for the social system of that country by the ruling circles of another. The principle of peaceful coexistence is directed at the maintenance and strengthening of peaceful relations between states amid the peaceful competition of the two systems in economic, scientific, technical, cultural and other fields of peaceful behavior.[14]

Peaceful coexistence is said to proceed from the premise that ideological differences are no bar to all-around collaboration, and that maximum advantage should be taken of the rationality of the international division of labor.[15]

The principle of the law of peaceful coexistence which requires international collaboration has a varied operation depending upon the type of states concerned.[16] It is invoked in relations with capitalist states in support of Soviet foreign policies and bids for greater economic and cultural ties, and to attack "cold war" policies, including the policies of quarantine, boycott, and controlled exports of strategic materials directed against socialist countries. In this latter

[13] "The Noble Aims of Soviet Foreign Policy," trans. from *Pravda* (August 8, 1965), in *CDSP*, XVII, No. 32, pp. 3–6; see 5.

[14] G. I. Tunkin, "Printsip Mirnovo Sosushchestvovaniia—General'naia Liniia Vneshnepoliticheskoi Deiatel'nosti KPSS i Sovetskovo Gosudarstva" [The Principle of Peaceful Coexistence—the General Line of the Foreign Policy of the CPSU and the Soviet State], *SGIP*, No. 7 (1963), pp. 26–37; see 33, 34.

[15] Zadorozhnyi, Mirnoe Sosushchestvovanie, *op. cit.*, *supra* note 1, p. 274.

[16] See the symposium entitled "Soviet Foreign Policy and the Contemporary World," *International Affairs*, No. 3 (1966), pp. 2–20, for a statement of Soviet collaboration and other foreign policy objectives vis-à-vis socialist, neutralist, and capitalist states.

connection it is said that the principle of the impermissibility of discrimination in economic relations is one of the most important principles of international law.[17] For example, increased Soviet interest in tourism is supported legally by the view that international tourism is one of the forms of international collaboration required of states with different social systems.[18] On the other hand, criticism is directed against Western states, principally the United States, for not desiring normal economic relations with socialist states.[19] Specifically, in 1964, the United States was criticized for its failure to cooperate with other states in the use of communication satellites for commercial purposes.[20] Similarly, in 1964, criticism was levelled against "Western closed economic blocs" (e.g., the Common Market) for violating the principle of the international division of labor, "the material foundation of peaceful co-existence between the two opposite [sic] socio-economic systems."[21] In levelling this criticism, the unfounded, but rather amusing, claim is made that Western discriminatory practices run counter to the best interests of the people of the states concerned as: "The large orders given Western powers by the Soviet Union reduce unemployment and raise employment and, with it, the living standard of the population in these countries."[22] In contrast, it is claimed that the corresponding economic organization of the socialist commonwealth, the Council for Mutual Economic Assistance, in no way isolates its members from the world economy and world trade, since the Council is developing international socialist division of labor to complement the international division of labor and to promote foreign trade with other countries.[23]

[17] *Mezhdunarodnoe Pravo* [International Law] ed. D. B. Levin and G. P. Kaliuzhnaia (Moscow: Publishing House "Legal Literature," 1964), pp. 329, 330.

[18] K. G. Borisov, "Mezhdunarodnopravovye Aspekty Mezhdunarodnovo Turizma" [International Legal Aspects of International Tourism], *SGIP*, No. 7 (1965), pp. 138–142; see 138.

[19] Zadorozhnyi, Mirnoe Sosushchestvovanie, *op. cit.*, *supra* note 1, p. 279.

[20] G. S. Stashevskii, "Sputniki Sviazi i Mezhdunarodnoe Pravo" [Communication Satellites and International Law], *SGIP*, No. 12 (1964), pp. 57–66; see 63–66.

[21] A. Bykov, "CMEA and International Economic Co-operation," *International Affairs*, No. 2 (1964), pp. 68–72; see 69.

[22] Zadorozhnyi, Mirnoe Sosushchestvovanie, *op. cit.*, *supra* note 1, p. 282.

[23] Bykov, *op. cit.*, *supra* note 21, p. 68.

In socialist relations with neutralist states, all-around political, economic, and cultural collaboration is desired to gain neutralist support for the policy and law of coexistence. Encouragement of this collaboration is evident in the support for national liberation and national and racial equality reflected in Soviet legal positions and, more tangibly, in the form of material assistance to the emerging nations and states. The principle of mutually advantageous international collaboration is the stated legal basis for the unselfish assistance rendered the newly independent states of Africa, Asia and Latin America.[24]

The world socialist system actively promotes the realization of the principles of sovereignty, equality, mutual advantage and friendship between peoples in international economic relations. The broadening of economic collaboration of the socialist countries with the countries of Asia, Africa and Latin America on the basis of these principles serves as an important factor in the independent economic and political progress of these new nation-states.[25]

Soviet economic and technical cooperation with the young independent states facilitates their efforts to build up independent national economies.

Guided by principles of equality and non-interference in the internal affairs of others, the Soviet Union does not attach any political strings which might infringe upon their sovereignty and offend their national dignity.[26]

---

[24] Zadorozhnyi, Mirnoe Sosushchestvovanie, *op. cit.*, *supra* note 1, p. 401. See also B. P. Kozintsev, "Sub'ekty i Kharakter Pravootnoshenii Voznikaiushchikh v Sfere Vneshneekonomicheskikh Sviazei SSSR s Razvivaiushchimisia Stranami" [The Subjects and Character of Legal Relationships in the Sphere of the External Economic Ties of the U.S.S.R. with the Developing Countries], *SGIP*, No. 4 (1965), pp. 72–82; and *Mezhdunarodnoe Pravo, op. cit., supra* note 17, pp. 348, 349.

[25] "Osnovnye Printsipy Mezhdunarodnovo Sotsialisticheskovo Razdelenia Truda" [The Basic Principles of International Socialist Division of Labor], *Pravda* (June 17, 1962), pp. 3, 4; see 3.

[26] "Soviet Economic Cooperation with Developing Countries," *Moscow News*, No. 42 (October 16, 1965), p. 3. See also "Sovmestnaia Bor'ba Bratskoe Sotrudnichestvo" [Joint Struggle, Fraternal Collaboration], *Pravda* (August 2, 1965), p. 1; Gleb Starushenko, "Internationalism—Steadfast Principle of Soviet Foreign Policy," *Moscow News*, No. 6 (February 5, 1966), p. 3; and I. Kapranov, "The U.S.S.R. and Industrial Development in the Newly Free States," *International Affairs*, No. 6 (1966), pp. 33–38.

A community of interest in peace and socialism is said to provide the basis for a greater degree of collaboration, reflecting a more progressive form of coexistence, than that extant in socialist relations with capitalist states.[27] Relationships of the latter with neutralist states are portrayed as exploitative and neo-colonial: "imperialist powers rob the countries of Asia, Africa and Latin America of about 20,000 million dollars annually by way of unequivalent exchange and profit on the invested capital."[28] Such exploitation is denounced on several grounds under the law of peaceful coexistence, i.e., as unequal arrangements and forms of neo-colonialism and indirect aggression.[29] The Soviets are, in effect, seeking to establish a legal basis for neutralist political, economic, and cultural collaboration with socialist states. The legal effort is supported by propaganda which extols such collaboration and discredits similar neutralist collaboration with capitalist states. The general effort is to enhance the acceptability of the policy and law of peaceful coexistence as a basis for the expansion of Soviet influence in the developing countries.

In the case of socialist countries, especially close collaboration and cooperation in political, economic, and cultural fields are subsumed under the legal principles of socialist internationalism and the concept of the socialist commonwealth of nations. The commonwealth, representing a new, higher type international relationship, is said to be necessary to defend the accomplishments of socialism and to maintain international peace.[30] The identity of social, economic and political systems, common ideology, and shared goals

[27] Bernard A. Ramundo, *The (Soviet) Socialist Theory of International Law*, (Washington, D.C.: Institute for Sino-Soviet Studies, The George Washington University, 1964), pp. 43–45. See also Tunkin, Voprosy Teorii, *op. cit.*, *supra* note 3, pp. 10–15.

[28] Konstantin Ivanov and Boris Batsanov, *What Disarmament Will Give to Developing Countries* (n.p., Novosti Press Agency Publishing House, n.d.), p. 32.

[29] "U.S. economic 'aid'. . .is a special form and method of global expansion by U.S. imperialism, an instrument of neo-colonialism, and subversion against the national-liberation movement, a policy designed to promote resistance to Socialism and the influence of Socialist ideas" (Y. Yelutin and M. Petrov, "American 'Aid': New Trends?", *International Affairs*, No. 6 (1966), pp. 50–56; see 50.).

[30] Tunkin, Voprosy Teorii, *op. cit.*, *supra* note 3, pp. 305 and 312, 313.

of the socialist states are said to create "the objective and natural basis for close, friendly, fraternal interstate relations."[31] The elements of community which make possible such relations require an unselfish attitude in pursuing national goals and interests.

> The Socialist nature of the CMEA [COMECON] countries prompts them harmoniously to combine national interests with the general interests and requirements of the Socialist countries in the great struggle for the victory of Socialism and Communism.[32]

Specifically it is said that one of the basic principles governing cooperation between socialist countries is "material benefit" which is to be determined not by "the narrow commercial view of profit-making, but. . .by achievements in the common cause of building Socialism and Communism."[33] In addition, the requirement for unity and solidarity in pursuing the common goal and generally advancing the collective interest of the socialist commonwealth is supposed to be given precedence in the formulation of national policy. The intended result is to place significant restraints upon national freedom of action for all but the largest member of the commonwealth.

Marxist preoccupation with the importance of the creation of an integrated economic base for the world system of socialism places special emphasis upon close economic collaboration as the indispensable condition for the success of socialist states, individually and collectively, in the building of socialism and communism. Current attempts at economic integration[34] are subsumed under the principle of international socialist division of labor which, Soviet

---

[31] V. I. Morozov, "Mnogostoronnie Soglasheniia—Deistvennaia Forma Ekonomicheskovo Sotrudnichestva Sotsialisticheskikh Stran" [Multilateral Agreements—An Effective Form of Economic Collaboration of Socialist Countries], *SGIP*, No. 12 (1963), pp. 75–85; see 75. See also "Nasha Obshchaia Tsel'—Kommunizm i Mir" [Our Common Goal—Communism and Peace], *Pravda* (July 3, 1965), p. 1.

[32] V. Morozov, "Equality: Cornerstone of the Socialist Countries' Economic Co-operation," *International Affairs*, No. 12 (1963), pp. 4–8; see 7.

[33] *Ibid.*, p. 6.

[34] I. Kapranov, "Socialist Economic Cooperation" (A Survey of Current Projects), *New Times*, No. 16 (April 20, 1966), pp. 5–7.

commentaries insist, is based upon the "sovereignty and full legal equality of all participants."[35] The term "socialist" however, reflects the special rationality served by the principle.

The further intensification of international socialist division of labor and increased specialization and cooperation in production, trade and scientific-technical collaboration are vitally important to each socialist country and the entire socialist commonwealth as a whole.[36]

In practice, however, the advantages of socialist division of labor have not always been apparent to socialist states called upon to sacrifice certain aspects of internal and external economic development to satisfy the needs of commonwealth economic integration.[37] The suggestion in the West that this constitutes a form of exploitation by the Soviet Union was confirmed during the 1963 Sino-Soviet polemical exchange by the following Chinese criticism:

It is absolutely necessary for socialist countries to practice mutual economic assistance and cooperation and exchange. Such economic cooperation must be based on the principles of complete equality, mutual benefit and comradely mutual assistance.

It would be great-power chauvinism to deny these basic principles and, in the name of "international division of labor" or "specialization," to impose one's own will on others, infringe on the independence and sovereignty of fraternal countries or harm the interests of their people.

---

[35] M. M. Boguslavskii, "Pravovye Formy Obespecheniia Mezhgosudarstvennoi Spetsializatsii i Kooperirovaniia Proizvodstva Stran-Chlenov SEV" [The Legal Forms for Securing Interstate Specialization and Coordination of the Production of Members of COMECON], *SGIP*, No. 8 (1966), pp. 3–11; see 4.

[36] "Kommiunike O Soveshchanii Pervykh Sekretarei Tsentral'nykh Komitetov Kommunisticheskikh i Rabochikh Partii i Glav Pravitel'stv Stran-Chlenov SEV" [Communique of the Meeting of First Secretaries of the Central Committees of the Communist and Workers' Parties and Heads of States Participating in COMECON], *Pravda* (July 28, 1963), p. 1. See also, A. Alekseev, "O Koordinatsii Narodnokhozaistvennykh Planov," *International Affairs*, No. 11 (1963), pp. 74–81; and M. Senin, "Forms and Methods in Relations between Socialist Countries," *International Affairs*, No. 5 (1966), pp. 12–18.

[37] See "COMECON Woes," *Time* (May 31, 1963), p. 78; "COMECON: Rotten Fruit," *Newsweek* (September 2, 1963), p. 38; J. A. Livingston, "Rumania's Spark of Self-reliance," *The Washington Post* (September 13, 1964), p. A-2; and "Red Common Market Seeks to Raise Output," *The Sunday Star* (September 26, 1965), p. A-9.

In relations among socialist countries it would be preposterous to follow the practice of gaining profit for oneself at the expense of others, a practice characteristic in relations among capitalist countries, or go so far as to take the "economic integration" and the "Common Market," which monopoly capitalist groups have instituted for the purpose of seizing markets and grabbing profits, as examples which socialist countries ought to follow in their economic cooperation and mutual assistance.[38]

Notwithstanding Soviet propaganda efforts to extol the equality, reciprocal benefit, and full respect for national sovereignty in socialist international relationships, it would appear that the governing principle of socialist internationalism, is little more than a euphemism for the institutionalization of great power control within the socialist commonwealth. The magnitude of the all-around collaboration required under this principle is intended to impose restraints upon the sovereign prerogatives of the smaller members of the commonwealth.

Thus, the law of peaceful coexistence provides for different degrees of international collaboration depending upon the states involved. There is, however, an element common to all formulations of collaboration—a careful attention to Soviet policy needs.

PEACEFUL CHANGE

The Soviets claim that peaceful coexistence is actually a law of peaceful change in the sense that it provides the legal basis and framework for the peaceful transition to world socialism. Commitment to the dialectical approach precludes Soviet acceptance of the maintenance of the status quo as an objective to be served by the international legal order. It is said that the immutable laws of social development, a type of socialist (Soviet) "natural or fundamental law," operate independently of man-made law and shape its development.[39] Tunkin holds that no law can conflict with the basic laws of social development and that law inconsistent with them, characterized as reactionary law, must give way to new, progressive

---

[38] Para. 21, Chinese letter of June 14, 1963, *Pravda* (July 14, 1963), p. 7. For trans. see *CDSP*, XV, No. 28, p. 12.

[39] Zadorozhnyi, Mirnoe Sosushchestvovanie, *op. cit.*, *supra* note 1, pp. 435, 436.

development.[40] Capitalist international law, to the extent reactionary in the Soviet view, is destined to disappear; whereas, the law of peaceful coexistence, which is fully consistent with the laws of social development, is "playing an active role in the destruction of the old system."[41] The new system, world socialism, gains in strength in its competition with capitalism under the legal umbrella of peaceful coexistence.[42]

Peaceful coexistence falls far short of being a meaningful vehicle for peaceful change in the traditional sense, since it is biased towards a particular goal. Peaceful coexistence, in recognizing and providing for only those changes which serve Soviet interests, is actually a strategy of conquest and capitulation, rather than a process for the accommodation of changed conditions and relationships. A national strategy cannot serve the broader interest of the family of nations in coping with change, the constant of international relations.

In still another, and perhaps more fundamental sense, peaceful coexistence cannot qualify as a meaningful formula for peaceful change. As in the case of the legal support it provides for the policies of peace, arms control, and peaceful settlement, peaceful coexistence lacks the all-inclusive prohibition against war essential to provide the element of peace in the concept of peaceful change. Peaceful coexistence fully condones the use of armed conflict in support of national liberation, the principal pressure for contemporary change. It also recognizes the permissibility of defensive war with a very loose conception of aggression to serve Soviet interests. Devoid of an all-embracing rejection of the use of force to effect change, peaceful coexistence is incongruous with the concept of peaceful change.

The Soviet view of the existence of inexorable laws of social development which are moving the world towards socialism prevents the operation of any system of nonsocialist, peaceful change, except in those cases where an accommodation (1) cannot be avoided by the

---

[40] Tunkin, Voprosy Teorii, *op. cit.*, *supra* note 3, pp. 223–227.
[41] Zadorozhnyi, Mirnoe Sosushchestvovanie, *op. cit.*, *supra* note 1, p. 484. In fact, it is said that the struggle for acceptance of the law of peaceful coexistence is a struggle of the new and progressive against the old and the reactionary in international law (*Ibid.*, pp. 345–352.).
[42] Tunkin, Voprosy Teorii, *op. cit.*, *supra* note 3, p. 213.

Soviet Union, or (2) can be utilized to serve "the cause of socialism." The basic positivism contained in Soviet positions which stress the importance of state consent—in connection with the formulation of international legal norms, the settlement of disputes, and other matters—reflects the desire to protect the Soviet Union from changes in international relationships of which it does not approve. Except where compelled by circumstances beyond its control, the Soviet Union can be expected to avail itself of this positivism to oppose any change which cannot be related to its policy objectives, thereby complicating mankind's search for a workable principle of peaceful change. The same Soviet attitude towards world law provides little hope that world peace can be achieved through law.

WORLD PEACE THROUGH LAW

In principle, Soviet jurists are not opposed to the concept of world peace through law. In fact, they claim that the Soviet Union and the socialist states have consistently been in the forefront of those who seek greater international legality.

...the states of the socialist world system are at the present time the chief support of international law and the main factor in its progressive development.[43]
The Soviet Union has consistently championed the strengthening of rational rules of international relations and their observance by all states without exception and the codification in international law of the principles of peaceful coexistence. This shows that the U.S.S.R. is working for the establishment of law and order in international relations.[44]

The effort of the Soviet Union has not, however, been the "search for an effective means of substituting the rule of law for rule by

[43] "V Assotsiatsii, Chetvertoe Ezhegodnoe Sobranie Sovetskoi Assotsiatsii Mezhdunarodnovo Prava" [In the Association, The Fourth Annual Meeting of the Soviet Society of International Law], *Sovetskii Ezhegodnik, 1961* (Moscow: Publishing House of the Academy of Sciences of the U.S.S.R., 1962), pp. 414–450; see 415.
[44] A. P. Movchan, "Kodifikatsiia Mezhdunarodnopravovykh Printsipov Mirnovo Sosushchestvovaniia" [The Codification of the International Legal Principles of Peaceful Coexistence], *Sovetskii Ezhegodnik, 1963* (Moscow: Publishing House "Science," 1965), pp. 15–30; see 30.

force. . .[and achieving] the goal of a world ruled by law" in the Western sense.[45] The basic Soviet effort has been directed toward answering the question "Whose law?", in a manner favorable to the policy objectives of the Soviet Union.[46]

The Soviets are vociferous champions of a special kind of legality. In their view, the international class struggle extends to the field of law with socialist and capitalist law vying for supremacy. As all states seek to shape international law to support their policies, so do camps or systems of states.[47]

They [bourgeois jurists] think that they will be able to shape the development of international law. . .and with the assistance of the United Nations Organization use it [law] for struggle against the socialist countries and the national liberation movement in the colonies.[48]

Soviet jurists claim that the growth of the forces of socialism, the decline of colonialism, and the expansion of international relations beyond relations between nations of the white race have transformed international law into a genuine, progressive world law.[49] The socialist and neutralist states are said to have played and to continue to play an important role in the transformation of international law.[50] It is claimed that socialist and neutralist states are in complete agreement that peaceful coexistence is the basis of contemporary international law.[51] The argumentation against old, capitalist international law, invoking prejudices of heritage and race, is

[45] World Peace Through the Rule of Law [Working Paper for the First World Conference, June 30-July 6, 1963, Athens, Greece] (Washington, D.C.: American Bar Association, 1963), p. 201.

[46] Y. Korovin, "Peace Through Law: Two Views," International Affairs, No. 7 (1963), pp. 100–102.

[47] Tunkin, Voprosy Teorii, op. cit., supra note 3, pp. 216, 217. See also Percy E. Corbett, Law in Diplomacy (Princeton: Princeton University Press, 1959), p. 101.

[48] Ibid., p. 204.

[49] Ibid., p. 210.

[50] A. P. Movchan, "O Znachenii Kodifikatsii Printsipov Mezhdunarodnovo Prava" [The Importance of the Codification of International Law], SGIP, No. 1(1965), pp. 46–55; see 48, 49, and 54.

[51] Ibid., p. 50. One of the resolutions adopted at the 1966 Havana Tricontinental Conference endorsed peaceful coexistence. ("Resolution Concerning Peaceful Coexistence" in "Documents of the First Conference of Solidarity of the Peoples of Asia, Africa and Latin America," Moscow News, Supplement to No. 6 [February 5, 1966], pp. 2–29; see 14, 15.)

bolstered by the view that the laws of social change, supreme and immutable, dictate that peaceful coexistence be the controlling law. The result is a Soviet position which will (*1*) recognize the existence of a world law only if it is the law of peaceful coexistence, or (*2*) in the absence of universal acceptance of that law, contend that world law will exist only after the victory of the law of the forces of peace and socialism over capitalist legal practices. In either case, Soviet support for world peace through law is dependent upon the governing law being the law of peaceful coexistence. Actually, the Soviets claim that the law of peaceful coexistence has already been accepted in principle (e.g., Charter of the United Nations) and that all that remains is to ensure compliance with that law in practice.[52] Of course, noncompliance is portrayed as a sin peculiar to the practice of capitalist states.

The Soviet position augurs ill for world peace through law as it is understood in the West. The Western ideal is an objective system of legal controls for the ordering of international relations; the Soviet, a tool for the realization of national objectives.[53] Even if there were the same approach to law and all states were ready to subordinate national interest to an international legal order, there would still be the gap of a lack of agreement as to the nature of that order (i.e., the absence of a generally accepted concept of community), without which a world system of law cannot be built.[54] In the Soviet view, there cannot be a community of capitalist and socialist states in this sense as the former are considered the "common enemy."[55] There can only be coexistence until the socialist system wins out. Unfortunately, coexistence, as distinguished from community, is too weak a foundation for the edifice of world law.[56]

[52] Tunkin, Voprosy Teorii, *op. cit.*, *supra* note 3, p. 214.

[53] Corbett, *op. cit.*, *supra* note 47, p. 101.

[54] *Ibid.*, pp. 101 and 107.

[55] Observer Article "A Compass to Steer By," *New Times*, No. 50 (December 15, 1965), pp. 2, 3; see 3.

[56] Corbett, *op. cit.*, *supra* note 47, pp. 101 and 107. See also Ann Van Wynen Thomas, *Communism versus International Law, Today's Clash of Ideals* (Dallas: Southern Methodist University Press, 1953), pp. 95, 96.

228

The law of peaceful coexistence is little more than a *lex sovietica* designed to shape international relationships in the Soviet interest.[57] The Soviets play the game of "pot calling the kettle black" by leveling the same charge against the United States approach to international law.

The doctrine of the primacy of international law, as interpreted by the Americans, is nothing but a cover-up for U.S. claims to world hegemony and the establishment of a *Pax Americana*, an imperialist American peace.[58]

Despite Soviet claims that the new law of peaceful coexistence provides the basis for world peace through law, it is clear that the formulation lacks the requisite objectivity and negation of the use of force to serve the claimed purpose. Western states, unprepared to accept a Soviet world order, can be expected to continue to resist acceptance of the new law. From the standpoint of world order, the Soviet approach and the Western reaction to it are significant because they tend to exaggerate the tendency toward lack of order which is already a part of the general attitude toward international law.

[57] See *Peaceful Coexistence—A Communist Blueprint for Victory* (Chicago: American Bar Association, 1964), p. 25.

[58] Korovin, *Peace Through Law, op. cit., supra* note 46, p. 101. See also Zadorozhnyi, Mirnoe Sosushchestvovanie, *op. cit., supra* note 1, p. 100.

CHAPTER THIRTEEN

CONCLUSION

Since the middle thirties, the Soviet Union has felt the need for international legal stability to ensure the realization of national developmental objectives. The price of stability has been acceptance of an international legal order which, because of its capitalist origins, was initially viewed as hostile to Soviet interests. The hostility attributed to traditional international law produced a defensism in Soviet international legal practice which continues until the present. The original Soviet defensive mechanism, extreme positivism and the claimed right to reject principles unilaterally characterized as non-progressive or reactionary, was simple, but crude. It earned for the Soviet Union a poor reputation for international legality and trustworthiness as a treaty partner. Accordingly, although formally a member of the family of nations, the Soviet state was viewed with suspicion and, as a practical matter, isolated from the mainstream of international relations.

As the Soviet Union matured, and its preoccupation with the problems and practical needs of national development all but replaced the tarnished dream of world revolution, the realities of international life were given primacy over the fantasy of international class struggle contained in the Marxist-Leninist scriptures. The realization that states are interdependent—the result of technological advances in all fields, especially weaponry—brought with it recognition of a Soviet stake in the status quo and a consequent need to work out an accommodation with the class enemy. The accommodation was complicated by the need to observe the ideological commitment to the forces of world revolution as an identifying link with the Marxist past. Soviet policy makers, influenced more by objective needs than ideological predilections, called for co-existence, i.e., a relaxation of the hostility of earlier policies and a refurbishing of the international legal image of the Soviet Union. The policy of peaceful coexistence, formally adopted at the Twentieth Party Congress of the Communist Party of the Soviet Union in 1956, reflects the primacy of practical foreign policy needs, with the inclusion of an appropriate ideological rationalization to maintain Marxist respectability.

Soviet international legal specialists were called upon to develop a supporting legal rationale for the new policy. Their efforts have produced the concept of a new international law of peaceful coexistence which is said to reflect, and take account of, the fact of international life that there is no policy alternative to coexistence. The new law, hardly a developed system, has not been accepted by the West because of the vagueness of its formulation and the consequent potential for mischief flowing from such vagueness.

The law of peaceful coexistence is artfully formulated because it appears to depart from the defensism of earlier formulations which sought to avoid international legal constraints upon flexibility in policy formulation through the technique of extreme positivism and unilateral characterization of the progressive. In effect, however, emphasis upon the prerogatives of sovereignty and the inclusion of the legally progressive in the new formulation ensure a continuation of the basic defensism of the Soviet approach to international law. At the same time, the law of coexistence, drawing upon the new socialist content claimed for it, is a most ambitious attempt to achieve legal flexibility for policy making. In military terms—and such terms have a special place in communist jargon—the current effort is to capture the international legal order rather than to provide defenses against its rein on Soviet foreign policies. The strategy for capture involves (1) an alliance with the neutralist states of Africa, Asia and Latin America, (2) seizure of the United Nations as the initial, principal objective, and (3) the use of new, specially-tailored legal concepts and, where necessary, the immutable laws of social development as the basic armament.

The new socialist content is said to be reflected in new progressive principles and a more progressive operation of traditional principles.

→>>≪←

Actually, socialist content is a Soviet euphemism for selectivity in the application of legal principles for the purpose of providing flexibility for the foreign policy of the Soviet Union and inhibiting the foreign policies of other states, capitalist and socialist alike. Selectivity is sought through the use of ambiguous formulations, permitting characterization in the Soviet interest; double standards in judging legal requirements and compliance therewith; new "socialist" concepts permitting avoidance or invocation of legal norms as needed; and a concept of *jus cogens* which, in the final analysis, is equated to the laws of social development derivable from Marxism-Leninism by the Soviet leadership. This selectivity has a dual operation. Minimally it is directed at selecting the norms binding upon the Soviet Union; maximally, the norms comprising the international legal order and, therefore, binding upon all states. In pursuing these variations of selectivity, the Soviet Union combines the conventional techniques of diplomatic initiative, pleasant sounding propaganda themes, and legal argumentation in an orchestrated effort. As compared with the international legal practice of other states, the Soviet effort is noteworthy because of (*1*) the attempt to capitalize upon a new international law recast in the Soviet image and interest, rather than to maneuver within the confines of traditional international law,[1] and (*2*) the special emphasis upon propaganda-diplomatic initiatives in seeking acceptance of the new law.

As international law shaped in a Soviet mold (in effect, a *lex sovietica*), peaceful coexistence represents the maximum Soviet position on international law. Circumstances—principally nonacceptance by the West of peaceful coexistence as a normative system and the objective need to coexist within the family of nations,

[1] It is not being suggested that Western states are law abiding and the Soviet Union is not. The difference is only one of degree. Although the former states show a greater willingness to submit to impartially formulated (and interpreted) general norms, there is a point at which national interest rather than legal mandate becomes controlling. The Soviets, for their part, reject out of hand all legal norms which are deemed hostile to the Soviet Union or restrain its sovereign prerogatives (See Percy E. Corbett, *Law in Diplomacy* [Princeton: Princeton University Press, 1959], pp. 106, 107). It would appear most correct to say that the Western states have a higher threshold of overriding national interest than the Soviet Union.

233

however, constrain the Soviet Union to continue to pursue a minimum position of seeking support for its insistence upon the prerogatives of state sovereignty and Soviet values in characterizing international legal situations as the *modus vivendi* in a world system where states generally seek flexibility within the parameters of traditional international law. The Soviet Union's pursuit of its minimum position simultaneously with proponency of the law of peaceful coexistence is possible because peaceful coexistence, the maximum position, includes the former as its basic premise. Both in seeking to close the gap between the desired (i.e., acceptance of peaceful coexistence as controlling the international legal order) and the presently attainable (support for positivism and Soviet characterizations of international legal principles and situations), and in operating within the gap, propaganda-diplomatic campaigns in support of legal positions are an essential feature of the Soviet approach to international law.

The policy and law of peaceful coexistence were reaffirmed at the Twenty-third Party Congress of the Communist Party of the Soviet Union in 1966, and it would appear at this writing that a change in formulation is not an immediate prospect. A *caveat* is in order, however, because the underlying premise of peaceful coexistence, a bipolar world of two ideologically opposed camps, is rapidly disappearing and a reformulation of the Soviet approach to international law may become necessary. It will be recalled that the Soviets had to adjust their formulation to take account of the existence of neutralist states. Treating these states, in effect, as part of the socialist camp for the purposes of the international class struggle, and thereby preserving the concept of bipolarity, is a simpler task than having to cope with a major fragmentation of the two camps, especially the implications of polycentrism in the socialist camp. Another factor bearing upon the stability of the coexistence formulation is that the policy of peaceful coexistence contemplates *detente* between East and West and not a series of confrontations on the issue of national liberation. Although the Cuban crisis did not result in any appreciable change in the policy of peaceful coexistence, a more serious confrontation could bring in its wake significant modifications. The point is that the law of peaceful coexistence, being based upon a general foreign policy line, has a built-in lack of permanency because it, like the policy it serves, is subject to the imperative of the need to accommodate the constancy of change. Although the vagueness and ambiguity of the principles of peaceful coexistence are designed to be sensitive to change within the parameters of the basic policy, a change in that policy would necessitate a corresponding change in legal formulation. Compelled to operate in such an unstable environment, Soviet international legal specialists have demonstrated either great wisdom or sheer frustration in devising a formulation which permits simultaneous pursuit of Soviet minimum and maximum international legal objectives.

SELECTED BIBLIOGRAPHY

Soviet Sources

Documents:

"Declaration of the Twelve Communist Parties in Power (November, 1957)" and "Declaration of the Representatives of the Eight-one Communist Parties (November-December, 1960)," in *The New Communist Manifesto*, ed. Dan N. Jacobs (2d. ed. Evanston, Illinois and Elmsford, New York: Row, Peterson and Company, 1962), pp. 169–182 and 11–47, respectively.

"Documents of the First Conference of Solidarity of the Peoples of Asia, Africa and Latin America," *Moscow News*, Supplement to No. 6 (February 5, 1966), pp. 2–29.

Gruliow, Leo (ed.), *Current Soviet Policies, II, The Documentary Record of the Twentieth Communist Party Congress and Its Aftermath*, New York: Prager, 1957.

———, *Current Soviet Policies, IV, The Documentary Record of the Twenty-second Congress of the Communist Party of the Soviet Union*, New York: Prager, 1962.

"Memorandum Sovetskovo Pravitel'stva o Merakh po Dal'neishemu Smiagcheniiu Mezhdunarodnoi Napriazhennosti i Ogranicheniiu Gonki Vooruzhenii" [Memorandum of the Soviet Government Concerning Measures for the Further Relaxation of International Tensions and Limiting the Arms Race], *Pravda* (December 8, 1964), pp. 1 and 4.

"Otkrytoe Pis'mo, Tsentral'novo Komiteta Kommunisticheskoi Partii Sovetskovo Soiuza, Partiinym Organizatisiiam, Vsem Kommunistam Sovetskovo Soiuza" [Open Letter of the Central Committee of the Communist Party of the Soviet Union to All Party Organizations and All Communist of the Soviet Union], *Pravda* (July 14, 1963), p. 2.

"Poslanie Predsedatelia Soveta Ministrov SSSR Uchastnikam Komiteta 18 Gosudarstv po Razoruzheniiu v Zheneve" [Communication of the Chairman of the Council of Ministers of the U.S.S.R. to the Participants in the Eighteen Nation Disarmament Committee at Geneva], *Pravda* (February 3, 1966), pp. 1–2.

"Report of the Central Committee of the Communist Party of the Soviet Union to the Twenty-third Congress of the CPSU," *Moscow News*, Supplement to No. 14 (April 2, 1966).

"Resolution of the Twenty-third Congress of the Communist Party of the Soviet Union on the Report of the Central Committee of the CPSU," *Moscow News*, Supplement to No. 16 (April 16, 1966), pp. 2–10.

Sobakin, V. K., *Sovremennoe Mezhdunarodnoe Pravo, Sbornik Dokumentov* [Contemporary International Law, Collection of Documents], Moscow: Publishing House "International Relations," 1964.

"Statement of the Twenty-third Congress of the C.P.S.U. Concerning U.S. Aggression in Vietnam," *Moscow News*, Supplement to No. 16 (April 16, 1966), pp. 11, 12.

Books and Monographs:

Bogdanov, O. V., *Vseobshchee i Polnoe Razoruzhenie (Mezhdunarodnopravovye Voprosy)* [General and Complete Disarmament (International Legal Problems)], Moscow: Publishing House "International Relations," 1964.

Chernogolovkin, N. V., *Krushenie Kolonializma i Mezhdunarodnoe Pravo* [The Downfall of Colonialism and International Law], Moscow: State Publishing House of Legal Literature, 1963.

Chkhikvadze, V. M. (ed.), *Entsiklopedicheskii Slovar' Pravovykh Znanii* [Encyclopedic Legal Dictionary], Moscow: Publishing House "Soviet Encyclopedia," 1965.

Engles, Frederick, *The Origin of the Family, Private Property and the State*, New York: International Publishers, 1942.

Fedorov, V. N., *Sovet Bezopasnosti OON* [The Security Council of the U.N.], Moscow: Publishing House "International Relations," 1965.

Fel'dman, D. I., *Sovremennaia Teoriia Mezhdunarodnopravovo Priznaniia* [Contemporary Theory of International Legal Recognition], Kazan': Publishing House of Kazan' University, 1963.

————, *Priznanie Gosudarstv v Sovremennom Mezhdunarodnom Prave* [The Recognition of States in Contemporary International Law] Kazan': Publishing House of Kazan' University, 1965.

International Law, Moscow: Foreign Languages Publishing House, ca. 1960.

Klimenko, B. M., *Demilitarizatsiia i Neitralizatsiia v Mezhdunarodnom Prave* [Demilitarization and Neutrality in International Law], Moscow: Publishing House of the Institute of International Relations, 1963.

————, *Gosudarstvennye Granitsy—Problema Mira* [State Boundaries and the Problem of Peace], Moscow: Publishing House "International Relations," 1964.

Kozhevnikov, F. I. (ed.), *Mezhdunarodnoe Pravo* [International Law], Moscow: Publishing House "International Relations," 1964.

Krasil'shchikova, S. A., *OON i Natsional'no-osvoboditel'noe Dvizhenie* [The U.N. and the National Liberation Movement], Moscow: Publishing House "International Relations," 1964.

Krylov, S. B., *Mezhdunarodnyi Sud* [The International Court], Moscow: State Publishing House of Legal Literature, 1958.

Kudriavstev, P. I. (ed.)., *Iuridicheskii Slovar'* [Legal Dictionary], 2d ed., Moscow: State Publishing House of Legal Literature, 1956.

Kuusinen, O. W., *Fundamentals of Marxism-Leninism*, 2d ed., Moscow: Foreign Languages Publishing House, 1961.

Ladyzhenskii, A. M., and Blishchenko, I. P., *Mirnye Sredstva Razresheniia Sporov mezhdu Gosudarstvami* [Peaceful Settlement of Disputes Between States], Moscow: State Publishing House of Legal Literature, 1962.

Lazarev, M. I., *Imperialisticheskie Voennye Bazy na Chuzhikh Territoriakh i Mezhdunarodnoe Pravo* [Imperialist Military Bases on Foreign Territories and International Law], Moscow: Publishing House of the Institute of Foreign Relations, 1963.

————, *Tekhnicheskii Progress i Sovremennoe Mezhdunarodnoe Pravo* [Technical Progress and Contemporary International Law], Moscow: State Publishing House of Legal Literature, 1963.

239

Lenin, *O Mezhdunarodnoi Politike i Mezhdunarodnom Prave* [Concerning International Relations and International Law], Moscow: Publishing House of the Institute of International Relations, 1958.

Levin, D. B., *Istoriia Mezhdunarodnovo Prava* [The History of International Law], Moscow: Publishing House of the Institute of International Relations, 1962.

Levin, D. B. and Kaliuzhnaia, G. P. (ed.), *Mezhdunarodnoe Pravo* [International Law], Moscow: Publishing House "Legal Literature," 1964.

Lisovskii, V. I., *Mezhdunarodnoe Pravo* [International Law], 2d ed. Moscow: State Publishing House "Higher School," 1961.

Lukin, P. I., *Istochniki Mezhdunarodnovo Prava* [Sources of International Law], Moscow: Publishing House of the Academy of Sciences of the U.S.S.R., 1960.

Menzhinskii, V. I. (ed.), *Voprosy Mezhdunarodnovo Prava* [Problems of International Law], Moscow: Publishing House of International Relations, 1963.

Minasian, N. M., *Istochniki Sovremennovo Mezhdunarodnovo Prava* [Sources of Contemporary International Law], Rostov: Publishing House of Rostov University, 1960.

———. *Sushchnost' Sovremennovo Mezhdunarodnovo Prava* [The Essence of Contemporary International Law], Rostov: Publishing House of Rostov State University, 1962.

Modzhorian, L. A., *Politika Neitraliteta* [The Policy of Neutrality], Moscow: Publishing House "Knowledge," 1962.

———, *Osnovnye Prava i Obiazannosti Gosudarstv* [The Fundamental Rights and Duties of States], Moscow: Publishing House "Legal Literature," 1965.

Morozov, G. I., *Sovet Ekonomicheskoi Vzaimopomoshchi—Soiuz Ravnykh* [The Council for Mutual Economic Assistance—A Union of Equals], Moscow: Publishing House "International Relations," 1964.

———, *Organizatsiia Ob'edinennykh Natsii* [The United Nations Organization], Moscow: Publishing House of the Institute of International Relations, 1960.

Ponomarev, B. N. (ed.), *Politicheskii Slovar'* [Dictionary of Political Terms], 2d. ed., Moscow: State Publishing House of Political Literature, 1958.

Sergeiev, S. D., *Ekonomicheskoe Sotrudnichestvo i Vzaimopomoshch' Sotsialisticheskikh Stran* [Economic Collaboration and Mutual Assistance of Socialist Countries], Moscow: The Publishing House of Foreign Trade, 1964.

Shiriaev, Iu. S. and Ladygin, B. M., *Problemy Sovershentsvovaniia Ekonomicheskovo Sotrudnichestva Stran—Chlenov SEV* [Problems of Improving the Economic Collaboration of the Countries Which Are Members of COMECON], Moscow: Publishing House "Economics," 1965.

Shurshalov, V. M. (ed.), *Mezhdunarodnopravovye Formy Sotrudnichestva Sotsialisticheskikh Gosudarstv* [Legal Forms of the Collaboration of Socialist States], Moscow: Publishing House of the Academy of Sciences of the U.S.S.R., 1962.

Sobakin, V. K., *Kollektivnaia Bezopasnost'—Garantiia Mirnovo Sosushchestovovaniia* [Collective Security—Guarantee of Peaceful Coexistence], Moscow: Publishing House of the Institute of International Relations, 1962.

Sovetskii Ezhegodnik Mezhdunarodnovo Prava, 1958–1963 [Soviet Yearbook of International Law, 1958–1963]. Moscow: Publishing House of the Academy of Sciences of the U.S.S.R. and Publishing House "Science" (1963 Yearbook), 1959–1963 and 1965, respectively.

Talalaev, A. N., *Iuridicheskaia Priroda Mezhdunarodnovo Dogovora*, [The Legal Nature of International Agreements]. Moscow: Publishing House of the Institute of International Relations, 1963.

Tunkin, G. I., *Problemy Mezhdunarodnovo Prava* [Problems of International Law]. Moscow: Publishing House of Foreign Literature, 1961.

————, *Voprosy Teorii Mezhdunarodnovo Prava* [Problems of the Theory of International Law]. Moscow: State Publishing House of Legal Literature, 1962.

Tuzmukhamedov, R. A., *Natsional'nyi Suvernitet* [National Sovereignty]. Moscow: Publishing House of International Relations, 1963.

Usenko, E. T., *Formy Regulirovaniia Sotsialisticheskovo Mezhdunarodnovo Razdeleniia Truda* [Regulation of Socialist International Division of Labor]. Moscow: Publishing House "International Relations," 1965.

Ushakov, N. A., *Suvernitet v Sovremennom Mezhdunarodnom Prave* [Sovereignty in Contemporary International Law], Moscow: Publishing House of the Institute of International Relations, 1963.

Viskov, S., *Za Mir bez Oruzhiia, za Mir bez Voin* [For a World Without Arms and War]. Moscow: The Publishing House of Social-Economic Literature, "Thought," 1964.

Zorin, V. A., and Morozov, G. I. (eds.), *OON i Aktual'nye Mezhdunarodnye Problemy* [The U.N. and Contemporary International Problems]. Moscow: Publishing House "International Relations," 1965.

Articles:

Alekseev, A., "O Koordinatsii Narodnokhozaistvennykh Planov" [On the Coordination of National Economic Plans], *Mezhdunarodnaia Zhizn'* [International Affairs], No. 11 (1962), pp. 74–81.

Al'tshuler, A. B., "Novaia Mezhdunarodnopravovaia Forma Ekonomicheskovo Sotrudnichestva (k Sozdaniiu Mezhdunarodnovo Banka Ekonomicheskovo Sotrudnichestva)" [A New International Legal Form of Economic Collaboration (Re The Creation of the International Bank of Economic Collaboration)], *Sovetskoe Gosudarstvo i Pravo* [Soviet State and Law, hereafter cited "SGIP"], No. 10 (1964), pp. 54–65.

Baskin, Iu. Ia., "Institut Priznaniia v Mezhdunarodnom Prave" [Recognition in International Law], *SGIP*, No. 2 (1966), pp. 158, 159.

Belayev, Y. and Tandit, V., "CMEA and the Six," *International Affairs*, No. 2 (1963), pp. 15–20.

Bobrov, R. L., "Mezhdunarodnoe Pravo i Istoricheskii Progress" [International Law and Historical Progress], *SGIP*, No. 12 (1963), pp. 3–11.

Bogdanov, O. V., "Security of States in a Disarmed World and International Law," trans. from *SGIP*, No. 9 (1963), in *The Daily Review* (Moscow), IX, No. 87 (November 12, 1963), pp. 1–12.

————, "Mezhdunarodno-pravovye Aspekty Osushchestvleniia Vseobshchevo i Polnova Razoruzheniia" [International Legal Aspects of the Realization of General and Complete Disarmament], *SGIP*, No. 6 (1963), pp. 87–99.

————, "O Znachenii i Soderzhanii Printsipa Razoruzheniia v Sovremennom Mezhdunarodnom Prave" [The Significance and Essence of the Principle of Disarmament in Contemporary International Law], *Sovetskii Ezhegodnik Mezhdunarodnovo Prava, 1961* [Soviet Yearbook of International Law, 1961] hereafter cited "*Sovetskii Ezhegodnik, 19—*"). Moscow; Publishing House of the Academy of Sciences of the U.S.S.R., 1962, pp. 94–117.

Borisov, K. G., "Mezhdunarodno-pravovye Aspekty Mezhdunarodnovo Turizma" [International Legal Aspects of International Tourism], *SGIP*, No. 7 (1965), pp. 138–142.

Bykov, A., "CMEA and International Economic Co-operation," *International Affairs*, No. 2 (1964), pp. 68–72.

Chernichenko, S. V., "Pravo Natsii na Samoopredelenie i Voprosy Grazhdanstva" [The Right of Nations to Self-determination and Problems of Citizenship], *SGIP*, No. 1 (1964), pp. 110–114.

Chkhikvadze, V. M., "Voprosy Mezhdunarodnovo Prava na XX Sessii General'noi Assamblei" [Problems of International Law at the 20th Session of the General Assembly], *SGIP*, No. 3 (1966), pp. 67–78.

Demichev, P. N. (trans.), "Leninism Is the Scientific Foundation of the Party's Policy," *Pravda* (April 23, 1965), in *Current Digest of the Soviet Press* (hereafter cited "*CDSP*"), XVII, No. 17, 3–8.

Durdenevsky, V. N., "Neitralitet i Atomnoe Oruzhie (V Svete Printsipa Mirnovo Sosushchestvovaniia)" [Neutrality and Atomic Weapons (In the Light of the Principle of Peaceful Coexistence)], *Sovetskii Ezhegodnik, 1960*, pp. 104–108.

Fedorov, V. N., "Istoriia Sozdaniia Soveta Bezopasnosti OON" (The History of the Creation of the Security Council of the

U.N.), in *Voprosy Mezhdunarodnovo Prava* [Problems of International Law], ed. V. I. Menzhinskii (Moscow; Publishing House of the Institute of International Relations, 1963), pp. 147–176.

Fel'dman, D. I., "O Nekotorykh Formakh i Sposobakh Mezhdunarodno-pravovo Priznaniia Novykh Gosudarstv" [Some Forms and Methods of International Legal Recognition of New States], *Sovetskii Ezhegodnik, 1963*, pp. 129–149.

Gaidukov, D. A., Review of *Mezhdunarodnoe Pravo* [International Law] (Moscow: State Publishing House of Legal Literature, 1951), *SGIP*, No. 7 (1952), pp. 67–77.

Galina, A., "Problema Neitraliteta v Sovremennom Mezhdunarodnom Prave" [The Problem of Neutrality in Contemporary International Law], *Sovetskii Ezhegodnik, 1958*, pp. 200–229.

Grevtsova, T. P., "Mezhdunarodnyi Dogovor v Sisteme Istochinikov Sovetskovo Vnutrigosudarstvennovo Prava" [International Agreements As Sources of Soviet Domestic Law], *Sovetskii Ezhegodnik, 1963*, pp. 171–179.

Ianovskii, M. V., "Sovetskie Soiuznye Respubliki—Polnopravnye Sub'ekty Mezhdunarodnovo Prava" [The Soviet Constituent Republics—Fully Competent Subjects of International Law], *SGIP*, No. 12 (1962), pp. 55–64.

"Internationalist Duty of Communists of All Countries" (trans.) *Pravda* (November 28, 1965), in *Moscow News*, Supplement to No. 49 (December 4, 1965), pp. 9–18.

"Iuridicheskaia Sila Rezoliutsii General'noi Assamblei i Ustav OON" [The Juridical Force of Resolutions of the General Assembly and the Charter of the U.N.], *SGIP*, No. 9 (1965), pp. 120–124.

Kalinychev, F. I., "Pravo Narodov na Mir" [The Right of Nations to Peace], *SGIP*, No. 3 (1961), pp. 3–15.

Karpets, I. I., "Pravo na Sluzhbu Mira" [Law in the Service of Peace], *SGIP*, No. 6 (1964), pp. 71–77.

Kartashkin, V. A., "Rol' Mezhdunarodnovo Suda OON v Mirnom Razreshenii Territorial'nykh Sporov" [The Role of the International Court of the U.N. in the Peaceful Settlement of Territorial Disputes], *Sovetskii Ezhegodnik, 1963*, pp. 501–503.

Kikot', A., "Pravovye Voprosy Sotrudnichestva Sotsialisticheskikh Stran v Oblasti Sel'skovo Khoziaistva" [Legal Problems of the Collaboration of the Socialist Countries in the Field of Agriculture], *SGIP*, No. 1 (1964), pp. 64–72.

Khlestov, O. N., "Razrabotka Norm Kosmicheskovo Prava" [Working Out the Norms of Space Law], *SGIP*, No. 8 (1964), pp. 67–77.

Klimenko, B. M., "Demilitarizatsiia Territorii v Svete Problemy Razoruzheniia" [The Demilitarization of Territory and the Problem of Disarmament], *SGIP*, No. 4 (1962), pp. 98–108.

———, "K Voprosu o Neitralizatsii Territorii v Sovremennom Mezhdunarodnom Prave" [The Problem of the Neutralization of Territories in Contemporary International Law] *Sovetskii Ezhegodnik, 1961*, pp. 208–219.

———, "Osnovnye Printsipy Sozdaniia Bez'iardernykh Zon" [The Basic Principles for the Creation of Nuclear–free Zones], *SGIP*, No. 12 (1964), pp. 110–115.

Korvin, E., "Likvidirovat' Posledstviia Kul'ta Lichnosti v Nauke Mezhdunarodnovo Prava" [Eliminate the Consequences of the Cult of the Individual in the Science of International Law], *Sotsialisticheskaia Zakonnost'* [Socialist Legality], No. 8 (1962), pp. 46–49.

———, "Peace Through Law: Two Views," *International Affairs*, No. 7 (1963), pp. 100–102.

———, "The Way to Peace" *International Affairs*, No. 11 (1964), pp. 73–75.

Kozintsev, B. P., "Sub'ekty i Kharakter Pravootnoshenii Voznikaiushchikh v Sfere Vneshneekonomicheskikh Sviazei SSSR s Razvivaiushchimisia Stranami" [The Subjects and Character of Legal Relationships in the Sphere of the External Economic Ties of the U.S.S.R. with the Developing Countries], *SGIP*, No. 4 (1965), pp. 72–82.

Lazarev, M. I., "Mezhdunarodnopravovye Voprosy Dvizheniia Narodov za Mir" [International Legal Aspects of the Peoples' Movement for Peace], *Sovetskii Ezhegodnik, 1963*, pp. 45–69.

————, "Zapreshchenie Inostrannykh Voennykh Baz na Chuzhikh Territoriiakh Normami Mezhdunarodnovo Prava" [Prohibition of Foreign Military Bases by Norms of International Law], *Sovetskii Ezhegodnik, 1962,* pp. 64–77.

————, "Vopros ob Inostrannykh Voennykh Bazakh i Vooruzhennykh Silakh na Chuzhikh Territoriiakh v Mezhdunarodnopravovoi Literature" [The Problem of Foreign Military Bases and Armed Forces Abroad in Writings on International Law], *Sovetskii Ezhegodnik, 1960,* pp. 371–380.

Levin, D. B., "Problema Sootnosheniia Mezhdunarodnovo i Vnutrigosudarstvennovo Prava" [The Problem of the Relationship Between International and Domestic Law], *SGIP,* No. 7 (1964), pp. 86–95.

————, "Ob Otvetstvennosti Gosudarstv v Sovremennom Mezhdunarodnom Prave" [The Responsibility of States Under Contemporary International Law], *SGIP,* No. 5 (1966), pp. 75–83.

"Marshal Sokolovsky on Art of War in Nuclear Age" (trans.) *Krasnaia Zvezda* [Red Star], in *CDSP,* XVI, No. 38, 14–18.

Melekhin, B. I., "Vozdeistvie Mirovovo Obschestvennovo Mneniia na Sovremennoe Mezhdunarodnoe Pravo" [The Influence of World Public Opionion on Contemporary International Law], *SGIP,* No. 2 (1964), pp. 75–83.

————, "Rol' Mirovovo Obshchestvennovo Mneniia v Formirovanii i Obespechenii Mezhdunarodnovo Prava" [The Role of World Public Opinion in Formulating and Ensuring International Legality], *Sovetskii Ezhegodnik, 1963,* pp. 498, 499.

Melnikov, D., "Neutrality and the Current Situation," *International Affairs,* No. 2 (1956), pp. 74, 75.

Mikhailov, B., "Konferentsiia Iuristov-Mezhdunarodnikov," [Conference of International Jurists], *SGIP,* No. 10 (1963), pp. 147–149.

Mironov, N. V., "Sootnoshenie Mezhdunarodnovo Dogovora i Vnutrigosudarstvennovo Zakona" [The Relationship Between International Agreements and Domestic Law], *Sovetskii Ezhegodnik, 1963,* pp. 150–170.

Modzhoryan, L. A., "Raspad Kolonial'noi Sistemy Imperializma i Nekotorye Voprosy Mezhdunarodnovo Prava" [The Break-up of the Colonial System of Imperialism and Some Problems of International Law], *Sovetskii Ezhegodnik, 1961*, pp. 36–49.

———, "Amerikanskie Doktriny Grabezha i Razboia: ot Monro do Zhonsona" [American Doctrine of Plunder and Brigandage from Monroe to Johnson], *SGIP*, No. 9 (1965), pp. 57–64.

Molodtsov, S. V., "Mirnoe Uregulirovanie Territorial'nykh Sporov i Voprosov o Granitsakh" [Peaceful Settlement of Territorial Disputes and Border Questions], *Sovetskii Ezhegodnik, 1963*, pp. 70–84.

———, "Frontiers and International Law," *International Affairs*, No. 4 (1964), pp. 9–14.

Morozov, G. I., "Poniatie i Klassifikatsiia Mezhdunarodnykh Organizatsii" [The Concept and Classification of International Organizations], *SGIP*, No. 6 (1966), pp. 67–76.

Morozov, G. I., and Pchelintsev, Y., "Behind the U.N. Financial Crisis," *International Affairs*, No. 6 (1964), pp. 23–29.

Morozov, V., "Equality: Cornerstone of the Socialist Countries' Economic Cooperation," *International Affairs*, No. 12 (1963), pp. 4–8.

Morozov, V. I., "Mnogostoronnie Soglasheniia—Deistvennaia Forma Ekonomicheskovo Sotrudnichestva Sotsialisticheskikh Stran" [Multilateral Agreements—An Effective Form of Economic Collaboration of Socialist Countries], *SGIP*, No. 12 (1963), pp. 75–85.

Movchan, A. P., "Kodifikatsiia Mezhdunarodnopravovykh Printsipov Mirnovo Sosushchestvovaniia" [The Codification of the International Legal Principles of Peaceful Coexistence], *Sovetskii Ezhegodnik, 1963*, pp. 15–30.

———, "O Znachenii Kodifikatsii Printsipov Mezhdunarodnovo Prava" [On the Importance of the Codification of the Principles of International Law], *SGIP*, No. 1 (1963), pp. 46–55.

Nedbailo, P. E. and Vasilenko, V. A., "Mezhdunarodnaia Pravosub'ektnost' Sovetskikh Soiuznykh Respublik" [The International Legal Personality of the Soviet Constituent Republics], *Sovetskii Ezhegodnik, 1963*, pp. 85–108.

Osnitskaya, G., "The Downfall of Colonialism and International Law," *International Affairs*, No. 1 (1961), pp. 38–43.

———, "Voina SShA v Indokitae—Gruboe Narushenie Mezhdunarodnovo Prava" [The U.S. War in Indo-China—A Flagrant Violation of International Law], *International Affairs*, No. 11 (1965), pp. 40–48.

"Osnovnye Printsipy Mezhdunarodnovo Sotsialisticheskovo Razdelenia Truda" [The Basic Principles of International Socialist Division of Labor], *Pravda* (June 17, 1962), pp. 3, 4.

Padbil', O. S., "Nekotorye Problemy Mezhdunarodnovo Meditsinskovo Prava" [Some Problems of International Medical Law], *Sovetskii Ezhegodnik, 1963*, pp. 303–307.

Pchelintsev, E. S., "Mezhdunarodno-pravovye Voprosy Ekonomicheskovo i Sotsial'novo Sotrudnichestva Gosudarstv" [International Legal Problems Concerning the Economic and Social Collaboration of States], *Voprosy Mezhdunarodnovo Prava* [Problems of International Law], ed. V. I. Menzhinskii (Moscow: Publishing House of the Institute of International Relations, 1963), pp. 177–217.

"Peaceful Coexistence and Revolutionary Struggle" (trans.) *Kommunist* [Communist] (March, 1963) in *The Daily Review* (Moscow), IX, No. 22 (March 26, 1963).

Piradov, A., "Bases and International Law," *International Affairs*, No. 5 (1964), pp. 98–99.

"Pravda on U.S.S.R. and National-Liberation Movement" (trans.) *Pravda* (June 28, 1965), in *CDSP*, XVII, No. 26, 3–5.

"Rech' Tovarishcha A. A. Gromyko" [The Speech of A. A. Gromyko], *Pravda* (April 3, 1966), pp. 4, 5.

Romanov, V. A., "Vseobshchee i Polnoe Razoruzhenie i Mezhdunarodnoe Pravo" [Universal and Complete Disarmament and International Law], *Sovetskii Ezhegodnik, 1960*, pp. 80–91.

Romashkin, P. S., "Agressiia—Tiagchaishee Prestuplenie protiv Mira i Chelovechestva" [Agression—The Most Heinous Crime Against Peace and Mankind], *SGIP*, No. 1 (1963), pp. 55–67.

Semyonov, K., "Geneva: Another Impass," *International Affairs*, No. 11 (1964), pp. 10–16.

Shimunek, Otakar, "Mezhdunarodnye Ekonomicheskie Otnosheniia i Sorevnovanie Dvukh Sistem" [International Economic Relations and Competition of the Two Systems], *Mezhdunarodnaia Zhizn'* (International Affairs), No. 12 (1962), pp. 23–31.

Shurshalov, V. M., "Mezhdunarodno-pravovye Printsipy Sotrudnichestva Sotsialisticheskikh Gosudarstv" [International Legal Principles of the Collaboration of Socialist States], *SGIP*, No. 7 (1962), pp. 95–105.

"Soviet Foreign Policy and the Contemporary World," *International Affairs*, No. 3 (1966), pp. 3–20.

Stashevskii, G. S., "Sputniki Sviazi i Mezhdunarodnoe Pravo" [Communication Satellites and International Law], *SGIP*, No. 12 (1964), pp. 57–66.

"The Noble Aims of Soviet Foreign Policy" (trans.) *Pravda* (August 8, 1965), in *CDSP*, XVII, No. 32, 3–6.

Talalaev, A. N. and Boiarshinov, V. G., "Neravnopravnye Dogovory kak Forma Uderzhaniia Kolonial'noi Zavisimosti Novykh Gosudarstv Azii i Afriki" [Unequal Treaties as a Form of Prolonging the Colonial Dependence of the New States of Asia and Africa], *Sovetskii Ezhegodnik*, *1961*, pp. 156–170.

Tokareva, P. A., "Mezhdunarodnye Economicheskie Organizatsii Sotsialisticheskikh Stran" [The International Economic Organizations of the Socialist Countries], *Sovetskii Ezhegodnik*, *1959*, pp. 169–180.

Tunkin, G. I., "Printsip Mirnovo Sosushchestvovaniia—General'naia Liniia Vneshnepoliticheskoi Deiatel'nosti KPSS i Sovetskovo Gosudarstva" [The Principle of Peaceful Coexistence—The General Line of the Foreign Policy of the CPSU and the Soviet State], *SGIP*, No. 9 (1963), pp. 26–37.

————, "The Twenty-second Congress of the CPSU and the Tasks of the Soviet Science of International Law," *Soviet Law and Government*. New York: International Arts and Sciences Press, Winter 1962/63, Vol. 1, No. 2, pp. 18–27.

————, "XXII S'ezd KPSS i Mezhdunarodnoe Pravo" [The Twenty-second Congress of the CPSU and International Law], *Sovetskii Ezhegodnik*, *1961*, pp. 15–35.

_____, "Remarks on the Juridical Nature of Customary Norms of International Law," 49 *California Law Review* 419–439 (1961).

_____, "The Soviet Union and International Law," *International Affairs*, No. 11 (1959), pp. 40–45.

_____, "Sorok Let Sosushchestvovaniia i Mezhdunarodnoe Pravo" [Forty Years of Coexistence and International Law], *Sovetskii Ezhegodnik, 1958*, pp. 15–49.

_____, "Organizatisiia Ob'edinennykh Natsii: 1945–1965 (Mezhdunarodno-pravovye Problemy)" [The United Nations Organization: 1945–1965 (International Legal Problems)], *SGIP*, No. 10 (1965), pp. 58–68.

_____, "Vstupitel'naia Stat'ia" [Introductory Article], *Sovetskii Ezhegodnik, 1959*, pp. 11–15.

Tunkin, G. I., and Nechaev, B. I., "Pravo Dogovorov na XV Sessii Komissii Mezhdunarodnovo Prava OON," [The Law of Treaties at the Fifteenth Session of the International Law Commission of the U.N.], *SGIP*, No. 2, (1964), pp. 84–92; *SGIP*, No. 3 (1965), pp. 70–77 (Sixteenth Session); and *SGIP*, No. 4 (1966), pp. 56–62 (Seventeenth Session).

Tuzmukhamedov, R. A., "Mirnoe Sosushchestvovanie i Natsional'no-osvoboditel'naia Voina" [Peaceful Coexistence and Wars of National Liberation], *SGIP*, No. 3 (1963), pp. 87–94.

_____, "Ustav Organizatsii Afrikanskovo Edinstva v Svete Mezhdunarodnovo Prava" [The Charter of the Organization of African Unity in the Light of International Law], *Sovetskii Ezhegodnik, 1963*, pp. 109–128.

Usenko, E. T., "Osnovnye Mezhdunarodno-pravovye Printsipy Sotrudnichestva Sotsialisticheskikh Gosudarstv" [The Basic International Legal Principles of the Collaboration of Socialist States], *SGIP*, No. 3 (1961), pp. 16–29.

_____, "O Iuridicheskoi Prirode Rekomendatsii Soveta Ekonomicheskoi Vzaimopomoshchi" [The Juridical Nature of Recommendations of the Council of Mutual Economic Assistance], *SGIP*, No. 12 (1963), pp. 86–94.

Usachev, I. G., "Moskovskii Dogovor o Chastichnom Zapreshchenii Ispytanii Iadernovo Oruzhiia i Mezhdunarodnoe Pravo" [The Moscow Treaty Concerning the Partial Prohibition of the Testing of Nuclear Weapons and International Law], *SGIP*, No. 3 (1964), pp. 72–78.

Ushakov, N. A., "Poslanie N. S. Khrushcheva i Mirnoe Uregulirovanie Territorial'nykh Sporov mezhdu Gosudarstvami" [N. S. Khrushchev's Letter and the Peaceful Settlement of Territorial Disputes Between States], *SGIP*, No. 5 (1964), pp. 3–10.

"V Assotsiatsii, Chetvertoe Ezhegodnoe Sobranie Sovetskoi Assotsiatsii Mezhdunarodnovo Prava" [In the Association, The Fourth Annual Meeting of the Soviet Society of International Law], *Sovetskii Ezhegodnik, 1961*, pp. 414–450.

Vasilyev, O., "World Peace, an International Law," *International Affairs*, No. 1 (1965), pp. 107–108.

Volosov, M. E., "Agressiia Amerikanskovo Imperializma protiv V'etnamskovo Naroda—Prestuplenie protiv Mira i Mezhdunarodnoi Bezopasnosti" [American Imperialist Aggression Against the Vietnamese People—A Crime Against Peace and International Security], *SGIP*, No. 6 (1965), pp. 134–136.

"Vysshii Internatsional'nyi Dolg Strany Sotsializma" [The Supreme International Duty of a Socialist Country], *Pravda* (October 27, 1965), pp. 3, 4.

"Za Vysokuiu Partiinost' v Sovetskoi Iuridicheskoi Nauke" [For a High Degree of Political Orientation in Soviet Legal Science], *SGIP*, No. 1 (1964), pp. 3–11.

Zhukov, G. P., "Demilitarizatsiia i Neitralizatsiia Kosmicheskovo Prostranstva" [Demilitarization and Neutralization of Outer Space], *SGIP*, No. 3 (1964), pp. 79–89.

Zorin, V. A. (trans.), "Disarmament Problems and Peking's Maneuvers," *Izvestiia* (June 30, 1964), in *CDSP*, XVI, No. 26, 11–13.

Non-Soviet Sources

Books and Monographs:

Anzilotti, Dionisio, *Corso di Diritto Internazionale* [Course on International Law]. 3d ed. revised Rome: Athenaeum, 1928.

Brierly, J. L., *The Law of Nations*. 5th ed. Oxford: Clarendon Press, 1955.

Briggs, Herbert W., *The Law of Nations*. 2d ed. New York: Appleton-Century-Crofts, Inc., 1952.

Claude, Inis L., Jr., *Swords Into Plowshares: The Problems and Progress of International Organization*. New York: Random House, 1956.

Corbett, Percy E., *Law in Diplomacy*. Princeton: Princeton University Press, 1959.

Dallin, Alexander, *et. al.*, *The Soviet Union and Disarmament*. New York, Washington, and London: Praeger, 1964.

————, *The Soviet Union at the United Nations* (An Inquiry into Soviet Motives and Objectives). New York: Praeger, 1962.

Fall, Bernard B. (ed.), *Primer for Revolt* (*The Communist Takeover in Vietnam*). New York and London: Praeger, 1963.

Friedmann, Wolfgang G., *The Changing Structure of International Law*. New York: Columbia University Press, 1964.

Grzybowski, Kazimierz, *The Socialist Commonwealth of Nations, Organizations and Institutions*. New Haven and London: Yale University Press, 1964.

Gardner, Richard N., *In Pursuit of World Order*. New York: Praeger, 1964.

Guins, George C., *Soviet Law and Society*. The Hague: Martinus Nijhoff, 1954.

Jenks, Wilfred C., *The Prospects of International Adjudication*. Dobbs Ferry, New York: Oceana Publications, 1964.

Kelsen, Hans, *The Communist Theory of Law*. New York: Praeger, 1955.

Kulski, W. W., *Peaceful Coexistence, An Analysis of Soviet Foreign Policy*. Chicago: H. Regnery Co., 1959.

Lapenna, Ivo, *Conceptions Sovietiques de Droit Internationale Public* [Soviet Conceptions of Public International Law]. Paris: A. Pedone, 1954.

McWhinney, Edward, *Peaceful Coexistence and Soviet-Western International Law*. Leyden: A. W. Sythoff, 1964.

Morelli, Gaetano, *Nozioni di Diritto Internazionale* [Theories of International Law]. 3d ed. Padua: Cedam, 1951.

Peaceful Coexistence, A Communist Blueprint for Victory. Chicago: American Bar Association, 1964.

Quadri, Rolando, *Diritto Internazionale Publico* [Public International Law]. 2d ed. Palermo: Priulla, 1956.

Ramundo, Bernard A., *The (Soviet) Socialist Theory of International Law*. Washington, D.C.: Institute for Sino-Soviet Studies, The George Washington University, 1964.

Rothstein, Andrew, *Peaceful Coexistence*. Hammondsworth, Middlesex, England: Penguin Books Ltd., 1955.

Schwarzenberger, George, *The Frontiers of International Law*. London: Stevens & Sons, Ltd., 1962.

Soviet Impact on International Law [External Research Paper 156]. Washington, D.C.: U.S. Department of State, Bureau of Intelligence and Research, May 1964.

Slusser, Robert M. and Triska, Jan F., *Calendar of Soviet Treaties, 1917–1957*. Stanford, California: Stanford University Press, 1959.

———, *The Theory, Law and Policy of Soviet Treaties*. Stanford, California: Stanford University Press, 1962.

Taracouzio, T. A., *The Soviet Union and International Law*. New York: Macmillan Company, 1935.

Theodor, Andreas, *Peaceful Coexistence, International Law and Ideology* (n.p.-n.d.).

Thomas, Ann Van Wynen, *Communism versus International Law*. Dallas: Southern Methodist University Press, 1953.

World Peace Through The Rule of Law [Working Paper for the First World Conference, June 30-July 6, 1963, Athens, Greece]. Washington, D.C.: American Bar Association, 1963.

Articles:

Brzezinski, Zbigniew K., "The Organization of the Communist Camp." *World Politics*, XIII (1960–1961), 175–209.

Chakste, Mintauts, "Soviet Concepts of the State, International Law and Sovereignty." 43 *American Journal of International Law* (hereafter cited "*AJIL*") 21–36 (1949).

Hazard, John N., "Legal Research on 'Peaceful Coexistence.'" 51 *AJIL* 63–71 (1957).

———, "Codifying Peaceful Coexistence." 55 *AJIL* 109–120 (1961).

———, "Coexistence Codification Reconsidered." 57 *AJIL* 88–97 (1963).

"Kosygin Says U.S. Policy Foments War and Forces Soviet Arms Budget Rise," *The New York Times* (December 8, 1965), pp. 1 and 20.

Lapenna, Ivo, "The Legal Aspects and Political Significance of the Soviet Concept of Co-existence." 12 *International and Comparative Law Quarterly* 737–777 (1963).

Lissitzyn, Oliver J., "International Law in a Divided World." *International Conciliation*, No. 542 (March 1963).

Livingston, J. A., "Rumania's Spark of Self-reliance." *The Washington Post* (September 13, 1964), p. A-2.

McWhinney, Edward, "Peaceful Coexistence and Soviet-Western International Law." 56 *AJIL* 951–970 (1962).

Ramundo, Bernard A., "Soviet Criminal Legislation in Implementation of the Hague and Geneva Conventions Relating to the Rules of Land Warfare." 57 *AJIL* 73–84 (1962).

————, Review of Kazimierz Grzybowski, *The Socialist Commonwealth of Nations*. New Haven and London: Yale University Press, 1964, in 17 *Journal of Legal Education* 476–479 (1965).

Shapiro, L. B., "The Soviet Concept of International Law." *Yearbook of World Affairs* II, (1948), 272–310.

Vali, Ferenc A., "Soviet Satellite Status and International Law," *The JAG Journal*, XV, No. 8 (1961), 169–172.

Zorza, Victor, "Warsaw Pact Improvement Is Red Aim." *The Washington Post* (September 15, 1965), p. A-12.

INDEX

-->>><<<--

"Active, positive neutrality." *See* Neutrality and neutralism
Administrative unions. *See* International organization
African Unity, Organization of. *See* Organization of African Unity
Aggression, 88, 90, 117, 130–131, 157–158, 168, 225; international responsibility for, 86, 119, 127, 139, 144, 210; as form of colonialism, *see* Colonialism. *See also* Racial aggression
—direct and indirect: 122–123, 133, 150, 221
Agreement theory of norm formulation, 25, 46–50, 61, 67, 73, 81–82, 102, 146–147, 189, 202, 217
Albania, 174, 191
Alliances, 11, 154, 163, 232
American States, Organization of. *See* Organization of American States.
Arab States, League of: 160, 173
Arbitration. *See* Judicial settlement
Arms control: 193–213; economic advantages, 199–200; functionalism, 195; policy, 193–200; relation to international law and order, 198–199, 202–203. *See also* Disarmament.
Arms race, illegality of, 31, 117, 200
Auxiliary sources of international law. *See* Sources of international law

Base rights arrangements: 57, 87, 94, 143, 209–211; legality of, 87, 94, 122, 149–150, 209–211; liquidation of, 18, 152, 155, 157, 196–197, 202, 209–211
—foreign: 18, 122, 148, 149–150
—Soviet: 191, 211
Bilateral agreements, preference for. *See* Treaties
Bipolarity, 234
Blocs, military. *See* Military blocs
Bourgeois jurists, 50, 60–61, 74, 85, 161, 164–65
"Breach of the peace," 157–158, 168–169

Brezhnev, 116
"Building of communism," vii, 7, 8, 11, 33, 40, 48–49, 88, 93, 104, 105, 112, 115, 162, 193, 200, 222
Bulgaria, 174, 176

Camp theory: 10, 111, 113, 165, 188, 194, 234; capitalist, 10, 15, 36, 87, 117, 181; socialist, 10, 16, 34, 35, 36, 49, 87, 104, 105, 181, 192, 234
"Capture" of the United Nations, 117, 170, 179, 232
Central Treaty Organization, 102, 152, 166, 171
Characterization, unilateral. *See* Law of peaceful coexistence
Charter of the United Nations. *See* United Nations
—as *jus cogens, see jus cogens*
China, People's Republic of. *See* People's Republic of China
Chinese, dispute with, 10, 88, 95, 114–115, 117, 215, 223–224
Civil and civil procedural codes, 40
Class struggle, international, 10, 11, 15, 19, 25–27, 42, 47, 87, 99, 106, 111–115, 117–118, 121, 178, 212, 227, 231, 234
Codification of international law, 13–14, 31–32, 46, 51, 95, 204–205
"Cold War," 115, 154, 166, 218
Collaboration: international, 27, 31, 32, 48, 97, 159, 166, 172, 216–224; legal obligation for, 216–217, 218–224; with neutralist states, 220–221; with capitalist states, *see* "Struggle and Cooperation"
—cultural: 216, 217–20
—economic: 216, 217–20
—political: 216–17, 218–24
—socialist: 10, 19, 32–34, 35, 83, 103–106, 121, 162, 176–77, 191–92, 221–22
Collective security: 151–158; as criterion of legality of arrangements, 31, 57, 149–150, 153–

255

158; definition, 151–152; European system, 174; legal principles of, 153–158; objective standard, 156; policy, 151–153; subjective standard, 155–156, 158

Collective self defense. *See* Self-defense

Colonialism, 141–150; as a form of aggression, 147–148; direct and indirect, 143; illegality of, 45, 134–135, 143–150; neocolonialism, 117, 141–143, 147–149; policy toward, 8, 11, 14, 30, 88, 98, 137, 141–143

Comintern. *See* Subjects of international law

Common Market. *See* European Economic Community

Commonwealth of nations, socialist. *See* Socialist commonwealth of nations

Communist and workers' parties, 12, 35, 83–85, 106, 118, 177, 191–192; meetings of national party leaders, *see* Sources of international law

Communist Party of the Soviet Union, 30, 40, 106, 115, 141; twentieth party congress, 2, 25, 111, 232; twenty-third party congress, 112, 116, 137, 141, 234

Communist society, world. *See* World communist society

"Contemporary international law," 21–22, 23–24, 48–49, 50, 51, 52, 102, 188

Content, socialist. *See* Socialist content

Council for Mutual Economic Assistance, 84, 160, 163, 173, 175–178, 219

Counterinsurgency, 136–137

Cult of the individual, 25, 38

Customary international law, 60–64; agreement of states, 46, 61–63; regional customary law, 63; "tacit agreement," 43, 61–62; effect of *jus cogens* upon, *see Jus cogens*

Czechoslovakia, 83, 17

Decisions of international tribunals. *See* Sources of international law

Declarations, Moscow. *See* Moscow Declarations of 1957 and 1960

Defensism in Soviet legal positions, 6–7, 18, 64, 71, 91, 97, 179, 226, 231–232

Defensive wars. *See* War

Demilitarized zones, 196, 205–206, 209

Democratic principles of international law, 18, 20, 31, 34–35, 99

Détente, 193, 231, 234

Diplomatic initiatives, 12, 17, 97, 120, 195–197, 233–234

Direct aggression. *See* Aggression

"Dirty war," Vietnam as, 126, 136

Disarmament, 30–31, 32, 76, 119, 155, 200–213; Eighteen-Nation Disarmament Committee, 17, 195, 196, 198, 211; general and complete, 14, 17, 115, 117, 131, 153, 155, 198, 201–202, 209; legal requirement for, 193, 200–202; Limited Test Ban Treaty, 10, 52, 194, 202, 205; nuclear, 17, 155, 195–197, 203–206; "strict international control," 203

Disarmed world, relations in, 131–132, 186, 211–212

Discrimination in economic relations, 218–219

Domestic law: relation to international law, 37–42, 161–162; dualism, 37, 39, 42; monism, 37; reference, reception, and transformation, 39, 41; as source of international law, *see* Sources of international law. *See also* Civil and civil procedural codes

Economic assistance: Soviet, 147, 220–221; Western, 57, 147–148, 149–150, 221

Economic collaboration, agencies of: International Bank, 173–174; Soviet-Rumanian Intergovernmental Commission, *see* Intergovernmental Commission for Economic Collaboration

Economic integration, 176–177, 222–223. *See also* International socialist division of labor

Economic penetration, 143

Economic planning, 27, 176

Eisenhower Doctrine, 96, 130

Equality of states, 30, 33, 34, 47–48,

50, 54, 62, 74–75, 92, 100, 154–155, 203
Equality of systems, 30, 47, 101
Ethical approach to law, 188, 226–227
European Economic Community, 172, 219, 224
"Export of revolution," 118, 133, 136

Force: use of, 25–27, 116–117, 123–124, 126–127, 130, 132, 146–147, 153, 225, 229
Foreign policy: basis for Soviet legal positions, 2, 5, 7–10, 11, 18, 19, 29, 32, 36, 44, 60, 61, 64, 73, 82, 92, 93, 94, 120, 152, 188, 200–201, 205, 206–207, 227, 232, 233–235; as source of international law, 68
Functionalism. See International organization; Arms control

General and complete disarmament. See Disarmament
General Assembly. See United Nations
General international law, 20–21, 22, 25, 31, 32, 35, 49, 60, 101
General principles of international law. See Sources of international law
German Democratic Republic, 100, 149, 154, 174
Globalism. See International organization
"Goulash communism," 200
Great powers, unity of action. See Unity of action of great powers

Havana Tricontinental Conference, 14, 32, 142, 227
Helsinki World Congress for Peace, National Independence and General Disarmament, 32
Hungary, 95, 174

Ideology, influence of, 10, 15–17, 19, 22, 29, 44, 47, 52, 113, 137, 179, 231–232
Immutable laws of social development, 8, 29–30, 48, 68, 159, 215, 224, 232; relation to *jus cogens, see Jus cogens*

Imperialism 8, 11, 14, 23, 34, 54, 75, 88, 89, 98, 106, 113, 123, 128, 138, 141, 171, 199, 208
India, 30, 182
Indirect aggression. See Aggression
Individuals. See Subjects of international law
Indivisibility of peace. See Peace
Insurgency, 124, 134–136, 137
"Inter-class law," 48
Interdependence of states, 15–16, 47, 64, 81, 113, 159–161, 178–179, 231
Intergovernmental Commission for Economic Collaboration, Soviet–Rumanian, 174
International class struggle. See Class struggle, international
International collaboration; See Collaboration: international
International Bank for Reconstruction and Development, 179
International Court of Justice, 41, 65, 71, 168, 185–189, 213; Statute of, 43, 64–66, 70–71
International division of labor, 218–219
International law: conventional, vii, 5, 31, 234; function and purpose, 7–10, 36; as "law of the jungle," 95; "old international law," 23, 100, 119–120, 143, 224–225, 227; primacy of, 37, 90–91, 164–165, 229; private, 27; progressive, 2, 6, 13, 14, 23, 28, 49, 59, 189, 217, 224–225, 227; relation to world government, 161–162; selective submission to, 6, 49, 189, 231–232; socialist, 17, 20–21, 22–24, 32–36, 48–49, 63; universality, 18–22, 25; withering away of, 85, 161. See also Sources of international law
International legal personality. See Subjects of international law
International medical law, 124–125, 203–205
International Monetary Fund, 179
International organization, 159–181; administrative unions, 160, 178; agreements of, 81–82; criteria of legality, 159–160, 165; functionalism, 81, 178–

179; globalism, 160–163; international legal personality, *see* Subjects of international law; regionalism, 105–107, 170–178; resolutions of, as sources of international law, *see* Sources of international law; supranational, 87, 90, 94–95, 160–162; universality, 163–170

International peace and security, maintenance of, 155–156, 166, 182, 187, 190

International socialist division of labor, 27, 104, 105, 176, 219, 222–224

International Telegraphic Union, 179

Internationalism, socialist. *See* Socialist internationalism

Intervention, concept of, 96–98, 100, 133–137, 156–157

Judicial settlement, 184, 185–189; arbitration 41, 185–186, 189, 191; nonsocialist third party judgment, 185, 187–189, 212. *See also* International Court of Justice

Jus cogens: Charter of the United Nations as, 51, 55, 166–168, 170–171; concept of, 29, 44–46, 55, 137, 147, 224–225, 233; effect upon customary law, 61, 64; relation to immutable laws of social development, 29, 44, 59, 224, 227–228; law of peaceful coexistence as, 12, 44, 48–49, 71, 137, 145, 227–228; relation to natural law, 44, 46, 59, 224; effect upon *pacta sunt servanda*, 58–60; effect upon sovereignty, 91–92; effect upon treaties, 45, 50, 55–60

Just wars. *See* War

Korean War, 128, 130, 166

Korovin, 25, 56

Kosygin proposal, 120, 196–197, 211

Land warfare, rules of. *See* Rules of land warfare

Law of peaceful coexistence: anti-colonial law as, 143–144; campaign on behalf of, 5, 8, 11–13, 17, 18, 21, 35, 40, 63, 120, 170; codification, 13–14, 31–32, 46, 51, 158, 166, 217, 226; component principles, 10, 20, 22–24; customary law, 13, 63–64; definitions, 24–27; embodiment in Charter of United Nations, 51–52, 163, 164–168, 170–173; as *jus cogens, see Jus cogens*; as law in being, 13–14, 19, 44, 46, 51, 63, 216; as "law in the service of peace," 9, 14, 118–121; as law of peaceful change, *see* Peaceful change; as "new" law, 5, 6, 11, 51, 89, 232; relation to policy of peaceful coexistence, 16, 28, 68, 86, 215–216, 227, 232, 234–235; positivism and unilateral characterization, 6, 7, 14, 27, 54–56, 69, 70, 71, 182–183, 231–232, 234; principle of peaceful coexistence, 10–11, 14, 20, 22, 28–32, 48, 59, 63, 67, 92, 203, 235; principle of socialist internationalism, 10–11, 14, 16–17, 20–21, 22, 27, 32–36, 48, 59, 63, 83–84, 102, 103–107, 176–177, 191–192, 221–224; as scientific law, 12–13, 16, 29; as progressive law, *see* International law; relation to Soviet foreign policy, *see* Foreign policy; substantive content, 28–36

"Law of the jungle." *See* International law

League of Arab States. *See* Arab States, League of

League of Nations, 164, 169

Legal offensive, 6–7, 8, 18, 153–158, 213. *See also* Sovereignty

Legality, socialist. *See* "Socialist legality"

Lenin, 53, 133, 177, 194

Lex sovietica, 229, 233

Limited Test Ban Treaty. *See* Disarmament

Maintenance of international peace and security. *See* International peace and security

Marshall Plan, 175

Marx, 137
Marxism–Leninism, 10, 12, 15–17, 26, 29, 36, 44, 68, 111, 114, 118, 121, 222, 231, 232, 233
Military Bases. *See* Base rights arrangements
Military blocs, 31, 57, 87, 102, 122, 152, 156, 157, 171–172, 175, 203
Military forces, withdrawal of, 122, 155
Monism. *See* Domestic law: relation to international law
Monroe Doctrine, 96, 130
Moscow Declarations of 1957 and 1960, 105
Multilateral agreements: aversion to, 51; growing use of, 51–52. *See also* Treaties
Multilateral force, 18, 196
Mutual benefit, 30, 34, 56, 92, 216

National interest, 8, 33–34, 36, 88, 104, 129, 192, 222, 228, 233
National liberation, 14, 15, 32, 45, 74–75, 77, 79, 87, 89, 95–96, 98, 112, 118, 122, 134–137, 141–150, 155, 161, 225, 233; relation to *jus cogens*, 137
National planning. *See* Economic planning
National sovereignty. *See* Sovereignty
Nationalization of the revolution, 1, 5, 231
Natural law. *See Jus cogens*
Neocolonialism. *See* Colonialism
Neutralist states, 2, 10–11, 14, 31, 49, 75, 79, 96, 97, 101, 106, 117, 135, 213, 220, 227, 232, 234
Neutrality and neutralism, 77, 94, 195, 205–209; "active, positive," 207–208; "nuclear," 207, 208–209
New international law. *See* Law of peaceful coexistence
New states: obligations of, 99, 146; recognition of, 100–101
Nonaggression, principle of, 30, 119, 122, 202
Nonalignment. *See* Neutrality and neutralism
Nonintervention, principle of, 30, 34, 56, 87, 89, 92, 95–96, 104–105, 156–157, 161

Norm formulation, agreement theory of. *See* Agreement theory of norm formulation
North Atlantic Treaty Organization, 102, 152, 155, 166, 171, 174, 196, 198, 209
Nuclear disarmament. *See* Disarmament
"Nuclear neutrality." *See* Neutrality and neutralism
Nuclear testing, legality of, 203–205
Nuclear warfare, 10, 14, 15, 112–115, 118, 122, 138, 194–195, 215; illegality of, 124–125, 127, 128, 138
Nuclear-free zones, 17, 195, 196, 198, 203, 205–206, 208, 209

Organization international. *See* International organization
Organization of African Unity, 160, 173
Organization of American States, 171–172
Outer Mongolia, 176, 178
"Outlaw state," Soviet Union as, 1, 231

Pacta sunt servanda, 53, 58, 59–60
Pakistan, 182
Panama, 57, 168
Pancha Shila, 30–31, 92
Pax americana, 229
Peace, 33, 35, 115–118; indivisibility of, 157–158; "law in the service of . . . ," *see* Law of peaceful coexistence; permanent peace, 121, 138; policy of Soviet Union, 15, 58, 88, 111–118; relationship to peaceful coexistence, 25, 26, 32, 97, 115, 117–118, 120–121; "right of nations to peace," 118–120; through law, *see* World peace through law; relationship to socialism and communism, 117–118, 120–121
Peace treaties, 55, 90, 126
Peace zone, 111, 117
Peace-keeping operations, cost of, 183–184
Peaceful change, 224–226; nonsocialist, attitude towards, 225–226;

support for socialist, 93–94, 224–225

Peaceful coexistence. *See* Policy of peaceful coexistence

Peaceful competition, 15, 117, 154, 195, 215–216, 218

Peaceful settlement, 181–192, 212–213, 225; effect of law of peaceful coexistence upon, 184–185; endorsement of, 14, 30–31, 112–114, 118–119, 128, 181–184; international organizations, role in, 182–184, 187, 189–190; judicial settlement, *see* Judicial settlement; preference for political settlement, 181–184, 185, 189–190; machinery within socialist commonwealth, 191–192; attitude towards traditional methods, 119–120, 182, 185.

People's Republic of China, 1, 30, 88, 95, 154, 166, 191

Personality, international. *See* Subjects of international law

Poland, 174

Polaris submarines, 211

Policy of peaceful coexistence, 25, 27, 32, 111–115; as arms control policy, 193, 194–198; inherent subjectivism of, 6–7, 158; law in support of, *see* Law of peaceful coexistence; legal requirements for, 29, 157; objective requirements for, 6, 16, 19, 29, 44, 114–115, 160–161, 215; "passive" and revolutionary approaches to, 6–7, 157, 215

Polycentism, 36, 84, 88, 234

Popular sovereignty. *See* Sovereignty

"Position of strength," policy of, 166

Positivism. *See* Law of peaceful coexistence

Pragmatic, purposeful approach to law, 52–60, 188, 226–227

Primacy of international law. *See* International law

Principle of peaceful coexistence. *See* Law of peaceful coexistence

Principle of socialist internationalism. *See* Law of peaceful coexistence

Private international law. *See* International law

Progressive international law. *See* International law

Proliferation of nuclear weapons, policy towards, 17, 114, 196, 198, 203

Propaganda: role of, 11–18, 32, 58, 71, 88, 89, 97, 99, 120, 125, 136–137, 138–140, 195, 198–199, 221, 233–234; war, prohibited, 30, 119, 123, 128

Racial aggression, 97, 141

Racial equality, Soviet Union as proponent of. *See* Soviet Union

Racism, 97, 123

Reaction, world forces of. *See* United States

Rebus sic stantibus, 53–54; effect of *jus cogens* upon, 54; interpretation of, 53–54

Reception. *See* Domestic law: relation to international law

Recognition of states. *See* New states

Reference. *See* Domestic law: relation to international law

Regional organization. *See* International organization

Responsibility of states, 127

Revolutionary activity, legal basis for, 75–76, 87, 94, 98, 148–149, 155–157

Rules of land warfare, 77, 138–140, 204

Rumania, 83, 174, 191, 223

Sanctions, use of force as. *See* Self-defense

Secretary General. *See* United Nations

Security, collective. *See* Collective security

Security Council. *See* United Nations

Self-defense, 128–133; collective, 133, 135; as sanction for violation of peaceful coexistence, 132; relation to wars of national liberation, 132–133, 145–147

Self-determination, principle of, 30–31, 56, 75, 78, 97, 98, 100, 130–132, 135–137, 143–149, 156–157; use of force, 146, 147, 225

Settlement, peaceful. *See* Peaceful settlement

Social development, immutable laws

of. *See* Immutable laws of social development

"Socialism in one country," 5

Socialist camp. *See* Camp theory

Socialist commonwealth of nations, 10, 16, 20, 27, 32, 33–34, 36, 42, 51, 83, 84–85, 88, 94, 102, 103–107, 112, 115, 121, 162–163, 173, 191–192, 221–224

Socialist content, vii, 33, 34, 48, 66, 103, 120, 204–205, 213, 232–233

Socialist internationalism. *See* Law of peaceful coexistence

Socialist international law. *See* International law

Socialist legality, 2, 40

Socialist objectivity, 130

Socialist unity, 36, 105–106, 192, 222

Sources of international law, 43–71; agreement of national party leaders, 84–85, 191–192; agreement of states, 43–50, 67–69, 70–71; auxiliary, 67–71; customary law, 43, 60–64, 66; domestic law, 65–66, 67, 69–70; decisions of international tribunals, 67, 70–71; foreign policy, *see* Foreign policy: general principles, 43, 64–67, 71; *jus cogens*, *see Jus cogens;* main, 43, 68; principal, 43, 52; resolutions of international organizations, 67, 69, 70–71; treaties, 43, 50–60, 66; treatises, 70–71

Southeast Asia Treaty Organization, 102, 152, 166, 171

Sovereignty, 30, 87–107, 117, 156–157; absolute, 91–92, 119; defensive use of, 87, 88–98; definition, 90–92; fundamental to law of peaceful coexistence, 45, 87, 88, 92–93; 97–98, 103, 106, 160, 165, 173, 186, 232, 234; as integrating force, 88, 103–107; relation to international legal personality, 75–80; effect of *jus cogens* upon, 55; national, 75–76, 77, 89, 98–100, 148–149, 192; offensive use of, 34, 87, 98–103; popular, 35, 50, 56–57, 75–76, 94, 101–103; relation to self-determina-

tion, 146; state, 34, 37, 38–39, 50, 73, 80, 85–86, 103–106, 123, 185–186, 212, 234

Soviet treaty practice: 51–60, 90; Soviet view, 53–54, 56, 58–59, 90, 102–103; Western view, 53, 54

Soviet Union: as defender of national liberation, 17, 88, 89, 99, 112, 122, 137, 142, 144, 194, 220; as defender of small states, 88, 89, 95, 99, 220; as leader in movement for humane rules of war, 139; as peace-loving state, 15, 17, 79, 88, 96, 112, 117, 119, 120, 125, 182, 193–195, 198; as proponent of arms control, 15, 17–18, 112, 117–118, 193; as proponent of legality, 2, 18, 53, 58, 95, 139–140, 169, 193, 226; as proponent of peaceful competition, 112, 113; as proponent of racial equality, 97, 142, 220; as proponent of self-determination, 88, 97

Specialized agencies of the socialist camp, 173–174

Stalin, 5, 9, 25, 111, 175

State of the entire people, 25

Status quo orientation, 2, 231

Statute of the International Court of Justice. *See* International Court of Justice

"Strict international control." *See* Disarmament

"Strong points," 210

"Struggle and cooperation," 9, 19, 25, 154, 217

Subjects of international law: 73–86; Comintern as, 82–83; component states of federation as, 78–79; definition, 73–74; individuals as, 27, 74, 80, 85–86, 89; international organizations as, 73, 74, 80–82; nations as, 26, 73, 74–75, 77, 80, 98, 146; aversion to pluralistic theory, 85–86; communist parties as, 82–85; states as, 73–80

Subversion, 133–134, 136–137

"Tacit agreement." *See* Customary law

Tacit consent, presumption of, 208–209

Tashkent Conference, 120, 182
Technological advances, 15–16, 60, 114, 160–161, 178, 231
Territorial integrity, 30, 34, 92–94, 145, 156–157, 204, 231
Tibet, 30, 95
Transformation. *See* Domestic law: relation to international law
Treaties, 50–60; as international legislation, 50–52; effect of *jus cogens* upon, *see Jus cogens*
—bilateral, 51
—colonial, 56–57, 168
—illegal, 54–60, 102–103
—multilateral, 51–52, 55, 60
—unequal, 47–48, 54, 56–57, 58, 90, 150, 210, 221
Troika proposal. *See* United Nations
Truman Doctrine, 96, 130
Tunkin, 8, 21, 30, 34, 35, 49, 67, 71, 81–82, 224

Universality. *See* International law; International organization
Universal Postal Union, 179
Use of force. *See* Force
Unequal treaties. *See* Treaties
Unilateral characterization. *See* Law of peaceful coexistence
United Nations, 81, 95, 97, 117, 152–162, 164–170, 182–183, 212–213, 227, 232; Charter of, 13, 31, 50–52, 55, 90, 95–96, 97, 126–127, 128–133, 135, 144, 146–147, 163, 165–170, 171, 173, 187, 209, 210, 216–217; General Assembly, 14, 51, 68, 69, 95–96, 181–184, 206; modification of, 166–167, 190–191, 213; Secretary General, 213; Security Council, 122, 129, 131, 167, 182–183, 187, 189–191; troika proposal, 213
United States: as rallying point for world forces of reaction, 96, 99, 136, 142, 143; as underminer of United Nations, 117, 152, 170, 171, 183
Uniting for Peace Resolution, 183
Unity of action of great powers, 31, 130–131, 153–154, 166, 183, 190

Veto in Security Council, 122, 129, 182–183, 190–191
Vietnam, 1, 26, 136, 138–139, 149
Vyskinsky, 25, 37

War, 111–139; aggressive wars, 116, 122, 193; defensive wars, 116, 125, 128, 225; as international sanction, *see* Self-defense; just wars, 116, 122, 158; lawful, 121–140; local and limited, 125; outlawing of, 112–117, 118–119, 122–128, 157–158, 182, 185, 209, 225; revolutionary, 116; unjust wars, 116; wars of national liberation, 116, 123–125, 132–133, 146–147
Warsaw Treaty Organization (Warsaw Pact), 84, 152, 155, 163, 173–175, 178, 196, 198, 209
Western treaty practice, 52, 53–54, 58–59, 90
Withering away of international law. *See* International law
World communist society, 10, 35, 84–85, 162
World forces of reaction. *See* United States
World government: aversion to non-socialist, 73, 80, 85, 87, 89, 90, 160–163, 187–188, 212; socialist attitude towards, 78–79, 162
World order, Soviet view of, 9–11, 27, 107, 189, 229
World peace through law, 226–229; Soviet approach, 226–228, 229; Western approach, 226–227, 228
World public opinion, 12, 32, 102, 123, 139, 144, 147
World socialism, forces of, 6, 8, 9, 89, 101, 111, 227
World socialist system, 89, 111, 137, 142, 157, 164, 177, 222
World victory of socialism, 7, 9, 14, 34, 36, 112, 215, 222, 228

Yugoslavia, 176, 191